Complete Latin American Spanish

Juan Kattán-Ibarra

For UK order enquiries: please contact Bookpoint Ltd,
130 Milton Park, Abingdon, Oxon OX14 4SB.
Telephone: +44 (0) 1235 827720. *Fax:* +44 (0) 1235 400454.
Lines are open 09.00–17.00, Monday to Saturday, with a 24-hour
message answering service. Details about our titles and how to order
are available at www.teachyourself.com

For USA order enquiries: please contact McGraw-Hill
Customer Services, PO Box 545, Blacklick, OH 43004-0545, USA.
Telephone: 1-800-722-4726. *Fax:* 1-614-755-5645.

For Canada order enquiries: please contact McGraw-Hill Ryerson Ltd,
300 Water St, Whitby, Ontario L1N 9B6, Canada.
Telephone: 905 430 5000. *Fax:* 905 430 5020.

Long renowned as the authoritative source for self-guided
learning – with more than 50 million copies sold worldwide – the
Teach Yourself series includes over 500 titles in the fields of languages,
crafts, hobbies, business, computing and education.

British Library Cataloguing in Publication Data: a catalogue record for
this title is available from the British Library.

Library of Congress Catalog Card Number: on file.

First published in UK 1994 as *Teach Yourself Latin-American Spanish*
by Hodder Education, part of Hachette UK, 338 Euston Road,
London NW1 3BH.

First published in US 1994 as *Teach Yourself Latin-American Spanish*
by The McGraw-Hill Companies, Inc.

This edition published 2010.

The *Teach Yourself* name is a registered trade mark of Hodder Headline.

Copyright © 1994, 2003, 2010 Juan Kattán-Ibarra

Typeset by MPS Limited, A Macmillan Company.

Printed in Great Britain for Hodder Education, an Hachette UK
Company, 338 Euston Road, London NW1 3BH, by MPS,
a Macmillan company.

The publisher has used its best endeavours to ensure that the URLs for
external websites referred to in this book are correct and active at the
time of going to press. However, the publisher and the author have
no responsibility for the websites and can make no guarantee that a
site will remain live or that the content will remain relevant, decent or
appropriate.

Hachette UK's policy is to use papers that are natural, renewable and
recyclable products and made from wood grown in sustainable forests.
The logging and manufacturing processes are expected to conform to
the environmental regulations of the country of origin.

Impression number   10 9 8 7 6 5 4 3 2 1
Year   2014 2013 2012 2011 2010

Acknowledgements

The author would like to thank Juan Luzzi Montes de Oca, from Chile, for his assistance in the preparation of the second edition of this book.

Every effort has been made to obtain permission for all material used. In the absence of any response to enquiries, the author and publisher would like to acknowledge the following for use of their material: *revista Tiempo Libre* (Mexico), *Oficina de Turismo* (Mexico), *diario El Mercurio, restaurante La cocina de Sebastián* (Chile), *restaurante Casa Brava, Mobli Market* (Colombia).

Thanks are also due to *Radio Mar FM* (Mexico), for use of material on the recording that accompanies this book.

Credits

Contents

Meet the author

I qualified as a teacher in Chile, where I began my teaching career, and then did postgraduate studies in foreign language teaching at Michigan State, Manchester and London Universities. I worked for several years at Ealing College in London, and also acted as an external examiner in Spanish for various London examination boards.

My first Spanish course was published in London in 1978, in a writing career which has lasted until today. I have written, or co-written, a number of courses in the Teach Yourself series, including **Complete Spanish, Complete Latin American Spanish, Perfect your Spanish, Essential Spanish Grammar** and **Speak Spanish with Confidence**. I am also an author or co-author of a number of books with other publishers, among them the BBC, Routledge and McGraw-Hill.

I am now a full-time author, and very much look forward to being your guide in the journey you are just about to begin into Latin American Spanish. **¡Vamos!**

Only got a minute?

Is this the right course for you? Whether you are new to Spanish or have already had some experience of it and are now looking for a course in Latin American Spanish, then this is the course for you. Once you start learning the language, you will be joining millions of people around the world who have chosen Spanish as their second language, the most popular language after English. Spanish, which most Latin Americans call **castellano** *Castilian*, is the native language of about 350 million people, most of them in the Americas.

Even if you are a complete beginner, you will be surprised at the many similarities that exist between Spanish and English. Spanish, like Italian, Portuguese, French, is derived from Latin, so many Latin-based words in English are similar to Spanish ones: **mayor** – *major*, **vehículo** – *vehicle*, **villa** – *villa*, etc. A number of Spanish words have found their way into English: siesta, fiesta, machismo, guerrilla, etc. Many others you will be able to guess from the similarity in their forms: **estación** – *station*, **nación** – *nation*, **libertad** – *liberty*, **diversidad** – *diversity*, etc. Perhaps you are already familiar with some Spanish words and expressions, but if not here are a few: **sí** *yes*, **no** *no*, **hola** *hello*, **por favor** *please*, **gracias** *thank you*, **adiós** *good bye*, **buenos días** *good morning*, **buenas tardes** *good afternoon/evening*, **señor** *Mr, sir*, **señora** *Mrs, madam*, **señorita** *Miss, madam*, etc.

You may be wondering whether by learning Latin American Spanish you will be able to communicate with Spanish speakers in Spain. The answer is yes. The differences between Latin American Spanish and that spoken in Spain are something like those which exist between British English and American, Australian or Canadian English. So you will be understood. Differences also exist between different Latin American countries, but again, these are no obstacle to communication.

5 Only got five minutes?

Complete Latin American Spanish has been designed with a double purpose in mind: firstly, to help you learn all the essentials of Spanish, so that you can communicate with speakers from any part of the Spanish-speaking world; secondly, to help you become familiar with those special features of Latin American Spanish which make it different from the Spanish of Spain. To achieve these aims the book has been structured into thirteen different units, each focusing on your specific communicative needs and on the constructions needed to express them.

You may not be familiar with Latin American Spanish and may be wondering in what ways this differs from the Spanish of Spain. In fact, the differences between the two are not unlike those that exist between British and American, Canadian or Australian English, or from that spoken in other parts of the world. Yet, despite such differences, speakers from all over the Spanish-speaking world can communicate with each other.

The features which distinguish Latin American Spanish from the Spanish used in Spain are mainly in the spoken language, particularly in pronunciation and intonation. Differences in vocabulary also exist, some more general, others specific to certain countries. A *mobile phone*, *cellphone* in American English, for example, is **un (teléfono) celular** in Latin America, and **un (teléfono) móvil**, in Spain, while a *computer* is **un computador** or **una computadora** in Latin America and **un ordenador** in Spain. Differences of this kind also exist between British and other variants of English, but one soon gets used to them and they are generally no obstacle to communication. A few minor differences in grammar also exist but even as a non-native speaker you will soon be able to identify them and they will not hinder your communication needs in any way. By and large, however, the grammar of Spanish is one and the same and there are no differences in spelling such as those you find between British and American English, as in 'neighbour, neighbor' or 'traveller, traveler'. Naturally, there are language variations within Latin America itself, just as there are differences within Spain, but not in the area of writing.

Latin American Spanish has borrowed a number of words from indigenous languages in the region. Some of these terms have found their way into Peninsular Spanish and even into other European languages. Words like **tomate, chocolate** and **maíz**, among others, have their origin in the Americas. Apart from Spanish words which have acquired a different meaning in Latin America, the region as a whole sometimes shows preference for one Spanish word instead of another. By and large, however, much of the Latin American lexicon is Spanish in origin, and most standard words used in Spain will be understood in Latin America.

Some variations in Spanish within Latin America have their roots in the Spanish colonization of the region; others stem from the influence of indigenous languages and from that of non-Spanish settlers, mainly African and European. This has given rise to distinctive linguistic areas within the region. The Spanish spoken in Mexico, for instance, sounds quite different from that spoken in the River Plate region, in countries like Argentina and Uruguay. This in turn differs from that of the Andean countries or that spoken around the Caribbean. In addition to using forms which will be understood in most Latin American countries, *Complete Latin American Spanish* also explains some of the main differences between various forms of Spanish, including references to specific countries or areas, for example Mexico and Central America, the Caribbean, the Southern Cone (Argentina, Chile and Uruguay), the River Plate (Argentina and Uruguay). Differences in pronunciation and intonation between major regions are demonstrated by means of the recordings which go with the course. Information on regional differences is given in the Pronunciation section in the back of the book.

If you are a complete beginner you may be wondering how far this course is going to take you on the way to achieving effective communication in Spanish. The aim of the book is to allow you to reach a stage at which you can deal effectively with all the main situations in which you might find yourself, either as a visitor in a Latin American country or in your dealings with Spanish speakers in your own country, whether making a hotel booking, asking the way, giving personal information, making a phone call, etc. But to achieve this you will need to work your way regularly through the course, without extensive gaps between one unit and another, reviewing material already learnt as often as you can. The more time you spend working on the course, the more fluent and accurate your Spanish will become. You should also try to find ways to improve your Spanish through other means, focusing on your own special interests. There are a number of things you can do to expand your competence in Spanish. Here are a few suggestions.

To increase your vocabulary place cards around your house with key words or short phrases you would like to learn and look at them from time to time. You will be surprised how many of them you will be able to remember later on. You can also do this to learn verbs and tenses. You will gain more from this exercise by focusing on a theme, for example food, clothing, travel and transport, occupations, etc. A good medium-size dictionary will help you to do this.

Get yourself a notebook and draw up vocabulary lists centred on a theme, just as you did with the cards above. List the English word first and then write down the Spanish next to it and try memorizing it. Once you have a reasonable number of words in your list, cover up the English while you look at the Spanish and give the English equivalent of each word. Then repeat the same process in reverse, giving the Spanish for each of the words in your list.

If you are not daunted by grammar and would like to know more about how Spanish works, buy yourself a grammar book. There are a number of user-friendly books on sale, some in the Teach Yourself series.

As you progress through the course and improve your understanding, try to read brief news items in Spanish. A good source for news is *BBC Mundo*, the Spanish web page of the BBC, in which you can either read or listen to news in Spanish. You should also try to get some Latin American and Spanish newspapers and magazines. You can use short news items for intensive reading, looking up some of the new words in your dictionary. You may find this difficult at first and you may be tempted to translate word for word, but with time and an increased vocabulary you should soon expand your capacity to understand written Spanish.

Listen to Latin American songs in Spanish using your MP3 or iPod, or get yourself some DVDs of Spanish films and listen to the Spanish while you read the English subtitles. With time you should be able to understand more and more without having to rely on the English all the time. Alternatively, try to find films in English with Spanish subtitles, and focus on the correspondence between the two languages.

If you have access to Internet at home, use it to find websites in Spanish on your favourite subjects, or try to make contact with Spanish-speaking people with whom you can chat or correspond. The options are wide in Internet as there are hundreds of websites to suit your own interests. In one of them, particularly, *La página del idioma español* (elcastellano.org), you will find ample information on the Spanish language and available resources, including direct access to major newspapers in all the main Spanish-speaking countries. The Taking it further section in the back of the book will be particularly useful if you are looking for sources of authentic Spanish, and if you intend to travel in Latin America or Spain or would like to study Spanish or find work in a Spanish-speaking country this section also includes a few useful websites.

10 Only got ten minutes?

Are you thinking of learning Spanish? If you are, you are making the right choice, because Spanish is one of the most widely spoken languages in the world, a status which shares with Mandarin Chinese and English. Like English, its use is not restricted geographically to one area. It is the official language of Spain and of nineteen countries in Central America, South America and the Caribbean. Mexico, with over 100 million people, is the largest Spanish-speaking country in the world, more than double the number of speakers in Spain. It is also spoken in the Spanish north African cities of Ceuta and Melilla and in the Canary Islands, off the west coast of Africa. This brings the total number of native speakers to about 350 million, most of them in *Hispanoamérica*, the Spanish-speaking countries of Latin America.

In Equatorial Guinea, a former Spanish colony on the west coast of Africa, Spanish is an official language together with French. It is also used in Andorra alongside Catalan, the official language, and in Gibraltar, where the official language is English. Around 34 million people of Hispanic origin in the United States use Spanish in their homes, making this the second language after English in that country.

Pockets of Spanish speakers still exist in the Philippines, a former Spanish colony, where Spanish enjoyed an official status until 1973. The imposition of English, however, following the United States annexation of the islands after the end of the Philippine-American war in 1913, led to the decline of Spanish. Spanish remains alive, however, in many people's names and surnames and in a large number of words and expressions of everyday use in Filipino, now an official language alongside English. Spanish vocabulary is also one of the main components of Chabacano, a creole language spoken by about 600 thousand people around the Philippine Islands.

Spanish has also left its imprint in Ladino, the Spanish spoken by Sephardic Jews who were expelled from Spain in 1492. The real number of Ladino speakers in the world now cannot be quantified, as this has been modified by the influence of the language of the host countries where the expelled people finally settled.

The enormous extension of the Spanish-speaking world, with speakers in Europe, Africa, the Americas and even in Polynesia, in the Pacific Ocean (in Easter Island, a Chilean territory), has led to a variety of accents and local usages. These differences, however, are no obstacle to communication, thus allowing Spanish speakers from all parts of the world to interact in all spheres of their lives and to share in a culture which has become increasingly richer.

This international status of Spanish, on the other hand, has led millions of people in different countries, in Europe, Asia and elsewhere, to choose Spanish as a second language and their numbers are increasing rapidly. Spanish is now the second most popular language after English. The motivations for learning it are manifold, ranging from purely personal reasons to travel, business, job requirements, academic needs or an interest in more specific aspects of Spanish and Latin American culture, such as music, dance, literature, etc.

As it happened with English, over the years Spanish has diversified, giving rise to different local variants. Castilian Spanish, el castellano (the language of the old Kingdom of Castile), of northern and central Spain, for example, sounds quite different from the Spanish spoken in areas such as Andalusia in southern Spain, Extremadura in the southwest, or in the Canary Islands, off the northwest coast of Africa. Although Castilian Spanish is considered by many to be the standard, most people in Spain now use other variants of Spanish and these differences are accepted in all social contexts. In spite of this, many people in Spain, and most Latin Americans, refer to their language as **castellano** instead of **español**.

In Latin America there are noticeable differences in speech and usage not only between the various countries but also within the same country. In an area as large as that which extends from

Mexico in the north to Chile and Argentina in the south, such differences are not just restricted to pronunciation but also to vocabulary, determined by a number of geographical and historical factors, among the second the influence of indigenous languages or even that of non-Spanish European immigrants, such as Italians in Argentina.

In spite of the large numbers of people who use Spanish as their native language in different countries and the great distance between Spain and the Americas, the grammar of Spanish has remained largely the same, except for a few differences which are easily identifiable. Written Spanish is the same in all parts of the Spanish-speaking world. A number of factors have contributed to this consistency, among these a long-standing shared literary tradition, the role of the press and communication technology, especially in more recent times, and that of the Real Academia Española (the Royal Spanish Academy), an official body with national academies in every Spanish-speaking country whose main function is to establish norms for Spanish usage, especially in relation with grammar, vocabulary and spelling.

Spanish and English: similarities and differences

Vocabulary

If you are a beginner in Spanish you may be wondering how difficult this will turn out to be or how different it is from English. Spanish is not in fact a difficult language to learn and there are many reasons for this. If you have never encountered Spanish before you will be surprised to find that there are many similarities between Spanish and English, especially in the area of vocabulary. Many of the words which are similar have their origins in Latin, from which Spanish derives (**visión** *vision*, **diario** *diary*, **mover** *to move*, etc.), while many others have their roots in Greek (**programa** *programme/ program*, **sistema** *system*, **escuela** *school*, etc.). You will be able to deduce the meanings of many Spanish words from the similarity or correspondence between certain forms, for example Spanish -ción, English -tion (**acción** *action*, **situación** *situation*), -ad -ty (**libertad** *liberty*, **universidad** *university*), -mente -ly (**especialmente** *especially*, **exactamente** *exactly*), -ista -ist (**artista** *artist*, **dentista** *dentist*). But some words which look the same have different meanings in Spanish and English: **actual** (current, present) – *actual*, **asistir** (to attend) – *to assist*, **carpeta** (folder, table cover) – *carpet*, etc.

These similarities between Spanish and English should help you to understand the meaning of some of the words you will find in your *Complete Latin American Spanish* course without having to look them up. Guessing meanings from the context in which the new words occur will be another ability you should develop as you progress in the course. You may feel at a loss at first but as you gain experience with Spanish you may even find yourself skipping the odd new word and trying to get the gist of what a text says, just as you do in your own language sometimes.

Grammar: the essentials

In terms of the grammar you are going to learn, you will find that English and Spanish have a number of characteristics in common, amongst them word order within sentences which, with a few exceptions, is very similar or almost identical in both languages, as in Patricia habla español Patricia speaks Spanish. But there are also some important differences, among them the following ones, which are dealt with in more detail in this book:

a Words which name things such as book, pound, etc. have gender in Spanish, that is they are either masculine or feminine. **Libro** *book*, for example, is maculine while **libra** *pound* is feminine. Most words ending in -o are masculine and most of those ending in -a are feminine. A few consonant endings can tell you whether a word is masculine or feminine, but generally this is not so, and the best thing is to learn each word with its gender, which in your dictionary and this book you will find signalled by m for masculine and f for feminine. Once you have made some progress with your *Complete Latin American Spanish* course you will begin to acquire a 'sense for gender' and may be able to determine, by its ending, whether a word is masculine or feminine.

b Many grammatical words change in Spanish depending on whether they go together with a masculine or a feminine word. The word for the, for example, is el for masculine and la for feminine: el libro the book, la libra the pound. The Spanish for *a* is **un** for masculine and **una** for feminine: **un rato** *a while*, **una rata** *a rat*. With time, you will acquire the capacity to make the necessary adaptations to a grammatical word in order to fit the gender of the accompanying word.

c In English you normally add -s to a word to make it plural. Spanish adds -s to words ending in a vowel, but -es to those ending in a consonant: **día** – **días** *day* – *days*, **tren** – **trenes** *train* – *trains*. In Spanish, the masculine plural form of words referring to people can be used to refer to males and females: **hermano** *brother*, **hermanos** *brothers* or *brothers and sisters*.

d In English, words which describe someone or something come before the word they qualify, while in Spanish such words usually come after the word they describe: **una persona interesante** *an interesting person* (literally, a person interesting).

e Unlike English, in which a word such as expensive does not change, in Spanish this must agree in gender (masculine or feminine) and number (singular or plural) with the word it qualifies: **un hotel caro/unos hoteles caros** *an expensive hotel/some expensive hotels*, **una casa cara/unas casas caras** *an expensive house/some expensive houses*.

Spanish verbs

If you look up the Spanish for words such as to speak, to eat, to live in a dictionary you will see that these, like all verbs in Spanish, can be grouped into three main categories according to their endings: -ar, -er and -ir verbs (**hablar** *to speak*, **comer** *to eat*, **vivir** *to live*, etc.) The largest group corresponds to -ar verbs.

Spanish, like English, uses changes in the verb to denote different times, as in **hablo** *I speak* (present), **hablé** *I spoke* (past). These changes are referred to as tense. In Spanish, the verb endings for each tense are dependent on three factors: time (past, present, future, etc.), category of the verb (-ar, -er or -ir) and person (**yo** *I*, **él** *he*, **ellos** *they*, etc.). English has a simpler verb system in which only the third person singular of the present tense is marked for person, by the ending -s (I work, you work, he/she/it works, etc.).

The majority of Spanish verbs follow a fixed pattern of change and so are called regular, but some behave in a different way and are called irregular. As most verbs are regular, once you know the forms for a particular tense, for example the present of hablar to speak, you will know how to form the present tense of hundreds of other verbs, so it is important that you learn the forms.

Three forms for you: tú, usted, ustedes

In Latin American Spanish there are three different forms for you: **tú**, **used** for addressing one person in a familiar or informal way: friends, family members, equals, such as colleagues, and younger people, even if you have not met them before; **usted**, used formally, as a sign of respect to address someone one does not know, an elderly person, a superior, etc.; and **ustedes**, used in formal or informal address to speak to more than one person. In Spain, a distinction is made when speaking to more than one person between **ustedes**, formal, and a fourth form, **vosotros**, which is informal. This can be said to be the main grammatical difference between Latin American and Peninsular Spanish. Verb endings associated with **vosotros** and other words related to it are not used in Latin America.

The use of vos

A few Latin American countries, notably Argentina and Uruguay, use **vos** instead of **tú** in familiar address. This is the norm in these two countries. In others, this usage is restricted to certain regions and social groups.

No need for I, you, he, she ...

An important difference between English and Spanish is that the words for I, you, he, she, etc., are usually omitted in Spanish, as the verb ending is usually sufficient to indicate the person, as in **hablo español** *I speak Spanish*, **hablamos inglés** *we speak English*. The -o in **hablo** indicates I, and the -amos in **hablamos** signals we. In formal address, usted is often kept for politeness.

Saying no and asking questions

To negate something in English you normally use forms like don't, doesn't, etc. In Spanish, all you need to do is to place the word no before the verb: **Hablo español** *I speak Spanish*, **No hablo español** *I don't speak Spanish*.

As for questions, in English you can ask these in a number of ways, for example Do you work?, You work, don't you?, You work? Spanish can also form questions in different ways, but the simplest way of doing it is by using the same word order as in a statement but with a rising intonation: **Trabajan mucho** *They work a lot*, **¿Trabajan mucho?** *Do they work a lot?*

All questions in Spanish are preceded by an inverted question mark: **¿qué pasa?** *what happens?*. Exclamations are also preceded by an inverted exclamation mark: **¡cuidado!** *look out!*

Latin American Spanish pronunciation

As it occurs in the English-speaking world, most of the countries in Latin America can be said to have their own pronunciation and intonation features. As a non-native speaker, you may not notice these differences at first, but increased familiarity with the spoken language will gradually allow you to distinguish them, perhaps not in terms of specific countries but in terms of larger areas or regions. More information on this will be found in the Pronunciation section in the back of the book.

Introduction

Welcome to *Complete Latin American Spanish*!

This is a complete communicative course in Latin American Spanish, which assumes no previous knowledge of the language. It is designed for beginners as well as those who, having done a general Spanish course or one based on Peninsular Spanish, now wish to learn the language spoken in Latin America. The emphasis is first and foremost on using Spanish, but we also aim to give you an idea of how the language works, so that you can create sentences of your own.

Although the course has been written especially for people studying on their own, the material and exercises will also lend themselves to classroom use. The 13 units which make up this book provide ample opportunity to learn and practise the language used in practical, everyday situations, such as introducing yourself and others, giving personal information, making travel arrangements, ordering food, shopping, etc. Those travelling in Latin America, for business or pleasure, will find the material in this course particularly useful.

The course covers all four of the basic skills – listening and speaking, reading and writing. If you are working on your own, the audio recording will be all the more important, as it will provide you with the essential opportunity to listen to the Spanish spoken in Latin America and to speak it within a controlled framework. You should therefore try to obtain a copy of the recording if you haven't already got one.

Use it or lose it!

Language learning is a bit like jogging – you need to do it regularly for it to be any good! Ideally, you should find a 'study buddy' to work through the course with you. This way you will have someone to try out your Spanish on. And when the going gets tough, you will have someone to chivvy you on until you reach your target.

Understanding authentic Latin American Spanish

Don't expect to be able to understand everything you hear or read straight away. If you listen to Latin American Spanish audio material, or watch a Latin American programme or film, or are able to get newspapers or magazines, you should not get discouraged when you realize how quickly native-speakers speak and how much vocabulary there is still to be learnt. Just concentrate on a small extract – either a video/audio clip or a short article – and work through it till you have mastered it. In this way, you'll find that your command of Spanish increases steadily. Look at the Taking it further section at the back of the book for sources of authentic Spanish.

The structure of this course

The course book contains

- ▶ 13 course units
- ▶ a Test yourself section at the end of each unit
- ▶ a reference section at the back of the book
- ▶ an audio recording (which you really need to have if you are going to get maximum benefit from the course)

The course units

The course units are structured in the following way:

Statement of aims

You will be told what you can expect to learn, both in terms of what you will be able to do in Spanish by the end of the unit, and in terms of the language points you will learn to handle.

Presentation of new language

The language is presented through a series of dialogues, two, or more. These are on the recording and also printed in the book. Some assistance with vocabulary is given before and after each dialogue including, where appropriate, regional variations of words used in the texts. The language is presented in manageable chunks, building carefully on what you have learnt in earlier units. Most dialogues are followed by listening comprehension exercises, and there are transcripts of these exercises at the back of the book.

Key phrases and expressions

Key phrases and expressions used in the dialogues and their English translations are listed in the Key phrases section.

Description of language forms

In the Grammar section you will learn about the forms of the language, thus enabling you to construct your own sentences correctly.

Practice

In this section you will be able to use the language that you have learnt. Some of the activities here require mainly recognition, but you are also encouraged, right from the start, to produce both in writing and in speech, following specific guidelines and models.

Information on Latin American Spanish and aspects of life and customs

At different stages in the course, you will find relevant information on language differences among the various countries, and about aspects of life and customs in Latin America. This information is given in English.

Insights

To help you get to grips with the new language and with the activities in the practise section, you will find, at various points in the unit, insights on how to deal with specific points as well as suggestions for further practice.

Test yourself

The aim of this section is for you to test yourself and judge whether you have successfully mastered the language in the unit.

Reference section

At the end of the book, there are sections that you can use for reference:

▶ a glossary of grammatical terms
▶ a grammar summary
▶ a list of irregular verbs
▶ a glossary of Latin American terms
▶ a pronunciation section
▶ transcripts of listening comprehension exercises
▶ a key to the activities and 'Test yourself'
▶ a Spanish–English vocabulary
▶ an English–Spanish vocabulary

▶ a 'taking it further' section
▶ an index of the grammar contents

How to use this course

Make sure at the beginning of each course unit that you are clear about what you can expect to learn.

Dialogues

Read the background information which is given before each dialogue. This sets the scene and the country. There are units based in Mexico (Units 1–4), Colombia (Units 5 and 6), Chile (Units 7–9), Argentina (Units 10 and 11) and Peru (Units 12 and 13). You will find information on the main pronunciation features in each of these countries in the Pronunciation section in the back of the book.

Read, or preferably listen to the dialogue first, before you look at the text, noting the new language forms and vocabulary. You can then check the key words and expressions which follow the dialogue before you read or listen to it again. Do this several times until you feel confident with it, then turn to the accompanying exercise to test what you have learnt. You will find the answers in the **Key to the activities**. If you need an explanation of new language points at this stage, study the relevant paragraphs in the **Grammar** section.

When you listen to the recording, pay special attention to the pronunciation and intonation of the native speakers and try to imitate them. Don't be content with just listening. Spanish may sound fast to you at first, but as you progress through the course you will find it easier to follow the speakers and imitate their speech.

Key phrases

Try learning the key phrases, as these constitute the substance of the unit. You can cover up the English translations and produce the English equivalents of the Spanish. If you find that relatively easy, go on to cover the Spanish sentences and produce the Spanish equivalents of the English. You will probably find this more difficult. Trying to recall the context in which words and phrases were used may help you learn them better.

Grammar

Here the grammatical content of the unit is explained in English and illustrated by means of examples, all with their English translation. The explanations are simple, but if you are daunted by grammar terminology, you can check the **Glossary of grammatical terms** to check the meaning of certain words.

In the **Grammar** section you will learn all major grammatical points, including all main tenses, from the frequently used present tense to the future and past tenses. You will also become familiar with the main grammatical differences between Latin American and Peninsular Spanish. Study the language points and note how they are used in the introductory dialogues as well as in the Practice exercises which follow.

Practice

Most of the exercises here are communicative in nature, requiring you to take an active part in them. Work through each one following the instructions that precede them. Some of them are listen-only activities and are there to help you increase your capacity to understand different forms of spoken Latin American Spanish. The temptation may be to go straight to the **Transcripts** in the back of the book, but try not to do this. The whole point of listening exercises is to improve your listening skills. You won't do this by reading first. The transcriptions are there to help you if you get stuck, or used as reading practice only if you do not have access to the recording. The recordings, many of which are authentic interviews, offer a good opportunity to hear speakers from different parts of Latin America.

As you work your way through the exercises, check your answers carefully in the **Key to the activities** at the back of the book. It is easy to overlook your own mistakes. If you have a study buddy it's a good idea to check each other's answers. Most of the activities have fixed answers, but some are a bit more open-ended.

Insights

Read the insights which you will find in the different sections of each unit, as these may help you to clarify some key language points as well as give you guidance on important cultural matters.

Test yourself

Work through the tests that you will find at the end of each unit and check your answers in the **Key to Test yourself**. If most of your answers are correct go on to the next unit, otherwise check the relevant sections in the unit again or your grammar book if you have one. Repeat the test again or do similar exercises until you feel confident that you have learnt the points that are being assessed.

Abbreviations used in this book

m = masculine, f = feminine; sing = singular, pl = plural; fam = familiar (or informal), pol = polite (or formal); lit = literally; Arg = Argentina; Mex = Mexico, QV = quick vocabulary, para. = paragraph.

México

Cuba

República Dominicana

Puerto Rico

Honduras

Guatemala

Panamá

El Salvador

Nicaragua

Venezuela

Costa Rica

Colombia

Ecuador

Perú

Brasil

Bolivia

Paraguay

Chile

Argentina

Uruguay

1

¿Cuál es su nombre?
What is your name?

In this unit you will learn
- *How to use simple greetings*
- *How to introduce yourself*
- *How to ask and give personal information*

1 En un hotel *At a hotel*

A tourist arrives at a hotel in Guadalajara, Mexico. Note the word
tengo *I have*, and the phrase **¿Cuál es su nombre?** *What is your
name?*, a formal way of asking someone's name.

Turista	Buenas noches.
Recepcionista	Buenas noches, señora. ¿Qué desea?
Turista	Tengo una reservación.
Recepcionista	¿Cuál es su nombre, por favor?
Turista	Ana González.
Recepcionista	Ah sí, es la habitación número quince.

Insight

'**Buenas noches**' means *'good night'*, literally *'good nights'*, but it can also stand for *'good evening'*, as in the dialogue above. '**Una**' is the word for *'a'*, and '**la**' means *'the'*, when used before a feminine word (see paragraphs 1 and 2 of Grammar): '**una reservación/reserva**' *'a reservation'*, '**la habitación**' *'the room'*. Before a masculine word use '**un**' or '**el**': '**un/el número**' *'a/the number'*.

¿qué desea? *can I help you?*
por favor *please*
quince *fifteen*

Formal or polite forms of address: señora, señorita, señor

Señora *Mrs, madam,* is used for addressing older and married women. A younger and unmarried woman will be addressed as señorita, *Miss.* These two words are used with the first name, the surname or the full name, e.g. señora María (Miranda). Señor *Mr, Sir,* used for addressing men, can only be used with the surname or the full name, not with the first name, e.g. señor (Gonzalo) Palma. In writing, señora, señorita and señor are normally abbreviated Sra., Srta., Sr., respectively. Generally speaking in Latin America, strangers and people providing services tend to use these words more often than in Spain, for example sí/no, señor/a *yes/no, sir/madam.*

2 En el bar *In the bar*

In the hotel bar, a man is looking for someone he has not met
before. Key phrases here are **¿es usted ...?** *are you?*, **soy** *I am*, **yo no
soy** *I am not*.

CD1, TR 1, 01:31

Señor	Buenos días, señorita.
Señorita	Buenos días.
Señor	¿Es usted la señorita Carmen Robles?
Señorita	No, yo no soy Carmen Robles. Soy Gloria Santos.
Señor	Disculpe.
Señorita	No se preocupe.

Insight

'**Buenos días**', used for saying *'good morning'*, means literally
'good days'. In some places (Argentina, Uruguay) you'll hear
'**buen día**' instead. Both expressions are sometimes used with
the word '**adiós**' for saying good bye: '**Adiós, buenos días**'
'Good bye, have a good morning/day'.

disculpe *I am sorry*
no se preocupe *that's all right (lit. don't worry)*

QV

Insight
La señorita, la señora, el señor

In indirect address, **señorita**, **señora** and **señor** are preceded
by the Spanish equivalent of *the*: **la** for feminine, **el** for
masculine, e.g. **¿Es usted la señorita Carmen Robles?** *Are you
Miss Carmen Robles?* **El** and **la** are not used in direct address,
for example greetings, e.g. **Buenos días, señorita.**

3 Mucho gusto *Pleased to meet you*

Señor Peña, a Chilean businessman, meets señor Palma, from Mexico.

CD1, TR 1, 02:03

Señor Peña	Buenas tardes. ¿Usted es el señor Gonzalo Palma?
Señor Palma	Sí, soy yo.
Señor Peña	Yo soy Luis Peña, de Chile.
Señor Palma	Encantado, señor Peña.
Señor Peña	Mucho gusto.
Señor Palma	Siéntese, por favor.
Señor Peña	Gracias.

Insight

Use '**encantado**' *'how do you do?/pleased to meet you'* if you are a man, and '**encantada**' if you are a woman. The alternative expression '**mucho gusto**' is used in the same way but it is invariable.

QUICK VOCAB

buenas tardes *good afternoon*
¿usted es ... ? *are you ... ?*
soy yo *it's me*
siéntese *sit down*
gracias *thank you*

Insight
Hand-shaking

In a situation like the one in the dialogue, people will normally shake hands. Hand-shaking is much more frequent in Latin America than in English-speaking countries. Even old friends and relatives will sometimes shake hands when meeting or leaving.

4 ¿Cómo se llama usted? *What is your name?*

Mónica Lagos and Raúl Molina, both from Mexico, meet at a conference and introduce themselves. Note the way in which they ask each other where they come from: **¿De dónde es usted?** *Where are you from?*, **Y usted, ¿de dónde es?** *And you? Where are you from?*

Señor Molina	Disculpe, ¿cómo se llama usted?
Señora Lagos	Me llamo Mónica Lagos. ¿Y usted?
Señor Molina	Mi nombre es Raúl Molina.
Señora Lagos	Encantada.
Señor Molina	Mucho gusto, señora.
Señora Lagos	¿De dónde es usted?
Señor Molina	Soy de Monterrey. Y usted, ¿de dónde es?
Señora Lagos	Yo soy de Puebla.

🔊 CD1, TR 1, 03:14

Insight

In Dialogue 2 above, **'disculpe'** was used to mean '*I'm sorry*'. In this dialogue it means '*excuse me*'. To ask someone's name formally use '**¿Cómo se llama usted'** (literally, '*What are you called? or What do you call yourself?*') or, as in Dialogue 1 above, '**¿Cuál es su nombre?**', both meaning '*What's your name?*'. In both cases the reply may be 'Me llamo ...' (literally, '*I'm called/I call myself*') or '**Mi nombre es ...**', '*My name is ...*'.

¿dónde? *where?*
(yo) soy de ... *I am from ...*

QV

Say it in Spanish

At a party in a Spanish-speaking country you meet someone. How would you answer these questions?:

a ¿Cómo se llama usted?   **b** ¿De dónde es usted?

5 ¿Cómo te llamas? *What is your name?*

All the people in the previous dialogues have used formal forms of address. **Usted,** *you,* is used to address a person formally. In this dialogue you will learn the familiar form of address, corresponding to **tú,** the familiar word for *you.* Observe the way in which Mark and Nora, two young people, address each other.

Nora	¿Cómo te llamas?
Mark	Me llamo Mark, ¿y tú?
Nora	Me llamo Nora. ¿De dónde eres?
Mark	Soy inglés, soy de Londres. Tú eres mexicana, ¿verdad?
Nora	Sí, soy mexicana, soy de Jalapa.

Insight

'**¿Cómo te llamas?**' is the familiar form for asking someone's name. An alternative familiar form you may also hear is '**¿Cuál es tu nombre?**', in which '**tu**' is the familiar word for '*your*', the formal equivalent being '**su**' (as in '**¿Cuál es su nombre?**', in Dialogue 1).

¿de dónde eres? *where are you from? (fam)*
inglés / inglesa *English (man/woman)*
tú eres ... ¿verdad? *you are ..., aren't you? (fam)*

Say it in Spanish

What questions would you ask to get these replies?
Use the familiar form.

a Me llamo Antonio García.
b Soy argentino. Soy de Buenos Aires.

6 Somos mexicanos *We are Mexican*

A Mexican couple meet a couple from Colombia. Key words and phrases here are **ustedes son** *you are*, and **somos** *we are*.

Colombiano	Ustedes son mexicanos, ¿no?	⌢ CD1, TR 1, 03:53
Mexicano	Sí, somos mexicanos. ¿Y ustedes?	
Colombiano	Somos colombianos.	
Mexicano	¿Y de qué parte de Colombia son?	
Colombiano	Somos de Bogotá.	

ustedes *you (pol, plural)*
¿y de qué parte de ...? *and what part of ...?*

QV

Key phrases

Greetings

Buenos días.	*Good morning.*
Buenas tardes.	*Good afternoon.*
Buenas noches.	*Good evening / night.*

Introducing yourself and exchanging greetings with people
you meet

Soy ...	*I am (name)*
Me llamo ... / Mi nombre es ...	*My name is ...*
Mucho gusto *(invariable).*	*Pleased to meet you.*
Encantado	*(if you are a man).*
Encantada	*(if you are a woman)*

Asking for personal information

¿Cómo se llama usted/te llamas?	*What's your name? (pol./fam.)*
¿Es usted ...? /¿Tú eres ...?	*Are you ...? (pol./fam.)*
¿De dónde es usted/eres tú?	*Where are you from? (pol./fam.)*
¿Es usted (mexicano/a)?	*Are you Mexican? (man/woman)*

Giving personal information

Me llamo (Pablo)/Mi nombre es (Eva).	*My name is (Pablo/Eva).*
Soy (John/Anne).	*I'm (John/Anne).*
Soy (inglés/inglesa).	*I'm (English). (man/woman)*
Soy de (Inglaterra/Londres).	*I'm from (England/London).*
Somos (americanos, de Nueva York).	*We're (American/from New York).*

Grammar

1 *Definite article: el, la the (sing)*

All nouns (words that name things or people) in Spanish are either
masculine (m) or feminine (f) and the word for *the* is **el** for singular
masculine nouns and **la** for singular feminine nouns.

el hotel *the hotel*   **la** habitación *the room*

2 *Indefinite article: Un, una a/an*

The word for *a* is **un** for masculine nouns and **una** for feminine nouns.

un hotel *a hotel*   una habitación *a room*

3 *Gender of nouns: masculine or feminine?*

Nouns ending in -**o** are usually masculine while nouns ending in -**a** are normally feminine:

el número *the number*   la visita *the visitor*

But there are many exceptions to the above rule, e.g. **el día** *the day*, **la mano** *the hand*, and there are many nouns which do not end in -**o** or -**a**, so it is advisable to learn each word with its corresponding article, **el** or **la** *the*, for example:

el nombre *the name*   **la tarde** *the afternoon*
el bar *the bar*   **la noche** *the evening / night*

Nouns which refer to people will normally agree in gender (masculine or feminine) with the person referred to, and to form the feminine of such nouns you may find it useful to remember these simple rules:

▶ Change the -**o** to -**a**.

   el mexicano (m) *the Mexican*   la mexicana (f) *the Mexican*

▶ Add -**a** to the consonant.

   el señor (m) *the gentleman*   la señora (f) *the lady*

▶ But if the noun ends in -**ista**, the ending remains the same for masculine or feminine.

   el recepcionista (m) / la recepcionista (f) *receptionist*

* Nouns ending in -e are mostly invariable.

el estudiante (m)/la estudiante (f) *student*

but

el jefe (m)/la jefa (f) *boss, manager*

4 Adjectives denoting origin, nationality or region

Adjectives are words which serve to qualify a person or a thing, for example a Mexican man, a good hotel. Adjectives of nationality, like many adjectives in Spanish, have masculine and feminine forms. To form the feminine from a masculine adjective of nationality or origin change the -o to -a or add -a to the consonant.

Masculine	Feminine
un señor mexicano	una señora mexicana
a Mexican gentleman	*a Mexican lady*
un turista inglés	una turista inglesa
an English tourist	*an English tourist*

Those adjectives which end in -a, -e, -í remain unchanged: 'un/una croata' 'a Croatian (man/woman)'; 'un/a inca' 'an Inca (man/woman)'; 'un/una árabe' 'an Arab (man/woman)', 'un/una estadounidense' 'a man/woman from the United States' ('los Estados Unidos'); 'un/a pakistaní/paquistaní' 'a Pakistani (man/woman)', 'un/a marroquí' 'a Moroccan (man/woman)'.

Other nationalities (m/f forms)

argentino/a	*Argentinian*
británico/a	*British*
colombiano/a	*Colombian*
cubano/a	*Cuban*
chileno/a	*Chilean*
escocés/escocesa	*Scottish*
galés/galesa	*Welsh*

inglés/inglesa	*English*
irlandés/irlandesa	*Irish*
norteamericano/a	*American*
(*also* **americano/a, estadounidense**)	
peruano/a	*Peruvian*
venezolano/a	*Venezuelan*

Note that adjectives of nationality in Spanish are written with small letters.

5 Subject pronouns: Yo, tú, él ... I, you, he ...

To say *I*, *you*, *he*, *she*, etc., use the following set of words, which are called *subject pronouns*:

Singular	
yo	*I*
tú	*you* (fam)
usted	*you* (pol)
él	*he*
ella	*she*

Plural	
nosotros/as	*we* (m/f)
ustedes	*you* (pl)
ellos	*they* (m)
ellas	*they* (f)

The main difference between Peninsular and Latin American Spanish is that the latter does not use the familiar plural form **vosotros/as** (*you*). Latin Americans use the plural form **ustedes** in familiar and formal address. In writing, **usted** and **ustedes** are normally found in abbreviated form as **Ud.** and **Uds.** or **Vd.** and **Vds.**

The feminine subject pronoun **nosotras** is used when all the people involved are women. If there are people of both sexes, you need to use the masculine form **nosotros**.

Generally, subject pronouns are omitted in Spanish, except for
emphasis or to avoid the ambiguity that may arise with **él, ella,
usted,** and the plural forms **ellos, ellas, ustedes,** which share the
same verb forms. Consider for example:

Es artista.   *He/she is an artist or You are an artist.*

If the context does not make it clear whether you are referring
to *he, she, or you,* you need to use the corresponding subject
pronoun, e.g. **Ella** es artista, *She's an artist.*

In the examples which follow the verb form is sufficient to indicate
the person you are referring to, and you would only use a subject
pronoun for emphasis or to establish some sort of contrast with
something said before.

Soy inglés	*I'm English.*
Yo soy chileno.	*I'm Chilean.*
Somos de Londres.	*We're from London.*
Nosotros somos de Santiago.	*We're from Santiago.*

6 Ser to be

Basic personal information, such as name, place of origin,
nationality, can be given with the verb **ser** (*to be*).

Soy Gonzalo Palma.	*I am Gonzalo Palma.*
Soy de Monterrey.	*I am from Monterrey.*
Soy mexicano.	*I am Mexican.*

The present tense forms of **ser** are as follows:

yo soy	*I am*
tú eres	*you are* (fam)
usted es	*you are* (pol)
él, ella es	*he, she is*

nosotros/as somos	*we are*
ustedes son	*you are* (pl)
ellos, ellas son	*they are* (m/f)

To say *it is*, as in *It is a hotel*, use the word **es** on its own: **Es un hotel.**

7 Negative and interrogative sentences

Negative sentences are formed by placing **no** before the verb:

Soy británico.	*I am British.*
No soy irlandés.	*I am not Irish.*

Interrogative sentences can be formed in three ways:

a By reversing the word order in the sentence.

Usted es boliviano.	*You are Bolivian.*
¿Es usted boliviano?	*Are you Bolivian?*

b By using the same word order as for a statement, but with a rising intonation.

¿Usted es ecuatoriana?	*Are you Ecuadorean?*

c By using the word **¿verdad?** (Lit. *true*) or the word **¿no?** at the end of the statement.

Tú eres uruguayo, ¿verdad?	*You are Uruguayan, aren't you?*
Ella es cubana, ¿no?	*She is Cuban, isn't she?*

Note that in writing, interrogative sentences carry two question marks, one at the beginning and one at the end of the sentence.

8 Written accent on question words

Note that question words such as **¿dónde?** *where?*, **¿cuál?** *what?*, *which?* carry a written accent.

9 Numbers

0	cero	21	veintiuno
1	uno	22	veintidós
2	dos	23	veintitrés
3	tres	24	venticuatro
4	cuatro	25	veinticinco
5	cinco	26	veintiséis
6	seis	27	veintisiete
7	siete	28	veintiocho
8	ocho	29	veintinueve
9	nueve	30	treinta
10	diez	31	treinta y uno
11	once	32	treinta y dos
12	doce	40	cuarenta
13	trece	45	cuarenta y cinco
14	catorce	50	cincuenta
15	quince		
16	dieciséis		
17	diecisiete		
18	dieciocho		
19	diecinueve		
20	veinte		

Before a masculine noun **uno** becomes **un** and before a feminine
noun **una**:

un señor   *one man*
una señora   *one woman*

Note that numbers from 21 to 29 are written as a single word in
Spanish.

Practice

1 It is early morning and you arrive in a hotel in Mexico
where there is a room booked in your name. Use the guidelines in
English to complete this conversation with the hotel receptionist.

Usted	*Say good morning.*
Recepcionista	Buenos días. A sus órdenes.
Usted	*Say you have a reservation.*
Recepcionista	¿Cuál es su nombre, por favor?
Usted	*Give your name.*
Recepcionista	Sí, es la habitación número veinte.
Usted	*Say thank you.*

2 You are in the bar waiting to meet señora Vargas, whom you
have not met before, when a gentleman approaches you. He has
obviously mistaken you for someone else. Use the guidelines to
complete your part of the conversation.

Señor	Buenas tardes.
Usted	*Say good afternoon.*
Señor	¿Es usted Emilio/a Zapata?
Usted	*No, say you are not Emilio/a Zapata. Say who you are.*
Señor	Disculpe.
Usted	*Say that is all right.*

3 Here comes the person you think you are expecting.

Señora Vargas	Disculpe, ¿cuál es su nombre?
Usted	*Say your name and where you are from.*
Señora Vargas	Yo soy Isabel Vargas, de Veracruz.
Usted	*Say pleased to meet you.*
Señora Vargas	Encantada.
Usted	*Ask señora Vargas to sit down.*
Señora Vargas	Gracias.

4 Here is an informal situation. You are at a party when a stranger approaches you and starts a conversation. Reply accordingly.

Desconocido/a	*Disculpa, ¿eres americano/a?*
Usted	…
Desconocido/a	¡Ah! ¿Y de qué ciudad eres?
Usted	…
Desconocido/a	¿Cómo te llamas?
Usted	…
Desconocido/a	Me llamo Mario.
Usted	…
Desconocido/a	El gusto es mío.

el gusto es mío

la ciudad city
desconocido/a stranger
el gusto es mío the pleasure is mine
a sus órdenes can I help you? (alternative to '**¿Qué desea?**')

5 You are on your first visit to Latin America and you want to meet people, so be prepared to use greetings and ask some simple questions to make the first contacts. How would you say the following in Spanish? (Use the polite form.)

    a Good afternoon.
    b What is your name?
    c Where are you from?
    d Are you Mexican?
    e What part of Mexico are you from?

6 Read the sentence here written
by Roberto Vera about himself, and then
write a similar line about yourself.

*Mi nombre es
Roberto Vera, soy
colombiano, de Bogotá.*

7 Read this form with information about Ana González, and the
line which follows.

Nombre:	Ana María
Apellidos:	González Ríos
Nacionalidad:	mexicana
Dirección:	calle Juárez 34, Monterrey

Ana María González Ríos es mexicana. Ana María es de
Monterrey.

Use the information in this box to write a similar statement about
Pablo Miranda Frías.

Nombre:	Pablo
Apellidos:	Miranda Frías
Nacionalidad:	venezolano
Dirección:	calle Bolívar 65, Caracas

el apellido *surname*
la nacionalidad *nationality*
la dirección *address*

Surnames
In Spain and in the Spanish-speaking countries of Latin America,
people have two surnames. The first surname is that of their father,
the second is their mother's. In Ana María's case above, for example,
González is her father's first surname and **Ríos** is her mother's first
surname. The second surname is used in more formal and official
situations. Married women add their husband's first surname,
preceded by the word **de** (*of*), to their own name or first surname.
For example, if Ana María marries a señor Barros, she will be called
Ana María de Barros or Ana María González de Barros.

8 Here are two recorded interviews with Mexican women and a brief introduction by someone from Panama. If you are using the recording, listen to each piece as many times as you want until you are confident that you understand what is being said. Then listen again, and as you do so, try to answer the questions below. If you are not using the recording, read the transcripts in the end of the book, then answer the questions. First study these new words:

el país   *country*   **para servirle**   *at your service*

    a What part of Mexico is Initia Muñoz García from?
    b What sentence has been used to express the following: *What country are you from?*
    c What part of Mexico is Clotilde Montalvo Rodríguez from?
    d What sentence has been used to express the following: *Where are you from?*
    e What city is Elizabeth from?
    f How does she express the following: My name is Elizabeth?

Test yourself

    1 Fill in the blanks with the missing verbs.
      a ¿Usted ____ el señor Antonio Pérez?
      b Tú ____ Carmen Díaz, ¿verdad?
      c Yo me ____ Teresa Rodríguez, ¿y usted?
      d Ustedes ____ cubanos, ¿no?
      e Nosotros ____ de La Habana.

    2 How would you express the following in Spanish?
      a I have a reservation.
      b What's your name? (formal, give two alternatives)
      c Where are you from? (formal)

d I'm from Santiago.

e Pleased to meet you (give two alternatives)

Test one focuses mainly on the use of **'ser'** *'to be'*, a verb which you will find in a number of other contexts, so it is important that you get it right from the start. Check your answers to both tests in the Key to test yourself before you decide whether you need some further study or are ready to go on to Unit 2, in which you will learn to ask for and give simple directions.

2

¿Dónde está?
Where is it?

In this unit you will learn
- *How to ask and say where places are*
- *How to ask and answer questions regarding the existence of something*
- *How to ask people how they are and say how you are*

---

1 En la recepción *In reception*

Carmen, a Mexican, has come to see her friend Gloria Martín at her hotel in Mexico City. Gloria is from Colombia. Key phrases here are **¿cuál es ...?** *which is ...?* and **está en ...** *she is in ...*

CD1, TR 2, 00:47

Carmen	Buenos días. ¿Cuál es la habitación de la señorita Gloria Martín, por favor?
Recepcionista	Un momentito. (*Looking at the register.*) La señorita Martín está en la habitación número cincuenta, en el quinto piso. Allí está el elevador.
Carmen	Gracias. Muy amable.

Insight

Note that '**¿cuál es ...?**' can mean '*what is ...?*' ('**¿Cuál es su nombre?**' '*What's your name?*') or '*which is ...?*' ('**¿Cuál es su habitación?**' '*Which is your room?*'). Observe also the use of '**estar**' which, like '**ser**' (Unit 1, Grammar paragraph 6), translates '*to be*', used here to express location (see paragraph 4a of Grammar).

un momentito *just a moment* (*diminutive from* '**un momento**')
el piso *floor*
quinto/a *fifth*
allí (*over*) *there*
el elevador / ascensor *lift*
muy amable *that's very kind*

QUICK VOCAB

---

2 En la habitación número cincuenta *In room fifty*

Gloria greets her friend Carmen. Key phrases here are **¿Cómo estás?** *How are you?*, **¿Cómo están?** *How are they?*, **Estoy bien** *I'm fine* (lit. *well*), **Están muy bien** *They are very well*.

Gloria	Hola, Carmen. ¿Cómo estás?
Carmen	Estoy bien, gracias. ¿Y tú, cómo estás?
Gloria	Muy bien. Siéntate. Me alegro mucho de verte otra vez.
Carmen	Yo también.
Gloria	¿Cómo están tus papás?
Carmen	Están muy bien.

CD1, TR 2, 01:14

QUICK VOCAB

hola *hello*
siéntate *sit down (fam)*
me alegro mucho de verte *I am very glad to see you (fam)*
otra vez *again*
también *too, also*
tus *your (fam, pl)*

---

3 ¿Dónde está la oficina? *Where is the office?*

Señor Alonso, a Colombian, has come to see señor Martínez, a Mexican businessman, at his office in Mexico City. A key phrase here is **¿dónde está ...?** *where is ...?*

Señor Alonso	Buenas tardes. ¿Dónde está la oficina del señor Martínez, por favor?
Recepcionista	La oficina del señor Martínez está al final del pasillo, a la izquierda.
Señor Alonso	Gracias.
Recepcionista	De nada.

> ## Insight
>
> **'Del'**, as in **'del señor ...'**, is the contraction of **'de'** + **'el'**; **'al'**, as in **'al final ...'** is the contraction of **'a'** + **'el'**.

What phrase has been used in the dialogue to say *Señor Martínez's office?*

la oficina *office*
al final de *at the end of*
el pasillo *corridor*
a la izquierda *on the left*
de nada *don't mention it*

---

4 En la oficina del señor Martínez *In señor Martínez's office*

Señor Martínez greets señor Alonso. Note here the formal greetings ¿Cómo le va?, ¿Cómo está? *How are you?*

Señor Martínez	¡Señor Alonso, buenas tardes!
Señor Alonso	Buenas tardes, señor Martínez.
Señor Martínez	Siéntese, por favor. Me alegro mucho de verlo. ¿Cómo le va?
Señor Alonso	Bien, gracias. ¿Y usted, cómo está?
Señor Martínez	Muy bien, gracias.

What expression does señor Martínez use to say *How are you?*

me alegro mucho de verlo *I am very glad to see you (pol)* QV

Insight

The familiar equivalent of the phrase above is **'me alegro mucho de verte'**, in which **'te'** *'you'* (fam), like **'lo'** *'you'* (pol), is attached to the verb.

---

5 Está a dos cuadras de aquí *It is two blocks from here*

At the hotel Las Américas (n° 2 on the map), a Mexican visitor asks the receptionist if there is an underground station, **una estación**

de metro, nearby, **por aquí**. A key word in this dialogue is **hay**, meaning *there is, is there?* or *there are, are there?*

Señorita	Buenas tardes.
Recepcionista	Buenas tardes, señorita. A sus órdenes.
Señorita	¿Hay una estación de metro por aquí?
Recepcionista	Sí, hay una, la estación de Cuauhtemoc. Está a dos cuadras de aquí, a la derecha, cerca del monumento a Cuauhtemoc.
Señorita	Muchas gracias. Muy amable.
Recepcionista	Para servirle. ¡Que le vaya bien!

Insight

The word **'cuadra'** is used in Latin America to mean *'block'*. To say how many blocks away, or how far a place is, use the word **'a'** followed by the distance: **'está a cinco cuadras de aquí'** *'it's five blocks from here'*, **'está a una hora de Buenos Aires'** *'it's an hour away from Buenos Aires'*.

a sus órdenes *may I help you?*
a la derecha *on the right*
muy amable *very kind*
cerca *near*
para servirle *don't mention it*
¡que le vaya bien! *have a nice day!*

Say it in Spanish

How would you say the following in Spanish? Study the dialogue again if necessary.

a Is there a bureau de change (**una casa de cambio**) nearby?
b Is there a bank (**un banco**) nearby?
c It is three blocks from here, on the left.
d It is four blocks from here, on the right.

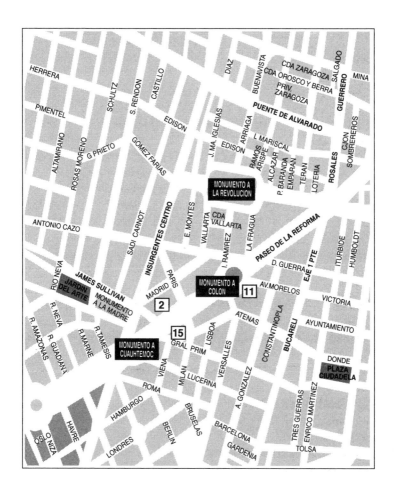

Insight

Notice the use of phrases such as **a sus órdenes, para servirle** lit. *at your service*, and **¡Que le vaya bien!** *Have a nice day!* Latin Americans, on the whole, and Mexicans in particular, are very polite, and you will encounter many such phrases when meeting Latin American people.

Key phrases

Asking and saying where places are

¿Dónde está la oficina / la habitación?	*Where is the office / room?*
Está al final del pasillo.	*It is at the end of the corridor.*
Está en el quinto piso.	*It is on the fifth floor.*
Está a la derecha / izquierda.	*It is on the right/left.*
Está a cinco cuadras / minutos de aquí.	*It is five blocks / minutes from here.*

Asking and answering questions regarding the existence of something

¿Hay una estación/un banco por aquí?	*Is there a station / bank nearby?*
Hay una/uno cerca de aquí.	*There is one near here.*

Asking people how they are and saying how you are

¿Cómo estás/está? *(fam/pol)*	*How are you?*
¿Cómo te / le va? *(fam/pol)*	
Estoy (muy) bien.	*I am fine / (very) well.*
¿Cómo están tus papás / padres?	*How are your parents?*
Están (muy) bien.	*They are (very) well.*

Grammar

1 *Definite article: los, las the (pl), and the plural of nouns*

a In Unit 1 you learnt the use of **el** and **la** *the* (m / f), with singular nouns. With plural nouns, you use **los** for masculine and **las** for feminine.

| el señor | *the gentleman* | los señores | *the gentlemen* |
| la señora | *the lady* | las señoras | *the ladies* |

b Most nouns form the plural by adding –s.

| el nombre | *the name* | los nombres | *the names* |
| la oficina | *the office* | las oficinas | *the offices* |

c Nouns ending in a consonant add **–es.**

| el hotel | *the hotel* | los hoteles | *the hotels* |
| la habitación | *the room* | las habitaciones | *the rooms* |

(See **Pronunciation** for notes on **Stress and accentuation**)

d Masculine nouns which refer to people may refer to both sexes in the plural.

el padre	*father*	los padres	*parents*
el hermano	*brother*	los hermanos	*brothers* or *brothers and sisters*
el hijo	*son*	los hijos	*sons* or *children* (sons and daughters)
el chico	*boy*	los chicos	*boys* or *children*

Insight

Nouns used in a general sense, just like those denoting something or someone unique or specific, must be preceded by the definite article in Spanish. Compare the following sentences: '**Las llaves están en la mesa**' *'The keys are on the table'*, '**Los hoteles son muy caros aquí**' *'Hotels are very expensive here'*.

2 Indefinite article: unos, unas some (pl)

The plural of '**un**' '*a*' (m) is '**unos**' and that of '**una**' '*a*' (f) is '**unas**'. Both translate '*some*'.

un hombre	a man
unos hombres	some men
una mujer	a woman
unas mujeres	some women

3 Del (de + el), al (a + el)

In the spoken and written language, **de + el** becomes **del** and **a + el** becomes **al**.

la casa **del** señor García	*señor García's house*
al final del pasillo	*at the end of the corridor*
al museo	*to the museum*

4 Estar to be

In Unit 1 you learnt the use of **ser** *to be,* to give personal information such as nationality, and place of origin, for example **Soy argentino, soy de Buenos Aires** *I'm Argentinian, I'm from Buenos Aires.* But Spanish has another verb meaning *to be*, which is **estar.** Try learning each use separately to avoid mixing them up. The notes below explain two main uses of **estar.**

a Using **estar** to express location and distance

Location and distance are normally expressed with **estar**

| El elevador / ascensor **está** allí. | *The lift is there.* |
| **Está** a dos cuadras de aquí. | *It is two blocks from here.* |

a Using **estar** to refer to a state or condition

To ask and answer questions about a state or condition, for example someone's health, use **estar.**

| **¿Cómo estás (tú)/está (usted)?** | *How are you?* |
| **Estoy bien, gracias.** | *I'm fine, thank you.* |

'**Estar**' and '**ser**' are two very important verbs in Spanish and they have a number of other uses, some of which will be dealt with in later units. A summary of their main uses will be found in the Grammar summary in the back of the book.

5 *The present tense of estar*

The following are the present tense forms of **estar**.

yo estoy	*I am*
tú estás	*you are* (fam, sing)
usted está	*you are* (pol, sing)
él, ella está	*he, she, it is*
nosotros/as estamos	*we are* (m/f)
ustedes están	*you are* (pl)
ellos/as están	*they are* (m/f)

Consider again the uses of **estar** in the dialogues and look at the examples listed under **Key phrases**.

6 *Hay there is, there are*

To say *there is* or *there are* and to ask questions regarding the existence of something, Spanish uses the single word hay, from the auxiliary verb **haber**.

¿**Hay** una estación de metro por aquí?	*Is there an underground station nearby?*
Sí, **hay** una.	*Yes, there is one.*
¿**Hay** habitaciones?	*Are there any rooms?*
No **hay**.	*There aren't any.*

The question '*where is ...?*', as in '*Where's a telephone?*' translates in Spanish as '¿**dónde hay ...?**', '¿**Dónde hay un teléfono?**'

7 Diminutives

Diminutives are very frequently used in Latin America, and you will need to recognize them when you hear them. Their main function is to give a more friendly tone to words or statements. Diminutives are usually formed with **-ito** (m) or **-ita** (f) added to the word, after removing the final **-o** or **-a**:

un rato – un ra**tito**	*a while*
ahora – ahor**ita**	*now, straight away*

(very frequent in Mexico and other countries)

Words ending in **-e** usually add **-cito** (m) or **-cita** (f):

un café – un cafe**cito**	*a coffee*
una calle – una calle**cita**	*a street*

Words ending in **-co** or **-ca** change **-c** into **-qu** and add **-ito** (m) or **-ita**:

un poco – un po**quito**	*a little*
la boca – la bo**quita**	*the mouth*

In some regions of Latin America you will hear the endings **-ico** or **-ica** instead of **-ito** and **-ita**, for example:

un momento – un momen**tico**	*moment*

8 Numbers

50	cincuenta	300	trescientos
60	sesenta	400	cuatrocientos
70	setenta	500	quinientos
80	ochenta	600	seiscientos
90	noventa	700	setecientos
100	cien	800	ochocientos

101	ciento uno	900	novecientos
200	doscientos	1000	mil
210	doscientos diez	1501	mil quinientos uno
		2000	dos mil

1.000.000	un millón
2.000.000	dos millones

Numbers which finish in -**cientos**, e.g. **doscientos, trescientos,** must change according to the gender of the noun which follows:

el peso (Latin Am. currency)	doscien**tos** pesos
la libra (pound)	doscien**tas** libras
el dólar (dollar)	doscien**tos** dólares

Cien (*one hundred*) does not change, e.g. cien pesos.

Note the way in which years are read in Spanish:

1850 mil ochocientos cincuenta
1999 mil novecientos noventa y nueve
2003 dos mil tres
2010 dos mil diez

Ordinal numbers (1st to 6th)

primero/a	**1st**
segundo/a	**2nd**
tercero/a	**3rd**
cuarto/a	**4th**
quinto/a	**5th**
sexto/a	**6th**

Ordinal numbers function as adjectives, therefore they must agree in gender (m/f) and number (s/pl) with the word they refer to, for example **el segundo piso** *the second floor*, **la segunda cuadra** *the second block*, **las primeras cuadras** *the first few blocks*. Before a masculine noun, **primero** changes to **primer**, and **tercero to tercer**, for example **el primer / tercer piso** *the first / third floor*.

Practice

1 A visitor has come to see a hotel guest.

Visita	¿Cuál es la habitación del señor Valdés, por favor?
Recepcionista	El señor Valdés está en la habitación trescientos diez, en el tercer piso.
Visita	Gracias.

Make up similar dialogues using the information below. See unit 1 for numbers from 0 to 50.

NOMBRE	HABITACIÓN	PISO
Sra. Marta Molina	220	2°
Sr. Cristóbal Salas	430	4°
Srta. Rosa Chandía	550	5°

2 On a visit to Mexico, you meet Carmen, a Mexican friend you have not seen for some time. Complete your part of the conversation with her, using the familiar form.

Ud.	*Say hello to your friend and ask her how she is.*
Carmen	Estoy bien, gracias. Y tú, ¿cómo estás?
Ud.	*Say you are very well. Ask her to sit down and say you are very glad to see her again.*
Carmen	Yo también.
Ud.	*You have met her parents; ask her how they are.*
Carmen	Están muy bien, gracias.

3 Señora Ramírez, a Latin American businesswoman, is visiting your company. She has come to see you in your office. Complete your part of this conversation with her, using the polite form.

4 Look at this dialogue between a receptionist and a hotel guest in Mexico.

Señor	Disculpe, ¿dónde están los teléfonos, por favor?
Recepcionista	Están al final del pasillo, a la izquierda, al lado del bar.
Señor	Gracias.
Recepcionista	Para servirle.

Now look at the plan of a hotel and make up similar dialogues. Choose appropriate words and phrases from the dialogue and from those listed below.

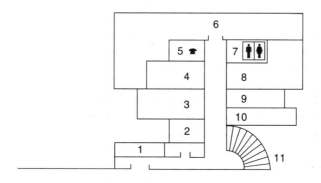

al lado de ... *next to* ...
a la derecha *on the right*
entre ... **y** ... *between* ... *and* ...
frente a ... *opposite* ...
pasado el / la ... *past the* ...
antes de ... *before* ...

QUICK VOCAB

KEY:

1 La recepción *reception*
2 El elevador/el ascensor *lift*
3 La agencia de viajes *travel agency*
4 El bar *bar*
5 Los teléfonos *telephones*
6 El comedor *dining-room*
7 Los baños *toilets*
8 El café *café*
9 La peluquería *hairdresser's*
10 La tienda de regalos *gift shop*
11 Las escaleras *stairs*

🔊 **CD1, TR 2, 03:25**

5 You will need to understand what people say to you when you inquire about a place or ask for directions. Listen to these conversations, then check your understanding by answering the questions.

In the first exchange, a man is seeking help from a young lady. Learn this new phrase, then listen to the conversation and answer the questions.

una casa de cambio (f) *bureau de change*

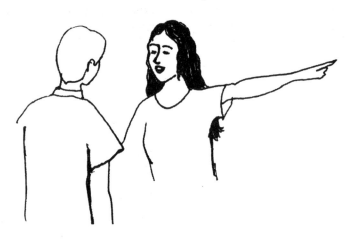

   a What is the man looking for?
   b Where can he find one?
   c How far is it?

In the second exchange, señor Ramos, a Colombian businessman, has come to see señor Silva at his office in Mexico City. Listen to the conversation and answer these questions.

   d Where is señor Silva?
   e What number is his office?
   f On which floor is it?
   g Where exactly is it?

6 You are visiting a Latin American city for the first time and you need to find your way around. What questions would you need to ask to get these replies?

   a Sí, hay una. La estación de Insurgentes.
   b Está a cuatro cuadras de aquí.
   c Sí, hay uno. El Hotel Reforma.
   d No, está cerca. A cinco minutos de aquí.
   e El Banco Nacional está en la plaza.
   f La calle Pánuco está a cinco cuadras de aquí.

Insight

In Spanish, distances are preceded by the preposition '**a**', the equivalent of '*away*' in English: '**a cuatro cuadras**' '*four blocks away*', '**a cinco minutos**' '*five minutes away*'.

el minuto *minute*
el banco *bank*
la calle *street*

7 Now you are going to hear a conversation between a Colombian and a Chilean tourist who is visiting Bogotá, the capital of Colombia. The tourist is looking for the station (**la estación**). Most streets in the centre of Bogotá carry numbers instead of names: streets going in one direction are called **carreras**, those running across are called **calles**. The questions below will help you to check comprehension.

QV

a pie *on foot*
más o menos *more or less*

True or false? ¿Verdadero o falso?

    a La estación está en la calle dieciséis.
    b Está al final de la carrera diecisiete.
    c Está a quince minutos a pie, aproximadamente.

◀) **CD1, TR 2, 04:46**

8 You are going to hear part of a conversation with Jorge Vera, a Mexican from Veracruz. Jorge introduces himself as the director of a modern languages centre. Listen to the conversation or, if you are not using the recording, read the transcript in the back of the book, then answer the questions below. First, familiarize yourself with these key words and then answer the questions below.

QUICK VOCAB

el centro de lenguas modernas *modern languages centre*
localizado *situated*
media cuadra *half a block*
una y media cuadra *one and a half blocks*
es decir *that is to say*
el parque *park*

   a How far is the modern languages centre from the main street?

   b How far is it from the main park?

9 You are planning to travel to Mexico and before you do so you decide to read a little about the country. Below is a description of Mexico City, known also as D.F. (Federal District). The following key words will help you to understand the text. Try to get the gist of it rather than translate it word for word. After you have read the passage answer the questions that follow.

un valle *valley*
tiene *it has*
la vida *life*
el lugar *place*
famoso/a *famous*
como *such as*
amplio/a *wide*
la avenida *avenue*
el barrio *district/neighbourhood*
el edificio *building*
la iglesia *church*
e *and (before 'i')*

QUICK VOCAB

México D.F.

La capital de México está situada en un valle de 2.240 m de altitud. Tiene una intensa vida cultural y artística y es el centro intelectual de Hispanoamérica. Aquí hay lugares históricos como el Zócalo, el Palacio Nacional, la Catedral Metropolitana, la capital azteca de Tenochtitlán o el famoso Museo Nacional de Antropología.

La Ciudad de México tiene 21 millones de habitantes. Es una ciudad moderna, con grandes avenidas y plazas animadas, barrios elegantes, mercados populares, edificios futuristas, residencias coloniales e iglesias barrocas.

Answer these questions in English:

a Where is the capital of Mexico situated?
b What does the text say about the city's cultural and artistic life?
c How does the text describe the city itself?

Insight

A number of words in the previous text are either exactly the same as or very similar to English words: **'capital'**, **'cultural'**, **'intelectual'**, **'situada'**, **'intensa'**, **'artística'**, etc. Can you identify others?

Test yourself

a How would you ask if there is a bureau de change nearby?
b How would you ask where Bolívar Street is?
c How would you ask where the telephones are?
d What does the following mean?: 'Hay uno a dos cuadras de aquí'.

e What does the following mean?: 'Está al final del pasillo, a la izquierda'.

f Your Spanish-speaking friend has just arrived. Say hello and ask her how she is.

g Fill in the missing verb: '(Yo) ____ muy bien, gracias'.

h Fill in the missing verb: '¿Cómo ____ su familia (*family*)?

i Fill in the missing question word: '¿ ____ es la habitación de la señora Miranda?'

j Fill in the missing question word: 'Buenas tardes. ¿ ____ le va?'

If most of your answers to this test were correct it means you are now able to ask and give simple directions and to exchange greetings such as '*hello*', '*how are you?*', '*I'm fine*', etc. If you feel confident with the new language get ready to learn the time and to talk about opening and closing times as well as meal times, which are the main subject of Unit 3.

3

Abren a las ocho
They open at eight

In this unit you will learn
- *How to ask and tell the time*
- *How to talk about opening and closing times*
- *How to talk about meal times*

1 ¿Qué hora es? *What time is it?*

Anne Barker, an English visitor who has just arrived in Mexico, wants to set her watch by the local time. She asks the hotel receptionist what time it is. The key phrase here is **¿Qué hora es?** *What time is it?*

CD1, TR 3, 00:47

Anne Barker	Buenos días.
Recepcionista	Buenos días, señora.
Anne Barker	¿Qué hora es, por favor?
Recepcionista	Son las ocho y media.
Anne Barker	Gracias.
Recepcionista	De nada.

QV

son las ocho y media *it's half past eight*

40

Ask and tell the time

a 2:30
b 6:30
c 10:30
d 11: 45
e 12:00
f 1:15

For other times see Key phrases and paragraph 1 of Grammar.

---

2 ¿Qué hora tiene usted? *What time do you make it?*

Another visitor is asking the time.

Señora	Perdón, ¿qué hora tiene usted?	
Recepcionista	Son diez para las nueve.	
Señora	Gracias.	
Recepcionista	Para servirle.	

♠ CD1, TR 3, 01:04

¿qué hora tiene usted? *what time do you have/make it?*
para servirle *you're welcome* (literally, *to serve you*)

---

3 Abren a las ocho *They open at eight*

A hotel guest has come down for breakfast, but the restaurant is closed. Key phrases here are **Está cerrado** *It is closed*, **¿A qué hora abren?** *What time do they open?*, **Dentro de ...** *Within ...*

Señorita	¿Dónde está el restaurante, por favor?
Recepcionista	*(pointing)* Está ahí, señorita, pero está cerrado.
Señorita	¿A qué hora abren?
Recepcionista	Abren a las ocho. Dentro de cinco minutos.
Señorita	Gracias. Muy amable.

CERRADO

Insight

'**Cerrado**', in '**está cerrado**' '*it is closed*', refers to '**el restaurante**', a masculine word, therefore it ends in **-o**. For a feminine word change the **-o** into **-a**: '**la panadería está cerrada**' '*the baker's is closed*'. To refer to more than one thing you need to add **-s**: '**los bancos/las tiendas están cerrados/as**' '*the banks/shops are closed*'.

los minutos *minutes*

¿a qué hora? *at what time?*

Ask and say it in Spanish

Example: el bar – 10.00

¿A qué hora abren el bar? Abren a las diez.

a el banco (*bank*) – 9.00
b el museo (*museum*) – 9.30
c la oficina de turismo (*tourist office*) – 10.00

---

4 En la tienda de regalos *At the gift shop*

A visitor needs to buy some presents to take home. He asks the shop assistant in the gift shop what time they close. Key words and phrases here are **¿A qué hora cierran?** *What time do you / they close?* and **cerramos** *we close.*

Cliente	Perdón, ¿a qué hora cierran?
Dependienta	Hoy cerramos a las siete y cuarto.
Cliente	Gracias.

la tienda *shop*
el regalo *gift, present*

QV

Insight

In '**cerrar**' the 'e' of the stem of the verb ('**cerr-**') changes into 'ie' in '**cierran**' but not in '**cerramos**'. Verbs which undergo such changes are known as stem-changing verbs. An explanation of this will be found in paragraph 6 of Grammar.

Ask in Spanish

Example: las tiendas

¿A qué hora cierran las tiendas?

a los bancos
b los museos
c las casas de cambio

5 ¿A qué hora es la cena? *What time is dinner?*

Another visitor is inquiring about dinner time.

CD1, TR 3, 01:58

Recepcionista	Buenas tardes, señorita.
Señorita	¿A qué hora es la cena, por favor?
Recepcionista	Es a las nueve.
Señorita	Y el restaurante, ¿dónde está?
Recepcionista	Está al fondo del pasillo.
Señorita	Muchas gracias.
Recepcionista	Para servirle.

QV

la cena *dinner*
al fondo *at the end, at the bottom*

Insight

Note the two forms of '*to be*' in Spanish: '**ser**' in '**¿a qué hora es la cena?**' '**es a las nueve**', and '**estar**' in '**¿dónde está?**' '**está al fondo del pasillo**'. To refer to the time use '**ser**'; to refer to a place use '**estar**'.

Ask and answer in Spanish

Example: la cena – 9.00

¿A qué hora es la cena? – Es a las nueve.

a el desayuno *(breakfast)* – 7.30
b el almuerzo *(lunch)* – 1.00
c la salida *(departure)* – 8.00

___

6 ¿A qué hora desayunas? *What time do you have breakfast?*

Raúl and Rosa, two Mexicans, talk about their meals. Key words and phrases here are **tomar el desayuno** *to have breakfast*, **almorzar** *to have lunch*, **comer** *to eat*.

Now, read the dialogue and answer these questions in English:

a What time does Rosa normally have breakfast?
b And Raúl?
c What time does Raúl normally have lunch?
d Where does Rosa normally have lunch?

Las comidas principales *Main meals*
Most Latin Americans have a light **desayuno** (*breakfast*),
consisting of **café** and **tostadas** or **pan tostado** (*coffee and toast*),
not very different from what you might have at home. But in
some countries, like Mexico, breakfast is often a more substantial
meal. **El almuerzo** (*lunch*) is the main meal in Latin America,
and in small towns people usually go home for lunch. In big
cities, restaurants normally offer quick, inexpensive meals for
working people. If this is what you want, ask for **el menú del día**
or **el plato del día** (*the menu of the day*), or **la comida corrida** in
Mexico. The alternative is to eat **a la carta** (choose from the menu),
which will cost you much more. **La cena** (*dinner*) is a light meal,
often consisting of **una sopa** (*soup*), **una ensalada** (*salad*), or
un sandwich.

The names associated with meals vary somewhat from region
to region. *To have breakfast* is **desayunar** in some places and
tomar (el) desayuno in others. The word for *lunch* is **la comida**
in certain countries, for example Mexico, where **el almuerzo** is
a mid-morning snack. In some regions **la comida** stands for the
evening meal, known also as **la cena** or **la merienda**. **La comida**
also means *meal*.

Key phrases

Asking and telling the time

¿Qué hora es / tiene?	*What time is it / do you make it?*
Es la una / Son las dos.	*It's one o'clock / two o'clock.*

Es mediodía/medianoche.	*It's midday/midnight.*
Son las cinco y cuarto.	*It's a quarter past five.*
Es un cuarto para las seis.	*It's a quarter to six.*
Son las seis menos cuarto.	
Son las ocho y media.	*It's half past eight.*
Son las nueve (y) veinte.	*It's twenty past nine.*
Son diez para las diez.	*It's ten to ten.*
Son las diez menos diez.	

Talking about opening and closing times

¿A qué hora abren / cierran?	*What time do you / they open / close?*
Abrimos / abren a las nueve.	*We / they open at nine.*
Cerramos / cierran a las siete.	*We / they close at seven.*
Está cerrado(a) / abierto(a)	*It's open / closed. (m/f)*

Talking about meal times

¿A qué hora es el desayuno / el almuerzo / la cena?	*What time is breakfast / lunch / dinner?*
Es a las siete / la una / las ocho.	*It's at seven / one / eight o'clock.*
¿A qué hora tomas el desayuno / desayunas? *(fam)*	*What time do you have breakfast?*
Tomo el desayuno / desayuno a las siete.	*I have breakfast at seven.*
¿A qué hora almuerzas / cenas? *(fam)*	*What time do you have lunch / dinner?*
Almuerzo/ceno a la una / las nueve.	*I have lunch/dinner at one / nine.*

Grammar

1 Asking and telling the time

To ask and tell the time, use **ser**, *to be*.

¿Qué hora **es**?	*What time is it?*
Es la una / la una y cuarto.	*It's one o'clock / a quarter past one.*
Es la una y media.	*It's half past one.*
Son las dos / tres menos diez.	*It's two o'clock / ten to three.*
Son las cinco / seis y cuarto.	*It's five o'clock / a quarter past six.*

In some countries you will hear the question **¿Qué horas son?** for **¿Qué hora es?** An alternative way of asking the time is to use **tener** *to have,* for example **¿Tiene hora?** *Have you got the time?* Some Latin American countries, among them Mexico and Chile, use phrases such as **Son (un) cuarto para las seis, Son veinte para las dos**, instead of **Son las seis menos cuarto, Son las dos menos veinte** *It's a quarter to six, It's twenty to two.*

2 At what time?

Notice also the use of **ser** in the following examples:

| **¿A qué hora es el desayuno?** | *What time is breakfast?* |
| **Es a las ocho.** | *It's at eight o'clock.* |

When we inquire about the time a place opens or closes or, more generally, about the time something takes place, the phrase **¿qué hora?** must always be preceded by the preposition **a: ¿A qué hora ... ?**

3 The days of the week

Días de la semana *Days of the week*

lunes	*Monday*	viernes	*Friday*
martes	*Tuesday*	sábado	*Saturday*
miércoles	*Wednesday*	domingo	*Sunday*
jueves	*Thursday*		

48

Notice that in Spanish the days of the week are written with small letters. To say *on Monday*, *on Tuesday*, etc., use the word **el** (*the*, m. sing): **el lunes, el martes.** To say *Mondays, Tuesdays,* etc., use the word **los** (*the*, m/pl): **los lunes, los martes.** To say *Today / Tomorrow is Friday / Saturday,* etc., use phrases like these: **Hoy es viernes, Mañana es sábado.** To ask what day it is today, say **¿Qué día es hoy?**

4 Three kinds of verbs

According to the ending of the infinitive (or dictionary form of the verb), Spanish verbs may be grouped into three main categories or conjugations: **-ar** (or first conjugation), **-er** (or second conjugation) and **-ir** (or third conjugation). For example:

tomar   *to take*
comer   *to eat*
abrir   *to open*

In Spanish, there are regular and irregular verbs. Regular verbs are those that follow a fixed pattern, which varies only according to certain grammatical categories, such as the ending of the infinitive (see above), *person*, for instance **yo** (*I*), **tú** (*you*, fam), **él** (*he*) (see grammar, Unit 1) or *tense*, for example present tense, future tense. Irregular verbs are those that do not follow a fixed pattern in their conjugation, for example **ser** *to be*.

5 The present tense

-ar verbs
In the present tense, all regular **-ar** verbs follow this pattern:

tomar	to take
yo tomo	*I take*
tú tomas	*you take* (fam, sing)

tomar	to take
Ud. toma	*you take* (pol, sing)
él, ella toma	*he, she, it takes*
nosotros/as tomamos	*we take*
Uds., ellos, ellas toman	*you take* (pl), *they take*

¿A qué hora tomas el desayuno? *What time do you have breakfast?*
Tomo el desayuno a las ocho. *I have breakfast at eight.*

-*er* verbs
Regular -**er** verbs are conjugated in the following way:

comer	to eat
yo como	*I eat*
tú comes	*you eat* (fam, sing)
Ud. come	*you eat* (pol, sing)
él, ella come	*he, she, it eats*
nosotros/as comemos	*we eat*
Uds., ellos, ellas comen	*you eat* (pl), *they eat*

Como en la universidad. *I eat in the university.*
Rosa come en casa. *Rosa eats at home.*

-*ir* verbs
Regular -**ir** verbs are conjugated like this:

abrir	to open
yo abro	*I open*
tú abres	*you open* (fam, sing)
Ud. abre	*you open* (pol, sing)
él, ella abre	*he, she, it opens*
nosotros/as abrimos	*we open*
Uds., ellos, ellas abren	*you open* (pl), *they open*

¿A qué hora abren? *What time do they open?*
Abrimos a las ocho. *We open at eight.*

Notice that the endings for **-er** and **-ir** verbs are the same, except in the first person plural **nosotros**.

6 *Stem-changing verbs: e > ie and o > ue*

Certain verbs undergo a change in the stem (the infinitive minus its ending). Stem-changing verbs (also known as radical-changing verbs) have the same endings as regular verbs. **Cerrar** (*to close*) is a stem-changing verb, in which -e changes into -ie. Notice that this change occurs only when the stem is stressed, therefore verb forms corresponding to **nosotros** (*we*) (**cerramos**, *we close*) are not affected by it.

cierro	*I close*
cierras	*you close* (fam, sing)
cierra	*you close* (pol, sing), *he, she, it closes*
cierran	*you close* (pl), *they close*

In later units you will encounter other verbs which change in the same way as **cerrar**.

Almorzar *to have lunch* is also a stem-changing verb, in which -o changes into -ue.

almuerzo	*I have lunch*
almuerzas	*you have lunch* (fam, sing)
almuerza	*you have lunch* (pol, sing), *he, she has lunch*
almuerzan	*you have lunch* (pl), *they have lunch*

In later units you will encounter other verbs which change in the same way as **almorzar**.

Practice

1 Ask and say the time, following the example.

¿Qué hora es? Son las seis y veinte.

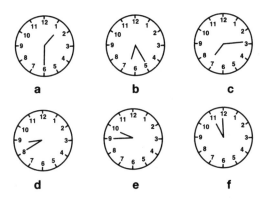

a   b   c

d   e   f

2 You are in Chile on business and want to make several phone calls abroad, so you need to be aware of time differences. Look at the information below and then answer the questions giving the correct time.

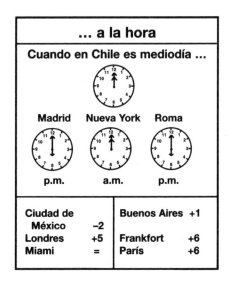

... a la hora

Cuando en Chile es mediodía ...

Madrid	Nueva York	Roma
p.m.	a.m.	p.m.

Ciudad de México	−2	Buenos Aires	+1
Londres	+5	Frankfort	+6
Miami	=	París	+6

En Chile es mediodía (*midday*).

   a ¿Qué hora es en la Ciudad de México?
   b ¿Qué hora es en Londres?
   c ¿Qué hora es en Buenos Aires?
   d ¿Qué hora es en París?

3 On your next visit to Mexico, don't miss the **Ballet Folklórico Mexicano,** a well-known group which presents the best of Mexican music and dance. Look at this advertisement for the ballet and the vocabulary which follows. Then answer the questions below.

BALLET FOLKLÓRICO MEXICANO
Dirección: Guillermo González

TEATRO DE LA DANZA
Detrás del Auditorio Nacional

ENERO | Jueves 14 y Viernes 15 / 20:00 hrs.
Sábado 16 / 19:00 hrs Domingo 17 / 12:00 hrs

In advertisements such as the one above, at railway stations, airports, on the radio, and so on, Spanish uses the 24-hour clock. Colloquially, however, people use phrases like the following to distinguish between a.m. and p.m.: **Son las dos de la tarde** *It's two o'clock in the afternoon,* **A las diez de la noche** *At ten o'clock at night.*

el teatro *theatre*   **enero** *January*
la danza *dance*   **detrás** *behind*

Read the advertisement again and answer these questions in Spanish.

   a ¿Dónde está el Teatro de la Danza?
   b ¿Cuántas funciones (*performances*) hay el viernes 15 (quince)?

c ¿A qué hora es la función el viernes?

d ¿A qué hora es la función el domingo 17 (diecisiete)?

4 Ask what time these places open and close.

la tienda *shop*   **el correo** *post office*

el supermercado *supermarket*   **el museo** *museum*

   a Ask what time the shops open.

   b Ask what time the supermarket opens.

   c Ask what time the post office closes.

   d Ask what time the museums close.

◀)) **CD1, TR 3, 03:27**

5 Jorge Vera from Mexico was asked what time the shops open in Veracruz, his home town. Listen to what he says, then answer the questions. Here are some key words used by Jorge:

la mañana *morning*   **para trabajar** *to work*

entonces *then*   **hasta** *until*

trabajan *they work*

Is it true or false? (**¿verdadero o falso?**)

   a Las tiendas abren a las ocho y media de la mañana.

   b Las tiendas cierran entre una y cuatro.

   c En la noche cierran a las siete.

6 You are on holiday in a South American country and you need to change some money. It is 2.30 p.m. and the nearest bureau de change (**casa de cambio**), La Internacional, which is two blocks from your hotel, does not open until 4.00. Use the information to write dialogues similar to the one that follows between yourself and a hotel receptionist.

Señorita	Disculpe, ¿qué hora tiene, por favor?
Recepcionista	Es un cuarto para las nueve. / Son las nueve menos cuarto.
Señorita	¿A qué hora abren los bancos?
Recepcionista	Abren a las nueve.
Señorita	¿Hay un banco por aquí?
Recepcionista	Sí, el Banco de la Nación está en la esquina.
Señorita	Muchas gracias. Muy amable.
Recepcionista	Para servirle. ¡Que le vaya bien!

disculpe *excuse me*
en la esquina *on the corner*

Practise with:

8:30/los supermercados/9:15/Supermercado Modelo/a dos cuadras de aquí

9:45/las panaderías/10:00/Panadería Selecta/segunda calle a la izquierda

7 A Spanish-speaking friend is asking you what time you have your meals. Answer his questions.
  a ¿A qué hora tomas el desayuno / desayunas normalmente?
  b ¿Y a qué hora almuerzas?
  c ¿Dónde almuerzas?
  d ¿Cenas muy tarde?? ¿A qué hora?

cenar *to have dinner*
muy tarde *very late*

◀ **CD1, TR 3, 03:50**

8 Jorge Vera and Clotilde Montalvo (Coty) were asked about the main meals and their times in México, their country. Listen to both conversations, and note the differences in the information given by each of them. Then answer the questions below. These key words and phrases will help you to understand:

QUICK VOCAB

dime *tell me*
¿cuál es el horario? *what are the times?*
cada *each*
opcionalmente *alternatively*
podríamos llamarle *we could call it*
poscena *after-dinner snack*
que puede ser *which can be*
si nos acostamos tarde *if we go to bed late*
la de mediodía *the midday one*
que varía *which varies*
en que se toma *when it is taken*
en adelante *onwards*

Now answer these questions in English:

a What are the times of the three main meals, according to Jorge?
b What time is the optional after-dinner snack?

Complete these sentences with the information given by Coty.

c La comida principal es la de —————.
d El almuerzo es entre ——— y —————.
e La cena es ————— .

Test yourself

1 Give the Spanish for the following times, using the 12-hour clock.

 a 10.25.
 b 11.45 (two alternatives)
 c 12.30.
 d 14.15.
 e 22.10.

2 Give the correct form of the verbs in brackets.

 a Ángela (*tomar*) el desayuno a las 7:30. Yo (*desayunar*) a las 8:00.
 b Pancho y María (*almorzar*) a la 1:00. ¿A qué hora (*almorzar*) usted?
 c Yo (*comer*) en la oficina. Mi esposa (*comer*) en casa.
 d Nosotros (*cenar*) a las 9:00 de la noche. ¿A qué hora (*cenar*) tú?
 e El restaurante está cerrado. (*abrir*) al mediodía y (*cerrar*) a las 3:00 de la tarde.

The focus in these tests is on the correct usage of the time and, grammatically, on a very important point: the use of the present tense to talk about things that happen regularly. Check your answers in the **Key to test yourself** and go back to the grammar notes if you feel you need to do some further study. Otherwise go on to Unit 4, in which you will learn to introduce people and to expand the language needed for talking about actions that happen regularly.

4

¿Qué haces?
What do you do?

In this unit you will learn
- *How to introduce people*
- *How to say where you live and what work you do*
- *How to talk about daily and spare-time activities*
- *How to ask and answer questions about age*

---

1 Te presento a mi hermana *Let me introduce you to my sister*

Jorge, a Mexican from Veracruz, introduces his friend Juan, a Chilean, to his sister.

Note the key phrases **Te presento a ...** *Let me introduce you to ...* (fam.), Vivo en ... *I live in ...*, **Trabajo en ...** *I work in ...*, ¿**Qué haces?** *What do you do?*

CD1, TR 4, 00:02

Juan	Hola, Jorge.
Jorge	Hola, Juan. Pasa. ¿Cómo te va?
Juan	Bien, gracias, ¿y tú, cómo estás?
Jorge	Pues, un poco cansado. Tengo mucho trabajo. Mira, te presento a mi hermana Luisa, que está aquí de vacaciones. Luisa, este es Juan, mi amigo chileno.

Luisa	Encantada.
Juan	Mucho gusto.
Luisa	¿De qué parte de Chile eres?
Juan	Soy de Santiago. ¿Y tú no vives en Veracruz?
Luisa	No, vivo en Cancún. Trabajo en una agencia de viajes. Y tú, ¿qué haces?
Juan	Soy arquitecto. Trabajo en una empresa constructora.

Insight

Words ending in **-ado** and which denote a state resulting from an action, as in **'Estoy un poco cansado'** *'I'm a little tired'*, change for gender (m/f) and number (sing/pl): **'Nora está cansada'**, **'Estamos cansados/as'**. Observe also **'Te presento a ...'** *'Let me introduce you to ...'*, in which the person being addressed comes first, in this case **'te'** *'to you'*, familiar. In formal address use **'le'**: **'Le presento a ...'** For an explanation of **'a'** in this sentence see Grammar, para 7.

pasa *come in*
pues ... *well ...*
este / esta *this*
mira *look*
las vacaciones *holidays*
vivir *to live*
la agencia de viajes *travel agency*
la empresa constructora *construction company*

QUICK VOCAB

trabajo en una agencia
de viajes

Say it in Spanish

What phrases are used in the dialogue to express the following?

a How are you? – Well, a bit tired.
b I have a lot of work.
c She is here on holiday.
d This is Juan.
e I work in a travel agency.

2 Empiezo a las nueve *I start at nine*

Juan asks Luisa about her work. First, practise the following key phrases: **¿Estás contenta?** *Are you happy?* (to a woman), **¿Cuál es tu horario de trabajo?** *What are your working hours?*, **Empiezo a las ...** *I start at ...*, **Termino a las ...** *I finish at ...*

CD1, TR 4, 01:10

Juan	¿Estás contenta de vivir en Cancún?
Luisa	Sí, es un lugar muy bonito y tiene un clima muy bueno.
Juan	Y tu trabajo, ¿qué tal?
Luisa	Es un trabajo interesante, aunque a veces pienso que trabajo demasiado.
Juan	¿Cuál es tu horario de trabajo?
Luisa	Empiezo a las nueve de la mañana y termino a las siete de la tarde.
Juan	¿Sin interrupción?
Luisa	No, cerramos al mediodía entre las dos y las cuatro.

Insight

In this dialogue, '**tener**' *'to have'*, '**pensar**' *'to think'*, '**empezar**' *'to begin, start'* and '**cerrar**' *'to close, shut'* are all stem-changing verbs, in which the **-e** of the stem changes into **-ie**, except in the '**nosotros**' form: '**emp*ie*zo, emp*ie*zas, emp*ie*za, empezamos, emp*ie*zan**'. '**Tener**' has an irregular first person singular: '**tengo**' *'I have'* (but '**t*ie*nes**', '**t*ie*ne**', etc.)

el lugar *place*
bonito/a *pretty*
tiene *it has*
bueno/a *good*
¿Qué tal? *What is it like?*
aunque *although*
a veces *sometimes*
demasiado *too much*
sin *without*

QUICK VOCAB

60

Read the dialogue again and answer these questions in English:

a Why does Luisa like Cancún?
b What time does she start and finish work?

---

3 ¿Qué haces los fines de semana? *What do you do at weekends?*

Luisa asks Juan about his spare-time activities. Note the following key verbs: **me levanto** *I get up,* **salgo** *I go out,* **me quedo** *I stay,* **voy** *I go,* **me acuesto** *I go to bed,* **hago** *I do,* veo *I watch,* **leo** *I read,* **escucho** *I listen.*

Luisa	¿Qué haces los fines de semana?
Juan	Por lo general, me levanto bastante tarde. A veces salgo fuera de Santiago, voy a la playa o al campo. Cuando me quedo en Santiago voy al cine o salgo a comer con mis amigos. Generalmente me acuesto muy tarde. Y tú, ¿qué haces?
Luisa	No hago nada especial. Normalmente veo la televisión, leo o escucho música.

CD1, TR 4, 02:07

QUICK VOCAB

por lo general *usually*
bastante tarde *quite late*
fuera de *out of*
la playa *beach*
el campo *countryside*
cuando *when*
con *with*
nada *nothing, anything*
los fines de semana *weekends*

Read the dialogue again and answer these questions in English:

a What does Juan do at weekends?
b What does Luisa do?

4 Tiene doce años *He is twelve years old*

Luisa tells Juan about her family. Note the following questions: **¿Eres casada?** *Are you married?*, **¿Cuántos años tienen?** *How old are they?* Note also how Luisa asks Juan whether he is single: **Tú eres soltero, ¿no?** *You are single, aren't you?*

Juan	¿Eres casada?
Luisa	Sí, soy casada. Tengo dos hijos.
Juan	¿Cuántos años tienen?
Luisa	Mi hijo mayor, José, tiene doce años, y la menor, Cristina, tiene diez. Tú eres soltero, ¿no?
Juan	Sí, soy soltero. Y tu esposo, ¿qué hace?
Luisa	Es maestro.

el hijo *son*
los hijos *children*
mayor *elder*
menor *younger*
esposo/a *husband/wife*
maestro/a *school teacher*

Read the dialogue again and answer these questions in English:

a How many children does Luisa have?
b What are their ages?

Key phrases

Introducing people

Este es Juan.	*This is Juan.*
Esta es Luisa.	*This is Luisa.*
Te presento a mi hermana / mi hijo *(fam)*	*Let me introduce you to my sister / son.*
Le presento a mi esposo / a (pol)	*Let me introduce you to my husband / wife*

Saying where you live and what work you do

Vivo en ...   *I live in ...*
Trabajo en ...   *I work in ...*

Talking about daily and spare-time activities

¿Cuál es tu horario de trabajo?   *What are your working hours?*
Empiezo / termino a las ocho   *I start/finish at eight in the*
  de la mañana / noche.   *morning / evening.*
¿Qué haces los fines de semana?   *What do you do at weekends?*
Por lo general / generalmente veo   *I usually watch television/*
  la televisión / leo / escucho   *read / listen to music / go to*
  música / voy al cine.   *the cinema.*

Asking and answering questions about age

¿Cuántos años tiene (él /   *How old is he / she / are you?*
  ella) / tienes (tú)?
Tiene / tengo doce años.   *He / she is / I am twelve years old.*
¿Qué edad tiene tu madre?   *What age is your mother?*
Tiene sesenta años.   *She's sixty years old.*

Grammar

1 *Possessives: mi, tu, su ... my, your, his ...*

To say *my*, *your*, *his*, *her*, etc. in Spanish, use the following set of words.

mi	*my*
tu	*your* (fam, sing)
su	*your* (pol, sing), *his, her, its*
nuestro/a	*our* (m/f)
su	*your* (pl), *their*

64

These words, which are called possessives, agree in number (sing/pl) with the noun that they accompany, but only **nuestro** (*our*) agrees in gender (m/f). Gender agreement is with what is possessed not with the possessor.

Mi hermana se llama Luisa.	*My sister is called Luisa.*
Mis hermanas se llaman Luisa y María.	*My sisters are called Luisa and María.*
¿Dónde está **nuestro** hotel?	*Where is our hotel?*
¿Dónde está **nuestra** habitación?	*Where is our room?*

Note that the form **vuestro** (*your*, pl/fam), corresponding to **vosotros** (*you*, pl/fam) used in Spain, is not normally used in Latin America. Notice also that **mi** *my* does not carry a written accent, unlike **mí** *me*, *as* in **para mí** *for me*, which must be written with an accent.

Insight

The ambiguity of '**su**' in '**su casa**', which can mean *'his/her/your'* (for '**usted**' or '**ustedes**')/*their house*', can be avoided with the following construction: '**la casa de él/ella/usted/ustedes/ellos**'.

2 Demonstratives: este/a, estos/as this, these

To say *this* and *these* in Spanish, use the following set of words, which vary for number (sing/pl) and gender (m/f).

este señor (*m*)	*this gentleman (next to you)*
esta señora (*f*)	*this lady (next to you)*
estos señores (*m*)	*these gentlemen (next to you)*
estas señoras (*f*)	*these ladies (next to you)*

In these examples, **este**, **esta**, etc. have been followed by nouns (e.g. **señor**, **señora**), in which case they are acting as adjectives. But they can also be used in place of a noun, functioning as a pronoun.

Esta es mi hermana.	*This is my sister.*
Este es mi hermano.	*This is my brother.*

To say *this*, when no gender is specified, use the neuter form **esto**.

¿Qué es esto?	*What is this?*
¿Cómo se llama esto?	*What is this called?*

For *that* and *those*, see Unit 6.

3 *Irregular verbs*

There are many verbs in Spanish which do not follow a fixed pattern, i.e. they are irregular. In the present tense, some verbs are irregular only in the first person singular. Some of them are also stem-changing.

hacer	*to do, to make*	**hago**	*I do, I make*
poner	*to put*	**pongo**	*I put*
salir	*to go out*	**salgo**	*I go out*
tener (e>ie)	*to have*	**tengo**	*I have*
venir (e>ie)	*to come*	**vengo**	*I come*
ver	*to watch, to see*	**veo**	*I watch, I see*

See also Irregular verbs at the back of the book.

No hago nada especial.	*I don't do anything special.*
Salgo a cenar.	*I go out for dinner.*
Veo la televisión.	*I watch television.*

4 *Tener to have*

Tener *to have* is irregular in the first person singular of the present tense. It is also a stem-changing verb, with the **e** of the stem changing into **ie** (see Unit 3).

tengo	*I have*
tienes	*you have* (fam, sing)
tiene	*you have* (pol, sing), *he, she, it has*
tenemos	*we have*
tienen	*you have* (pol/fam), *they have*

Tener has a number of uses, among them the following ones:

a To express age

¿Cuántos años **tienes**? *How old are you?*
Tengo cuarenta años. *I'm forty years old.*
Patricia **tiene** treinta y seis. *Patricia is thirty six.*

b To express possession, including family relationships

Tengo dos hijos / hermanos. *I have two children / brothers.*
Tiene una casa muy grande. *He / she has a very large house.*

c To refer to obligations

Tengo mucho trabajo. *I have a lot of work.*

d To ask the time (see Unit 3)

¿**Tiene** hora? *Have you got the time?*

e To express availability

¿**Tiene** una habitación? *Have you got a room?*

f In a number of phrases in which it translates *to be* in English.

Tengo frío/calor.	*I'm cold/hot.*
¿Tienes hambre/sed?	*Are you hungry/thirsty?*
Tiene miedo/razón.	*He/she is afraid/right.*

5 *Ir to go*

Here are the present tense forms of **ir** (*to go*), a verb which is very irregular.

voy	*I go*
vas	*you go* (fam. sing)
va	*you go* (pol. sing), *he, she, it goes*
vamos	*we go*
van	*you go* (pl), *they go*

Voy a la playa.	*I go to the beach.*
¿Vas al cine?	*Do you go to the cinema?*

For **ir** a + infinitive, as in **Voy a estudiar español** *I'm going to study Spanish*, see Unit 7, Grammar, para 1.

6 *Reflexive verbs*

A reflexive verb is one that has **-se** added to the infinitive, e.g. **levantarse** *to get up*. Normally, **se**, as in this example, is not expressed at all in English, but it sometimes translates into English as *oneself*, for example **mirarse** *to look at oneself*. Many verbs in Spanish are reflexive where their English equivalents are not.

In the examples from dialogue 3 **me levanto** *I get up*, **me acuesto** *I go to bed*, **me quedo** *I stay*, **me** can be said to correspond to the English word *myself*. Words like **se** and **me** are called reflexive pronouns and these precede the conjugated verb. Here is a verb fully conjugated:

levantarse	*to get up*
me levanto	*I get up*
te levantas	*you get up* (fam. sing)

levantarse	to get up
se levanta	you get up (pol. sing), he, she, it gets up
nos levantamos	we get up
se levantan	you get up (pl), they get up

The plural familiar form **os levantáis** *you get up* has been omitted, as this is not normally used in Latin America.

Remember that in a dictionary, reflexive verbs are listed with **-se** on the end of the infinitive, for example: **divertirse** *to enjoy oneself*, **quedarse** *to stay*, **acostarse** *to go to bed*.

7 Personal a

In the sentence **Te presento a mi hermana** *Let me introduce you to my sister*, **mi hermana**, the person being introduced, is the direct object of the sentence. Before noun direct objects referring to people, Spanish uses the preposition **a**. This is known as the *personal* **a**. Note the use of the personal **a** in the following examples:

Veo **a** Luisa los lunes.	*I see Luisa on Mondays.*
Quiere mucho **a** sus padres.	*He / she loves his / her parents very much.*

But:

Veo la televisión todos los días.	*I watch television everyday.*
Quiere mucho su trabajo.	*He/she loves his/her work very much.*

8 Formation of adverbs

Adverbs are used to provide information about verbs, adjectives or other adverbs:

Ceno **normalmente** en casa.	*I usually have dinner at home.*
Es **extremadamente** difícil.	*It's extremely difficult.*
Habla **realmente** bien.	*He / she speaks really well.*

Adverbs can be formed by adding -**mente** to the adjective.

general	*general*
generalmente	*generally, usually*
normal	*normal*
normalmente	*normally*
Normalmente escucho música.	*I normally listen to music.*
Generalmente voy al teatro.	*I usually go to the theatre.*

If the adjective ends in -**o**, change the -**o** to -**a** and add -**mente**.

claro	*clear*
claramente	*clearly*
lento	*slow*
lentamente	*slowly*
Habla claramente.	*He / she speaks clearly.*
Progresa lentamente.	*He / she is progressing slowly.*

In a sentence with two or more adverbs in -**mente**, only the last one takes the ending -**mente**.

Habla clara y lentamente.   *He / she speaks clearly and slowly.*

A large number of adverbs are single words or group of words not formed from adjectives, for example **siempre** *always*, **nunca** *never*, **por lo general** *usually*, **a menudo** *often*, **ahora** *now*, **mañana** *tomorrow*, **bien** *well*, **mal** *badly*, and so on.

Insight

Overuse of adverbs ending in -**mente** may seem clumsy in Spanish. The alternative is to use phrases like **de manera** or **de forma** *in a way*, followed by the feminine form of the adjective: **de manera/forma rápida** (for **rápidamente**) *in a quick way*, **de manera/forma extraña** (for **extrañamente**) *in a strange way*.

Practice

1 An informal introduction

Raúl Riveros, from Mexico, is introducing his father to his friend María Elena.

Raúl	Hola, María Elena. ¿Cómo te va?
María Elena	Muy bien, y tú, ¿cómo estás?
Raúl	Bien, gracias. Te presento a mi papá.
	(Addressing his father.) Esta es María Elena.
Señor Riveros	Encantado.
María Elena	Mucho gusto.

Note that Latin Americans normally use **papá** *father* and **mamá** *mother* in this context. Spaniards would normally use **padre** and **madre** instead.

Raúl is now visiting María Elena, who introduces him to Señora de García, her mother (**su mamá**). Rewrite the dialogue above making the necessary adaptations.

2 A formal introduction

You are on business in Latin America, and after greeting señor Molina, manager of Hispanometal, you introduce your colleague John Evans to him. After exchanging greetings with John Evans, señor Molina offers you a seat. Write a dialogue based on this situation. Then compare your version with the model dialogue in the **Key to the activities**.

el gerente de ...	*the manager of* ...
mi colega	*my colleague*
siéntense	*sit down (pl)*

3 Latin Americans tend to be more direct in their questions when they meet people for the first time. For instance, they often ask people about their work, so here is your chance to practise.

a On a train journey in Latin America you meet Carlos, a student from Uruguay. He uses the familiar form to address you, so you do likewise.

Ud.	*Ask Carlos where he lives.*
Carlos	Vivo en Montevideo. ¿Y tú?
Ud.	*Say where you live and then ask him what work he does.*
Carlos	Soy estudiante. Estudio ingeniería en la Universidad de Montevideo. ¿Y tú?
Ud.	*Say what you do.*

QV

estudiar *to study*   **la ingeniería** *engineering*

b During an excursion you meet María and her husband José. They use the polite form to address you.

Ud.	*Ask them where they are from.*
María	Somos de Colombia. Y usted, ¿de dónde es?
Ud.	*Say what country you are from and then ask them where they live.*
José	Vivimos en Medellín.
Ud.	*Ask them what work they do.*
María	Mi marido es médico y yo soy periodista.
Ud.	*Don't wait to be asked! Say something about your own work or occupation.*

QV

el marido *husband*   **el/la periodista** *journalist*
el médico *doctor*

🔊 **CD1, TR 4, 03:28**

4 Listen to Coty Montalvo, from Mexico, talking about her work. The key words which follow will help you to understand what Coty says, while the questions below will help you check comprehension.

regresar *to come back*
seguir laborando *to continue working*

Answer true or false (verdadero o falso):

    a Coty empieza a trabajar a las nueve de la mañana.
    b Sale a almorzar a la una.
    c Termina de trabajar a las siete.

5 Imagine you are writing in Spanish to someone about your own activities. Use the following guidelines and some of the words below to express these ideas:

Say what you do.
Say what days you work or what days you go to school or university.
Say what time you start and what time you finish.
Say where you normally have lunch.
Say what you usually do after work / school.
Say what you usually do at the weekend.

estudiar *to study*
ir al colegio / a la universidad *to go to school / university*
salir de compras *to go out shopping*
limpiar la casa *to clean the house*
ir al teatro / a conciertos *to go to the theatre / concerts*
después de trabajar / de clases *after work / school*
salir a caminar / correr *to go out and walk / run*
regar (e > ie) el jardín *to water the garden*
leer el periódico *to read the newspaper*
cocinar *to cook*

....

Insight

After the preposition in phrases such as '**después de**' '*after*', '**antes de**' '*before*', Spanish uses the infinitive whereas English uses the **-ing** form of the verb: '**después de desayunar**' '*after having breakfast*', '**antes de salir de casa**' '*before leaving the house*'.

....

6 Coty was asked how she normally spends her holidays. Listen to what she says then answer the questions below. First, look at this new vocabulary:

aprovecho *I take the opportunity*
los sobrinos *nephews and nieces*
la frontera *border, frontier*
los Estados Unidos *United States*
el viaje *journey*
largo *long*
hasta allá *to there*
lo disfruto *I enjoy it*
muy de vez en cuando *very rarely*

Now answer these questions in English:

   a Where does Coty normally go on holiday?
   b Why does she enjoy the long journey?

7 Read this information about Luisa Álvarez, then use the information in the box to write a similar passage about Antonio Fernández, his children and his wife (**su mujer** or **esposa**).

Luisa Álvarez es mexicana y trabaja como secretaria en una agencia de viajes. Luisa es casada y tiene dos hijos, José y Cristina. Su hijo José tiene doce años y su hija Cristina tiene diez. El marido de Luisa se llama Pablo. Pablo es maestro.

Nombre:	Antonio Fernández
Nacionalidad:	nicaragüense
Profesión:	técnico, empresa textil
Estado civil:	casado
N° de hijos:	3
Edades:	Adela (24 años), Mario (21), Domingo (19)
Casado/a con:	María Rosa Poblete
Profesión:	ama de casa

nicaragüense *from Nicaragua*
el técnico *technician*
la empresa textil *textile company*
el estado civil *marital status*
la edad *age*
ama de casa *housewife*

🔊 **CD1, TR 4, 05:06**

8 Coty, whose full name is Clotilde Montalvo Rodríguez, now talks about herself and her family. Listen to what she says, or read the transcript in Listening comprehension transcripts, and as you do so, fill in the box below with the information given by her. First, look at these key words:

Centro Cultural de Lenguas Modernas *a languages school in Veracruz, Mexico*
manejar *to drive*
la carretera *main road*
el chofer de carretera *coach or lorry driver*

....

Insight

Most Latin Americans use **manejar** for *to drive*. The alternative word is '**conducir**' ('**conduzco, conduces, conduce**', etc.), which is used in Spain.
....

Name:	Clotilde Montalvo Rodríguez
Age:	....
Marital Status:	....
Profession:	....
Husband's Profession:	....
Nº of children:	....
Age(s):	....

9 During a stay in a Latin American country you meet someone. Like many Latin Americans often do, he/she asks you about yourself and your family. Answer the relevant questions.

    a ¿Es usted casado/a o soltero/a?

    b ¿Tiene hijos? ¿Cuántos?

    c ¿Tiene hermanos? ¿Cuántos?

    d ¿Cuántos años tiene(n) su(s) hijo(s) o hermano(s)?

    e ¿Dónde vive usted?

Test yourself

1 Choose from the verbs below and change them into their appropriate form to complete the sentences below.

tener, hacer, terminar, ser, ir, empezar, vivir, trabajar

    a Yo ____ en Bogotá con mi familia, mi hermana ____ en Medellín y mis padres ____ con mi abuela en Cali.

    b '¿Cuál es tu horario de trabajo?' – '(Yo) ____ a las 8:30 y ____ a las 5:30 de la tarde'.

    c Me llamo Marisol Lagos, ____ treinta y cinco años, ____ casada y ____ dos hijos.

    d '¿Qué ____ su esposo?' – 'José ____ maestro, ____ en una escuela.'

    e '¿Qué ____ (tú) los fines de semana?' – 'Normalmente (yo) ____ a casa de mis padres'.

2 How would you say the following in Spanish?

    a 'Let me introduce you to my wife' (fam, sing) – 'This is Carlos' – 'Pleased to meet you.' (said by Carlos)

    b I get up at seven and usually go to bed at eleven.

    c I usually stay at home, I watch television, read or listen to music.

    d We have three children. Our eldest son is six years old and our youngest daughter is four.

    e I'm an engineer and work for a company. My wife is a nurse and works in a hospital.

If most of your answers were correct, congratulations! Among other things, these tests assess your ability to talk about things you do regularly, using different present tense forms. If you are still uncertain about some of these forms, stop to revise them before you go on to the next unit. Paragraphs 3 to 6 of the Grammar are especially important.

5

Una mesa para dos

A table for two

In this unit you will learn
- *How to express wishes and preferences*
- *How to order food and drink*

---

1 En el avión *On the plane*

🔊 **CD1, TR 5, 00:02**

James Parker is flying from London to Bogotá with a South American airline. Lunch is now being served and James has to choose from the menu below. Two key words in this dialogue are **prefiero** *I prefer* and **quiero** *I want*.

la ensalada mixta *mixed salad*
el bistek de lomito *fillet steak*
las arvejas con mantequilla *green peas with butter*
el arroz blanco *plain rice*
los filetes de pescado *fish fillets*
las legumbres mixtas *mixed vegetables*
las papas fritas *fried potatoes*
el queso *cheese*
las galletas *biscuits*
el pastel de durazno *peach cake*

> *Almuerzo*
> ENSALADA MIXTA
>
> Y
>
> BISTEK DE LOMITO
> ARVEJAS CON
> MANTEQUILLA
> ARROZ BLANCO
>
> O
>
> FILETES DE PESCADO
> LEGUMBRES MIXTAS
> PAPAS FRITAS
>
>
>
> QUESO Y GALLETAS
> PASTEL DE DURAZNO
> CAFÉ o TÉ

Insight

Words related to food vary considerably between different
Latin American countries. It may be confusing sometimes,
even for native speakers, as the same word can have different
meanings in different countries. Don't be discouraged by
all the various names. You don't need them as part of
your active vocabulary, unless you are spending time in a
particular country.

Azafata	¿Qué menú prefiere, señor?
James	Prefiero el filete de lomito.
	(The stewardess hands James his food tray.) Gracias.
Azafata	¿Qué va a tomar?
James	Quiero vino tinto, por favor.

(Contd)

*Azafata is **aeromoza** in some countries.

Insight

'**Preferir**' *'to prefer'* and '**querer**' *'to want'* are both stem-changing verbs: **-e** changes into **-ie**. Note also the phrases '**¿Qué va a tomar?**' *'What are you going to drink?'* and '**¿Va a tomar café?**' *'Are you going to have coffee?'*, in which the construction **ir** + **a** + infinitive corresponds to the English *to be going* + infinitive. More on this in Unit 7.

tomar *(here) to drink, have*
el vino tinto *red wine*

Say it in Spanish

Use the guidelines below to fill in your part of the conversation with a flight attendant.

Azafata	¿Qué menú prefiere?
Usted	*Say you prefer fish fillets.*
Azafata	¿Y qué va a tomar? Tenemos vino tinto, vino blanco, cerveza, jugo, agua mineral...
Usted	*Say what you want.*
	(After lunch, the flight attendant comes round with coffee and tea)
Azafata	¿Va a tomar café o té?
Usted	*Say whether you want coffee or tea.*

Names for fruit and vegetables

Differences in vocabulary between Latin America and Spain and within Latin America itself are common in the area of fruit and vegetables. Here are some examples:

Latin America	Spain	
la papa	**la patata**	*potato*
el durazno	**el melocotón**	*peach*
las arvejas / los chícharos	**los guisantes**	*peas*
(Mexico and Central America)		
los frijoles / los porotos	**las judías /**	*beans*
(Southern Cone countries)	**las alubias**	

See also Unit 6 and the **Glossary of Latin American** terms at the back.

---

2 Una mesa para dos *A table for two*

James Parker and a Colombian associate in Bogotá go to a restaurant for dinner. Key words and phrases here are **pueden** *you can,* **¿Nos trae ...?** *Will you bring us ...?,* **para mí** *for me.*

Mesera	Buenas noches.
Señor Donoso	Buenas noches. ¿Tiene una mesa para dos?
Mesera	*(Pointing to a table)* Sí, pueden sentarse aquí si desean.
Señor Donoso	Sí, está bien. ¿Nos trae la carta, por favor? *(The waitress brings them the menu.)* Gracias.
Mesera	¿Van a tomar un aperitivo?
James	Para mí no, gracias.
Señor Donoso	Para mí tampoco.
Mesera	Bien, ya regreso.

Insight

'**Poder**' '*can, to be able to*', is a stem-changing verb (**o>ue**). Note also the request '**¿Nos trae ...?**' '*Will you bring us ...?*', where Spanish uses the present tense and English the future with 'will'. In Spanish, the pronoun, in this case '**nos**' '*us*', precedes the verb, translating literally '*Us you bring ...?*'. (See Grammar, para 3.)

mesero(a) / camarero(a) *waiter / waitress*
sentarse (e > ie) *to sit*
si desean *if you wish*
¿Van a tomar ...? *Are you going to have ...?*
tampoco *neither*
Ya regreso *I'll be straight back*
regresar *to come back*

Say it in Spanish

How would you express the following in Spanish?

a Have you got a table for three?
b I want an apéritif.
c Will you bring us a bottle of (**una botella de**) red wine, please?

3 ¿Cómo lo quiere? *How would you like it?*

James and señor Donoso order their food. First, try learning these
key phrases: **Yo quiero ...** *I would like*, **¿Me trae ...?** *Will you bring
me ...?*, **Para mí ...** *For me ...*, **Tráiganos ...** *Bring us...*

Mesera	¿Qué van a pedir?
James	Yo quiero una sopa de verduras para empezar.
Mesera	Una sopa de verduras …¿Y qué más?
James	Quiero pollo.
Mesera	El pollo, ¿cómo lo quiere?
James	Lo quiero asado.
Mesera	¿Con qué lo quiere? ¿Con arroz, con puré…?
James	Con arroz. Y me trae una ensalada mixta también, por favor.
Mesera	¿Y para usted, señor?
Señor Donoso	Para mí, crema de espárragos, y carne guisada con papas.
Mesera	Las papas, ¿las quiere fritas, doradas …?
Señor Donoso	Fritas.
Mesera	¿Y qué van a tomar?
Señor Donoso	Una botella de vino tinto.
Mesera	Tenemos un vino chileno muy bueno.
Señor Donoso	Sí, tráiganos un vino chileno.

una botella de
vino tinto

Insight

Two important things to notice here: first, the Spanish for
'*it, them*', as in '**¿Cómo lo quiere?**' '*How would you like it?*'
and '**¿Las quiere fritas …?**' '*Would you like them fried …?*';
second, the position of such words in Spanish before the verb,
translating literally '*How it you would like?*' and '*Them you*

(Contd)

would like fried …?' But note '**tráiganos**' '*bring us*', a command form, where '**nos**' '*us*' must follow the verb. (See Grammar, para 3.)

¿Qué van a pedir? *What are you going to order?*
la sopa de verduras *vegetable soup*
para empezar *to start*
el pollo asado *roast chicken*
¿Con qué lo quiere? *What do you want it with? (pol)*
la crema de espárragos *asparagus soup*
la carne guisada *stewed meat*
las papas fritas / doradas *fried / golden potatoes*

Insight

Note that in questions, prepositions come first in Spanish, whereas in English they normally go at the end of the sentence: '**¿Con qué lo quiere?**' '*What do you want it with?*', '**¿Para cuándo las quiere?**' '*When do you want them for?*'.

Say it in Spanish

You are in a restaurant in a Spanish-speaking country. How would you say the following?

a Will you bring me a vegetable soup?
b I want roast chicken with mashed potatoes.
c Will you bring us a mixed salad?
d Coffee for me, please.

4 ¿Qué van a comer de postre? *What are you going to have for dessert?*

James Parker and señor Donoso order a dessert, **un postre**. Note the expression **yo quisiera** *I would like.*

Mesera	¿Qué van a comer de postre?
Señor Donoso	¿Qué tiene?
Mesera	Tenemos helados, fruta, flan, pastel de queso …
James	Yo quiero una ensalada de fruta.
Señor Donoso	Para mí un helado de chocolate.
Mesera	¿Van a tomar café?
James	Yo no, gracias.
Señor Donoso	Sí, yo quisiera un café.

Insight

'A chocolate ice cream' is '**un helado de chocolate**' in Spanish (literally, 'an ice cream of chocolate'). Similarly, 'a fruit salad' is '**una ensalada de fruta**' and 'cheesecake' is '**un pastel de queso**'.

¿Qué van a comer …? What are you going to eat …?
el flan crème caramel
el pastel de queso cheesecake

Say it in Spanish

Use the guidelines below to complete your conversation with the waitress.

Mesera	¿Qué va a comer de postre?
Usted	*Ask whether she has ice-cream.*
Mesera	Sí, tenemos helado de chocolate, de vainilla, de mango y de papaya.
Usted	*Say which one you prefer, and say you would like coffee too.*

5 ¿Nos trae la cuenta, por favor? *Will you bring us the bill, please?*

Señor Donoso and señor Parker order the bill, **la cuenta**.

Señor Donoso	¿Nos trae la cuenta, por favor?
Mesera	Sí, un momento, señor. En seguida se la traigo.

Insight

Note again that, as in the previous dialogues, the pronouns come before the verb: '**¿Nos trae la cuenta?**' *'Will you bring us the bill?'* and '**Enseguida se la traigo**' *'I'll bring it to you straight away'*. In the second sentence '**se**' translates '*to you*' and '**la**' '*it*' ('**la cuenta**'). (See also Grammar, para 4.)

Key phrases

Expressing wants and preferences

Quiero/quisiera vino blanco / tinto.	*I want/would like white / red wine.*
Prefiero café / té / agua mineral.	*I prefer coffee / tea / mineral water.*

Ordering food and drink

¿Me / nos trae la carta / la cuenta?	*Will you bring me / us the menu / bill?*
Tráigame/nos una botella de vino, por favor.	*Bring me / us a bottle of wine, please.*
Quiero carne/pollo/pescado.	*I would like meat / chicken / fish.*
Lo/la quiero asado(a) / frito(a) (m/f).	*I would like it roast / fried.*

Lo / la prefiero con puré / arroz /   *I prefer it with mashed potatoes /*
una ensalada *(m/f).*   *rice / a salad.*
Para mí, una sopa de verduras /   *For me, a vegetable soup / a vanilla*
un helado de vainilla.   *ice-cream.*

Grammar

1 *Expressing wants and preferences: querer to want, preferir to prefer*

To say what you want, use **querer** *to want,* and to say what you prefer, use **preferir** *to prefer.* These two verbs are stem-changing, the e of the stem changing into ie (e > ie): **yo quiero / prefiero, tú quieres / prefieres, usted / él / ella quiere / prefiere, ustedes / ellos / ellas quieren / prefieren.**

¿Qué **quieres / prefieres**   *What do you want /*
comer / tomar?   *prefer to eat / drink?*
Quiero / prefiero papas   *I want / prefer chips /*
fritas / una cerveza.   *a beer.*

2 *Poder to be able to, can*

Poder is a stem-changing verb in which the o of the stem changes into ue (o > ue): **yo puedo, tú puedes, usted / él / ella puede, ustedes / ellos / ellas pueden. Poder** can be used in requests, as when ordering food and drink, but it has other uses as well.

¿Puede traerme / nos la carta?	*Can you bring me / us the menu?*
¿Pueden reservarme / nos una mesa?	*Can you book me / us a table?*
Pueden sentarse aquí.	*You can sit here.*

3 Direct object pronouns

a Lo / la, los / las it, *them*
To say *it* or *them*, as in *How do you want it / them?*, use **lo** when reference is to a masculine word, and **la** for feminine. In the plural use **los** and **las**.

¿Cómo quiere el pescado?	*How do you want the fish?*
Lo quiero a la plancha.	*I want it grilled.*
¿Con qué quiere la carne?	*What do you want the meat with?*
La quiero con papas.	*I want it with potatoes.*
¿Cómo quiere las papas?	*How do you want the potatoes?*
Las quiero fritas.	*I want them fried.*

Lo, la, los, las can also refer to people:

Lo/La quiero mucho.	*I love him/her very much.*
Los/las veo a menudo.	*I see them often.*

These words are known as *direct object pronouns* (see Glossary of grammatical terms) and they normally come before the verb, but in sentences with a finite verb (e.g. **puede** *you / he / she can*) followed by an infinitive (e.g. **traer** *to bring*) or a gerund (e.g. **preparando** *preparing*), the pronoun can either precede the finite verb or be attached to the infinitive or the gerund.

¿Puede traer la carta, por favor?	*Can you bring the menu please?*
¿Puede traer**la**, por favor? *or* ¿**La** puede traer, por favor?	*Can you bring it, please?*
Estoy preparando el almuerzo.	*I'm preparing lunch.*
Estoy preparándo**lo**. *or* **Lo** estoy preparando.	*I'm preparing it.*

(For *gerunds* see Unit 10.)

Object pronouns follow positive imperatives but precede negative one.

Traiga el vino.	*Bring the wine.*
Tráig**alo**.	*Bring it.*
No **lo** traiga.	*Don't bring it.*

(For *imperatives* see Unit 12)

b me, te, nos *me, you (fam), us*
Direct object pronouns corresponding to **yo** *I*, **tú** *you* (fam), nosotros *we*, are **me, te, nos**, respectively.

| **Me** / **te** / **nos** invita. | *He is inviting me / you / us.* |
| **Me** / **te** / **nos** conocen. | *They know me / you / us.* |

Me, te and **nos** can also function as indirect object pronouns. See 4 below.

4 Indirect object pronouns

Me *me, to me*, nos *us, to us*…
a To say *me, to me, us, to us*, etc., as in *Will you bring me a salad?*, *Will you bring us the menu?*, use the following set of words, which are called *indirect object pronouns* (see Glossary of grammatical terms). In requests such as the above, these are followed by a verb in the present tense.

me	*me, to me, for me*
te	*you, to you, for you* (fam, sing)
le	*you, to you, for you* (pol, sing)
le	*him, to him, for him*
le	*her, to her, for her*
nos	*us, to us, for us*
les	*you, to you, for you* (pl)
les	*them, to them, for them*

¿Me pasa la sal?	*Will you pass me the salt?*
¿Te preparo un café?	*Shall I prepare a coffee for you?*
Ahora le / les traigo el postre.	*I'll bring you the dessert right now.*
¿Nos reserva una mesa?	*Will you reserve a table for us?*

Note that le and les are used for both masculine and feminine.

b In sentences with two object pronouns, one direct and the other indirect, the indirect object pronoun comes first.

| ¿Me trae la ensalada? | *Will you bring me the salad?* |
| ¿Me la trae? | *Will you bring it to me?* |

c Le and les become se before lo / la, los / las.

| Enseguida le doy la cuenta. | *I'll give you the bill right away.* |
| Enseguida se la doy. | *I'll give it to you right away.* |

5 Para mí, ti, él, ella ... For me, you, him, her ...

a Para mí, para usted ... *for me, for you* ...

To say *for me, for you, for him*, etc. use **para** followed by **mí** *me* and **ti** *you* (fam) for the first and second person singular, and **usted, él, ella, nosotros/as, ustedes, ellos/as** with all other persons.

Para mí, pescado con papas fritas.	*For me, fish and chips.*
¿Y para ti?	*And for you? (fam)*
¿Y para usted, señor?	*And for you, sir? (pol)*

With the exception of **con** *with*, which in the first and second person singular ('yo', 'tú') give '**conmigo**' '*with me*' and '**contigo**' '*with you*' (fam), other prepositions (words like *from, in, without, to*, etc.) follow the same rule as **para**.

| **Él va sin mí.** | *He is going without me.* |
| **Ellos vienen sin ella.** | *They are coming without her.* |

b Notice the use of **para** in these sentences:

¿Tiene una mesa para dos?   *Have you got a table for two?*
Quiero una sopa para empezar.   *I want a soup to start with.*

6 Agreement of adjectives

In Spanish, adjectives (words like *big*, *small*, *long*) must agree in gender (masc/fem) and number (sing/pl) with the word they refer to. Here are some examples taken from this unit.

una ensalada mixta   *a mixed salad*
legumbres mixtas   *mixed vegetables*
un pollo asado   *a roast chicken*
pollos asados   *roast chickens*

Note that in Spanish, adjectives normally follow the noun that they qualify, but for emphasis or special effect some adjectives can precede the noun. Neither of the adjectives above can be used in this position, so unless you are certain, stick to the above rule.

Practice

1 You are on business in Bogotá, and today you are having lunch with a Colombian colleague at Casa Brava, so you decide to telephone the restaurant to make a reservation. Complete your part of the conversation, below, with the restaurant manager.

Jefe	*(Al teléfono)* Restaurante Casa Brava, buenos días.
Ud.	*Answer the greeting and say you would like to book a table for two.*
Jefe	Para hoy, ¿verdad?
Ud.	*Yes, for today.*
Jefe	¿Y para qué hora?
Ud.	*For half past one.*
Jefe	¿A nombre de quién?
Ud.	*Say in what name you want the reservation.*

CASA BRAVA

Km. 4.5 Vía a la Calera
Tel: 6124106

Está decorado con buen gusto,
originalidad, sencillez. La calidad
de su cocina es excelente y el
servicio es especialmente amable.

En la noche el ambiente es alegre
de fiesta. Pero durante el día es
apacible y acogedor. Ideal para un
almuerzo de negocios.

¿A nombre de quién? *In whose name?*

2 You arrive at Restaurante Casa Brava with your colleague and you are met by the head waiter.

Mesero	Buenas tardes.
Ud.	*Answer the greeting and say you have a reservation for half past one.*
Mesero	¿Cómo se llama usted?
Ud.	*Give your name.*
Mesero	Sí, su mesa es esa, la que está junto a la ventana.

esa *that one (f)*
junto a *next to*
la ventana *window*

3 You now are ready to order. First, study the menu opposite, then write a dialogue between you and your companion and the **mesera**, using some of the phrases in which follow the menu and those you learnt in dialogue 3. You can then compare what you have done with the model dialogue in the **Key to the activities**.

Restaurante
Casa Brava

PARA EMPEZAR
Cocktail de camarones
Aguacate relleno
Empanadas

SOPAS Y CREMAS
Sopa de verduras
Sopa de tomate
Crema de espárragos
Crema de zapallo
Sopa o crema del día

CARNES Y PESCADOS
Chuletas de ternera
Chuletas de cerdo
Carne asada
Pollo asado
Filete de pescado
 a la plancha
Pescado frito

POSTRES
Duraznos o mangos
 en almíbar
Flan de vainilla
Fresas con crema
Pastel de fresas
Helados

los camarones *shrimps*
el aguacate relleno *stuffed avocado*
la sopa de zapallo *pumpkin soup*
la chuleta *chop*
la ternera *veal*
a la plancha *grilled*
los duraznos en almíbar *peaches in syrup*
la fresa *strawberry*
la crema *cream*
el pastel *cake*
los champiñones *mushrooms*
pollo en salsa de mostaza *chicken in mustard sauce*
el soufflé de calabaza *pumpkin soufflé (a hot soufflé containing*
  pumpkin, eggs and seafood, served with sauce)
no queda *we don't have any left*
el jugo *juice*

Insight

'**Empanadas**', *'turnovers or pasties'* will be found in most Spanish-speaking countries. Most will contain minced meat and different kinds of vegetables, depending on the region. In some places you will find them with *tuna* ('**atún**'), (*'chicken'*) **pollo** or *cheese* ('**queso**'). '**Empanadas**' are usually served as a starter or a snack. To order one you can say: '**Quiero una empanada de** (**atún, pollo**, etc.)'.

¿Qué desean comer?
Para empezar tenemos ...
También tenemos sopas y cremas.
¿Y qué más?
¿Con qué lo / la quiere?
¿Y para usted señor/a?
¿Algo más?
¿Qué van a tomar?
¿Qué desean de postre?
¿Van a tomar café?

4 At a table next to you, a Colombian is ordering food. What food has she ordered? Listen to her conversation with the waiter then complete the order below, as the waiter might have done. First, look at these new words.

Mesa –
_____
_____
_____
_____

_____
_____
_____
_____

_____
_____
_____
_____

5 You are going out for a meal with an English-speaking colleague who is travelling in Latin America with you. Your colleague has spotted the advertisement below for a restaurant and would like to know more about it. Look at the key words before you read the advertisement, then answer your colleague's questions.

el sabor *taste*
la atención *service*
el precio *price*
acogedor *warm, welcoming*
sabrá *you will know*
a cuerpo de rey *like a king*

QUICK VOCAB

ser atendido como un príncipe *to be served like
  a prince*
pagar *to pay*
el plebeyo *commoner*

LA COMBINACIÓN PERFECTA…!

¡Sí! Ahora **Sebastián** tiene la combinación perfecta para convertirse en su restaurante favorito. Los mejores pescados, mariscos y deliciosas carnes en un acogedor ambiente. Visítenos y sabrá lo que es comer a cuerpo de rey, ser atendido como un príncipe y pagar precios de plebeyo.

LA COCINA DE SEBASTIÁN

José Domingo Cañas 1675
(Esq. M. Eyzaguirre –
Nuñoa)
Reservas: 2091565

Now answer these questions in English:

a Why is Sebastián the 'perfect combination'?
b What sort of food do they serve?

6 The passage below looks at the contribution of the *New World* – el **Nuevo Mundo** – to the European diet. As you read the text, try answering the following questions with the help of the key words below:

  a Which two main products came to Europe from the Americas?
  b According to the text, what is difficult to imagine?

La contribución del Nuevo Mundo a la dieta europea

Algunos productos que hoy en día son esenciales en la dieta europea, son en realidad originarios de las Américas. Los más importantes son la papa y el tomate. Pero hay muchos otros, entre ellos los frijoles, las habas, el chile, los aguacates, los cacahuetes, los damascos ('chabacanos' in Mexico, 'albaricoques' in Spain and some other countries), las papayas, el chocolate, etcétera. Es difícil imaginar la cocina europea sin algunos de estos productos, especialmente la papa y el tomate.

Insight

The words '**aguacate**' '*avocado*' and '**cacahuete**' '*peanut*' are derived from náhuatl, a language spoken by indigenous people in southern Mexico and parts of Central America. In some South American countries, among them Peru, Chile and Argentina, '**el aguacate**' is known as '**la palta**', and '**el cacahuete**' as '**el maní**'.

algunos *some*
hoy en día *nowadays*
son originarios de *they come from*
el frijol *bean*
el haba *broad bean*
el damasco *apricot*

QUICK VOCAB

7 The passage which follows deals with Latin American food. Look at the key words before you read the text, then check your comprehension by answering the questions which follow the passage.

Insight

This text is longer than others you have encountered in this book. Try to get the gist of what it says rather than translate

(Contd)

it word for word. Many of the words are similar to those in English and you should have little difficulty in guessing their meanings. You don't need to learn all the new words either, as this is an exercise in understanding and its main purpose is to help you increase your passive vocabulary.

variada *varied*	**el plato** *dish*
el pan de maíz *maize bread*	**como en** *as in*
la base *basis*	**el mar** *sea*
a base de carne *with meat*	**la carne de vaca** *beef*

La cocina hispanoamericana es muy variada y está basada fundamentalmente en los productos típicos de cada país o región. La dieta de los mexicanos, por ejemplo, es muy diferente a la de los colombianos o a la de los argentinos. Lo más típico de México son las tortillas, un pan de maíz, que es la base de muchos platos mexicanos. Otro ingrediente básico en la dieta mexicana es el chile. México es un país muy grande y existen platos típicos de cada región, muchos de ellos a base de carne. En la costa se come mucho pescado y mariscos.

En los países centroamericanos se comen muchos platos a base de maíz. El arroz con pollo es un plato típico en muchos países del Caribe y de América del Sur, entre ellos Colombia. Pero en Colombia, como en otros países sudamericanos, la cocina es muy variada y los restaurantes presentan una gran variedad de platos nacionales e internacionales. En el Perú y Chile, por ejemplo, se comen muchos productos del mar. En la Argentina y el Uruguay se come preferentemente carne de vaca.

Answer these questions in English:

a What is the most typical food in Mexico?
b What is the staple food in Central America?
c Name a typical dish in many Caribbean and South American countries.
d What do Argentinians and Uruguayans prefer to eat?

Test yourself

1 Fill in each blank with a suitable pronoun: *lo, la, las, me, nos, se*

   a 'El pollo, ¿con qué ____ quiere?' – '____quiero con papas'.

   b 'Y las papas, ¿cómo ____ prefiere?' – ' ____ prefiero fritas'.

   c Quisiera un café. ¿Y ____ trae la cuenta también, por favor?

   d ¿La cuenta? En seguida ____ ____ traigo.

   e Una mesa para dos, por favor. ¿Y ____ trae la carta, también?

2 You and your partner are having a meal in a restaurant. How would say each of the following?

   a Pork chops with mixed vegetables for me.

   b I would like grilled fish with mashed potatoes.

   c (¿Y para beber?) A mineral water and a beer, please.

   d Will you bring us a vanilla ice-cream and a fruit salad?

   e Can you bring me a coffee, please?

Are you ready to order your meal now? Many of the phrases used in this unit and in the tests are set phrases which only require changes in vocabulary. If most of your answers were correct, go on to Unit 6 which focuses on shopping. But if you are unhappy with your performance, especially with the grammar in Test 1, go back to paras 3 and 4 of the Grammar section.

6

¿Cuánto vale?
How much does it cost?

In this unit you will learn
- *About shopping*
- *How to describe things*
- *How to express comparisons*
- *How to express likes and dislikes*

---

1 ¿Cuánto vale? *How much does it cost?*

Mario, a Colombian, is buying a briefcase, **un maletín**. Try learning these key phrases first: **Quisiera ver ...** *I would like to see ...*, **Me gusta** *I like it*, **¿Cuánto vale?** *How much does it cost?*, **Es un poco caro** *It is a little expensive.*

Mario	Buenos días. Quisiera ver ese maletín que está en la vitrina.
Vendedora	¿Este?
Mario	Sí, ese, el negro.
	(Mario examines the briefcase.)
Vendedora	Es un maletín muy bonito y muy elegante.
Mario	¿Es de cuero?
Vendedora	Sí, todos los artículos que vendemos son de cuero.
Mario	Me gusta mucho. ¿Cuánto vale?
Vendedora	Doscientos cincuenta mil pesos.
Mario	Es un poco caro. ¿No tiene otro más barato?
Vendedora	Sí, ese de color café es más barato. Vale ciento veinte mil pesos.
Mario	Ese no me gusta mucho.
Vendedora	No tenemos otro.
Mario	Bueno, voy a llevar el negro. ¿Puedo pagar con tarjeta de crédito?
Vendedora	Claro que sí.

Insight

'**Me gusta (ese maletín)**' '*I like (that briefcase)*' translates literally as '*(that briefcase) is pleasing to me*'. In this sentence, the subject of the sentence is '**ese maletín**' '*that briefcase*', not the person who likes it, therefore you cannot use 'yo' '*I*'. (See Grammar, para 2.)

la vitrina / el escaparate *shop window*
el cuero *leather*
el artículo *article*
vender *to sell*
otro/a *another (one), other*
más barato *cheaper*
café *brown*
llevar *to take*
pagar *to pay*
la tarjeta de crédito *credit card*
claro que sí *certainly*

QUICK VOCAB

Say it in Spanish

You go into a shop to buy a suitcase, **una maleta**. How would you express the following in Spanish?

a I would like to see that (**esa**) suitcase.
b It is a little expensive. Have you got a cheaper one?
c I don't like that (suitcase) very much.
d I'm going to take the black one.
e May I pay with traveller's cheques (**cheques de viaje**)?

Latin American currency

The currency used in Colombia is **el peso. Pesos** are also used in Argentina, Chile, Cuba, the Dominican Republic, Mexico and Uruguay. The rate of exchange, **el cambio,** of the peso in relation to the dollar, the euro, the pound and other currencies is not the same in all countries which use this currency. The unit of currency in Paraguay is **el guaraní,** in Peru **el sol,** in Bolivia **el boliviano,** and in Venezuela **el bolívar.** Costa Rica and El Salvador use **el colón,** Nicaragua **el córdoba,** Guatemala **el quetzal,** Honduras **la lempira** and Panama **el balboa** and the American dollar, **el dólar.** Ecuador and Puerto Rico also use American dollars.

The standard word for money is **el dinero,** but in many Latin American countries you will hear the more informal word **la plata** (literally *silver*), for example **No tengo plata** *I have no money,* **Es mucha plata** *It's a lot of money.*

---

2 ¿Me lo puedo probar? *May I try it on?*

Clara, a Colombian, is buying a sweater, **un suéter**. First, try learning these key phrases: **¿Me lo puedo probar?** *May I try it on?*, **Me queda un poco pequeño** *It is a bit small for me,* **¿Tiene uno más grande?** *Have you got a larger one?*

Vendedor	A la orden.
Clara	*(Pointing to some sweaters)* Quisiera ver esos suéteres, por favor.
Vendedor	¿Qué talla tiene usted?
Clara	Talla ocho.
Vendedor	Bueno, tenemos en blanco, azul, verde, rojo y amarillo.
Clara	El verde me gusta más. Es muy bonito. ¿Me lo puedo probar?
Vendedor	Claro que sí. *(Clara tries the sweater on.)*
Clara	Este me queda un poco pequeño. ¿Tiene uno más grande?
Vendedor	Sí, aquí tiene uno en la talla diez, en el mismo color. *(Clara tries on the other sweater).*
Clara	Sí, este me queda bien. ¿Cuánto vale?
Vendedor	Cuarenta mil pesos.
Clara	Sí, lo voy a llevar.
Vendedor	¿Va a pagar en efectivo?
Clara	Sí, en efectivo.

Insight

'**Probarse**' '*to try on*' is a reflexive verb (Unit 4, para. 6). In '¿**Me lo puedo probar?**', '**me**' stands for '*myself*', and '**lo**' translates '*it*' ('*el suéter*').

'**Quedar**' in this context means '*to fit*', '*to suit*'. In '**Me queda un poco pequeño**' '*It's a bit small for me*' (literally, '*it fits me ...*') '**quedar**' is in the third person singular, as it agrees with the subject '**el suéter**'.

a la orden *can I help you?*
la talla *size*
más *more*
más grande *bigger*
mismo/a *same*
pagar en efectivo *to pay cash*

Los colores *colours*
amarillo/a *yellow*   **naranja** *orange*
azul *blue*   **negro** *black*
blanco/a *white*   **rojo/a** *red*
gris *grey*   **rosa** *pink*
café / marrón *brown*   **verde** *green*

Insight

Colours are masculine in Spanish: '**el amarillo**', '**el azul**', etc. Note also that only those colours which end in **-o**, like '**amarillo**', change in the feminine: '**la camisa amarilla**'; other colours, including those ending in **-a** remain unchanged: '**la corbata azul**' '*the blue tie*', '**el vestido naranja**' '*the orange dress*'. If the word they qualify is plural, add **-s** to those colours ending in a vowel and **-es** to those ending in a consonant: '**los sombreros negros**' '*the black hats*', '**los zapatos azules**' '*the blue shoes*'.

Say it in Spanish

During a holiday in a Spanish-speaking country you decide to buy some trousers, **unos pantalones**. Fill in your part of the conversation with the shop-assistant.

Vendedor	Buenas tardes. ¿Qué desea?
Ud.	*Say you would like to see the trousers which are in the shop window.*
Vendedor	¿Esos?
Ud.	*Yes, those ones.*
Vendedor	¿Qué talla tiene usted?
Ud.	*Say what size you wear.*
Vendedor	Los tenemos en negro, gris, café y blanco.
Ud.	*Say what colour you want them in.*
Vendedor	Aquí tiene usted.
Ud.	*Ask if you can try them on.*
Vendedor	Sí, sí, pase por aquí, por favor.

3 En el mercado *At the market*

Silvia, a Colombian, is buying some vegetables at the market.
Colombians use **libras** *pounds*, instead of **kilos**. First, try learning
these key phrases: **deme** *give me*, **¿Qué precio tienen?** *How much
are they? / What is the price?*, **Eso es todo** *That's all*, **¿Cuánto es?**
How much is it?

🔊 CD1, TR 6, 02:52

Vendedor	A la orden, señora.
Silvia	¿Cuánto valen las papas?
Vendedor	Doscientos cincuenta pesos la libra.
Silvia	Deme tres libras.
	(The stallholder weighs the potatoes and puts them in a bag.)
Vendedor	¿Algo más?
Silvia	Sí, ¿qué precio tienen las lechugas?
Vendedor	Treinta pesos cada una.
Silvia	Quiero dos. Y los tomates, ¿cuánto valen?
Vendedor	Doscientos cincuenta pesos la libra.
Silvia	Deme libra y media.
Vendedor	¿Algo más?
Silvia	No, eso es todo. ¿Cuánto es?
Vendedor	Son mil ciento ochenta y cinco pesos.
Silvia	Hasta luego, gracias.
Vendedor	Hasta luego.

Say it in Spanish

You are in a market buying some fruit and vegetables. How would you express the following in Spanish?

a How much are the tomatoes?
b What's the price of the mangoes (**los mangos**)?
c Give me two pounds / kilos.
d I want one and a half kilos.

4 En la oficina de correos *At the post office*

Silvia is sending a postcard, **una postal**. Key words here are **mandar** *to send*, **la estampilla** *stamp*, **el buzón** *postbox*, and **afuera** *outside*.

Silvia	¿Cuánto vale mandar una postal a Inglaterra?
Empleado	Mil doscientos pesos.
Silvia	Quiero dos estampillas de mil doscientos y cinco de seiscientos pesos.
	(The clerk gives Silvia the stamps and she pays for them.)
	Gracias. ¿Dónde está el buzón?
Empleado	Está afuera.

Insight

Another word for '**la estampilla**' '*stamp*' is '**el sello**', which is the word used in Spain. '**Postal**' is a short for '**la tarjeta postal**' '*postcard*'. In everyday language, in most places in Latin America, '**la oficina de correos**' '*post office*' is '**el correo**'. In Peru it is known as '**el Serpost**'.

Say it in Spanish

You are travelling in Latin America and you want to send some letters home. How would you say the following in Spanish?

a Where is the post office?
b How much does it cost to send a letter (**una carta**) to ...?
c I'd like three eight hundred *peso*-stamps.

Key phrases

Shopping

Quisiera ver esa maleta / ese suéter.	*I'd like to see that suitcase / sweater.*
Quiero dos kilos / libras.	*I want two kilos / pounds.*
Deme un kilo y medio / uno / una.	*Give me one and a half kilos / one.*
¿Tiene otro/a?	*Have you got another one?*
¿Cuánto vale/n?	*How much is it / are they?*
¿Cuánto cuesta/n?	

¿Qué precio tiene/n?	
¿Cuánto es?	*How much is it (all)?*
¿Puedo pagar con tarjeta de crédito / cheques de viaje?	*May I pay with a credit card / traveller's cheques?*
Voy a pagar en efectivo.	*I'll pay cash.*

Describing things

Es un poco caro(a) / pequeño(a) / grande.	*It is a bit expensive /small / big.*
Es / son (muy) bonito/s.	*It is/they are (very) nice / pretty.*
¿Es / son de cuero?	*Is it / are they made of leather?*

Expressing comparisons

ese / Esa es más grande / pequeño(a).	*That is bigger / smaller.*
¿Tiene algo más barato / uno(a) más barato(a)?	*Have you got something cheaper / a cheaper one?*

Expressing likes and dislikes

Me gusta/n (mucho)	*I like it / them (very much)*
No me gusta/n.	*I don't like it / them.*

Grammar

1 *Demonstratives*

a ese/a, esos/as *that, those*

To say *that* and *those* in Spanish we use the following set of words:

that	**those**
ese (m)	esos (m)
esa (f)	esas (f)

Quisiera ver ese maletín.	*I would like to see that briefcase.*
Quisiera ver esos suéteres.	*I would like to see those sweaters.*

Ese, esa, etc., can also function as pronouns, in place of a noun. You may sometimes find them written with an accent, which is discouraged by the Real Academia de la Lengua.

Ese de color negro.	*That black one. (masc)*
Me gusta esa.	*I like that one. (fem)*

To say *that*, as in *That is all, What is that?*, we use the word **eso**, which is neuter:

Eso es todo.	*That is all.*
¿Qué es eso?	*What is that?*

b aquel, aquella, aquellos, aquellas *that, those*

Spanish has a second set of demonstratives meaning 'that' and 'those', which are used to refer to things which are more distant. Like those above, they can function as pronouns, meaning 'that one', 'those ones'.

Aquel equipaje.	*That luggage.*
Aquella maleta negra.	*That black suitcase.*
Me gustan aquellos zapatos/aquellos.	*I like those shoes/those ones.*

The neuter form is aquello.

Aquello no vale nada.	*That is worth nothing.*

2 Me gusta I like (it)

To express likes and dislikes in Spanish, we use the verb **gustar** (literally *to please*), preceded by an object pronoun (words like *me, you, him, her*) (see Unit 5).

me gusta	I like (it)
te gusta	*you like (it)* (fam, sing)
le gusta	*you like (it)* (pol, sing)
	he, she likes (it)
nos gusta	*we like (it)*
les gusta	*you like (it)* (pl)
	they like (it)

These phrases translate literally into English as *it pleases me*, *it pleases you*, *it pleases him*, etc. Therefore the verb remains in the third person singular. To say *I like them*, *you like them*, *he likes them*, use the third person plural of the verb (**gustan**):

me gustan	*I like them*
te gustan	*you like them*
le gustan	*you like, he, she, likes them*

To say what you like to do, use the appropriate form of **gustar** followed by the infinitive. Look at these examples:

| **Me gusta viajar.** | *I like to travel.* |
| **Nos gusta jugar al tenis.** | *We like playing tennis.* |

If **gustar** is preceded by a name, for example Carmen, this must be preceded by the preposition **a**:

| **A Carmen le gusta la comida mexicana.** | *Carmen likes Mexican food.* |
| **A Julio le gustan las zapatillas.** | *Julio likes the trainers.* |

For emphasis or contrast with something that has been said before, use the following set of pronouns after **a**: **mí** (for 'yo'), **ti** (for 'tú'), él, ella, usted, nosotros, ellos:

¿A ti también te gustan?	*Do you like them too?*
A mí no. A mí me gustan las otras.	*I don't (like them). I like the other ones*
A él/ella tampoco.	*He/She doesn't (like them) either.*

3 Comparisons

To express comparisons in Spanish (e.g. cheaper, bigger), we simply place the word **más** (*more*) before the adjective. Here are some examples:

Ese es más barato.	*That is cheaper.*
Esos son más caros.	*Those are more expensive.*
Esos suéteres son más grandes.	*Those sweaters are bigger.*

To say that something is '*smaller, longer*', etc. than something else use '**más que**' '*more than*'.

El vestido azul es más pequeño que el blanco.	*The blue dress is smaller than the white one'.*
Los pantalones negros son más largos que los grises.	*The black trousers are longer than the grey ones.*

A few adjectives form the comparative form in an irregular way: '**bueno**' '*good*' – '**mejor**' '*better*'; '**malo**' '*bad*' – '**peor**' '*worse*'; '**grande**' '*big*', '*large*' – '**mayor**' or '**más grande**' '*bigger*', '*larger*'.

Estos tomates son mejores.	*These tomatoes are better.*
Mi talla es mayor que la de Gloria.	*My size is larger than Gloria's.*

To say that something is '*the prettiest*', '*the most comfortable*', etc. use **el/la/los/las más** followed by the adjective:

Su chaqueta es la más bonita.	*His/Her jacket is the prettiest.*
Mi apartamento es el más cómodo.	*My apartment is the most comfortable.*
Este vino es el mejor.	*This wine is the best.*

4 Ser to describe things

To describe things, we normally use the verb **ser** *to be*:

Es un maletín muy bonito.	*It's a very nice briefcase.*
Es muy elegante.	*It is very elegant.*

Son bonitos.	*They are nice.*
Es de cuero / fibra sintética.	*It is made of leather / synthetic fibre.*

este suéter es demasiado grande

5 *Todo all, whole*

Todo agrees in number (sing / pl) and gender (m / f) with the noun it refers to, functioning as an adjective.

Todo el día	*The whole day*
Todos los días	*Every / each day.*
Toda la gente	*All the people*
Todas las tiendas	*All the shops*

'**Todo**' can also function as a pronoun, meaning '*all*' or '*everything*' in the singular, or '*everybody*', '*everyone*', '*all (of them)*' in the plural.

Eso es todo.	*That's all.*
¿Tienes todo?	*Have you got everything?*
Todos lo conocen.	*Everybody/Everyone knows him.*
Todos hablan español.	*All of them speak Spanish/They all speak Spanish.*

6 *Otro another (one), other*

Like **todo** above, **otro** agrees in number and gender with the noun it refers to, and it can go with a noun or in place of a noun.

Otro color	*Another colour*
Otros pantalones	*Other trousers*
Otra falda	*Another skirt*
Otras camisas	*Other shirts*
Deme otro	*Give me another one*

Practice

1 You are on holiday in Bogotá and before going back home you decide to buy a present for someone. Choose one of these articles and then play your part in this conversation with a shop assistant.

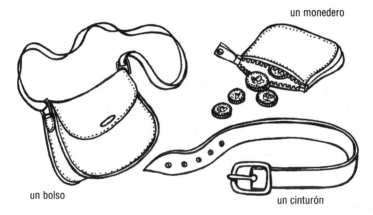

un monedero

un bolso

un cinturón

Ud.	*Tell the shop assistant which article you would like to see from the shop window.*
Vendedora	¿Cuál? ¿Este?
Ud.	*That one, the brown one.*
Vendedora	Aquí tiene usted.
Ud.	*Say it is very nice and ask if it is made of leather.*
Vendedora	Sí, es de cuero. Sólo vendemos artículos de cuero.
Ud.	*Ask how much it costs. The price given by the shop assistant seems a bit high, so ask if they have a cheaper one.*
Vendedora	No, este es el más barato que tenemos. Es muy fino. Es un cuero de muy buena calidad.
	(Contd)

Insight

To refer to the material which something is made of Spanish uses the construction '**ser**' + '**de**': '**es/son de cuero/plástico/plata/oro**' '*it is/they are leather/plastic/silver/gold*'.

2 Clothes seem to be cheaper in Colombia than back home, so you decide to buy something for yourself. Choose from one of these items and then play your part in the conversation with the shop assistant.

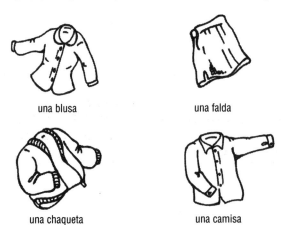

una blusa   una falda

una chaqueta   una camisa

la blusa *blouse*	**la falda** *skirt*
la camisa *shirt*	**la chaqueta** *jacket*

Ud.	*Tell the shop assistant what you would like to see.*
Vendedor	¿Qué talla tiene usted?
Ud.	*Say what size you are.*
Vendedor	¿En qué color la prefiere?
Ud.	*Ask what colours they have.*
Vendedor	Las tenemos en negro, gris, blanco, beige y naranja.
Ud.	*Say you prefer it in white.*
Vendedor	Aquí tiene usted una blanca.
Ud.	*Say you don't like the style (**el modelo**) very much. Ask if they have others.*
Vendedor	*(Showing you other items)* Sí, estas son diferentes. ¿Le gustan?
Ud.	*Yes, you like those more.*
Vendedor	Aquí tiene una en blanco.
Ud.	*Ask if you can try it on.*
Vendedor	*(Pointing to the fitting room)* Sí, allí está el probador.
Ud.	*Say it fits very well and ask how much it costs.*
Vendedor	Esa cuesta treinta y cinco mil pesos.
Ud.	*Yes, you are going to take it.*
Vendedor	¿Cómo va a pagar?
Ud.	*Say you are going to pay cash (with ready money).*

¿En qué colores…? *What colours…?*

Insight

To say '*the white/black/blue one*' use phrases like the following: '**el/la blanco/a**', '**el/la negro/a**', '**el/la azul**'. Note that '**azul**', which ends in a consonant, does not change for masculine or feminine.

Unit 6 ¿Cuánto vale? How much does it cost?   115

◄ CD1, 6, 04:28

3 You go shopping again. This time you buy several things, and while waiting to have them wrapped, you overhear a conversation between a Colombian customer buying shoes (**unos zapatos**) and a shop assistant. Listen to the conversation, and as you do so, complete the box below with details of the purchase. First look at these new words:

QV

¿Podría decirme ...? *Could you tell me ...?*
¿cuáles? *which ones?*
el descuento *discount*
el número *size (of shoes)*

artículo	precio	precio con descuento	color	número
zapatos				

◄ CD1, TR 6, 05:05

4 'Next time you want to buy men's clothes, why don't you try Almacenes García? They have big discounts for you.' Listen to this radio advertisement, and try to understand what discounts are being offered and on what articles of clothing. First look at these key words, then answer the questions below.

QUICK VOCAB

los almacenes *department store*
por fin de temporada *for end of season*
la manga larga *long sleeve*
la manga corta *short sleeve*
el caballero *gentleman*
los pantalones *trousers*
las promociones *special offers*

Now answer these questions in English:

> **a** What sort of shirts are on offer?
> **b** What discounts are they giving on men's trousers?

c What phrases have been used in the advertising to express the following: *all men's trousers and special offers are not included?*

5 You are in a market buying some fruit and vegetables. Study these key words first and then do the exercise opposite.

los aguacates *avocados*   **las zanahorias** *carrots*
los mangos *mangoes*   **las lechugas** *lettuces*
los duraznos *peaches*   **los repollos** *cabbages*

How would you express the following in Spanish?

   a How much are the avocados?
   b Have you got mangoes?
   c What is the price of the peaches?
   d I would like a kilo of carrots.
   e Give me one lettuce.
   f I want two cabbages.
   g That is all.
   h How much is it?

6 Here is an incomplete dialogue between a Colombian post-office clerk and a customer who is sending a letter (**una carta**) to the United States. Fill in the missing words.

Cliente	¿Cuánto cuesta _____ una carta _____ los Estados Unidos?
Empleado	Mil _____
Cliente	Deme una _____ de mil y cuatro _____ seiscientos.
Empleado	¿Algo más?
Cliente	_____ es todo. ¿Cuánto _____?
Empleado	Son _____ pesos.
Cliente	¿Dónde está el _____?
Empleado	Está afuera, _____ la derecha.

7 Understanding figures in Spanish may not be easy at first, so here is a chance to practise. First, look at the advertisement for furniture, below, and try reading each of the prices a few times until you feel sure that you can say them fluently. Luis Nuñez, from Bogotá bought several pieces of furniture from the shop, and now the shop assistant is adding up the price. As you listen to the figures, make a list of the items bought by Luis and write down the total amount he paid. First, look at the new vocabulary below.

los saldos *sales*
la feria *market*
al costo *cost price*
las ofertas *offers*
de contado *cash*
el descuento *discount*
el sofá-cama *sofabed*
la alcoba *bedroom*
la nevera *refrigerator*
la lavadora *washing machine*
el equipo de sonido *stereo system*
la cama *bed*

Test yourself

1 Fill in the blanks with *ese, esa, esos, esas* or *eso*, as appropriate
   a ¿Cuánto valen ____ pantalones?
   b Quisiera ver ____ cinturón, por favor.
   c ¿Qué es ____?
   d Quiero un kilo de ____ papas.

2 Fill in the blanks with a suitable form of *todo* or *otro*.
   a '¿Quiere algo más?' - 'No, eso es ____.'
   b ____ la fruta es de muy buena calidad.
   c Esta chaqueta me queda pequeña. ¿Tiene ____ más grande?
   d Este modelo no me gusta. ¿Tiene ____ más moderno?

3 How would you say the following in Spanish?
   a I like all of them. They are cheaper too.
   b I like that handbag. What about you? (fam.)
   c Ema likes playing tennis, and so do I.
   d We don't like that hotel very much. The other one is better.

Are you ready to do your shopping now and say whether you like or do not like something? If most of your answers were correct go on to Unit 7 in which you will learn to talk about the future, otherwise go back to the Grammar section again.

7

Planes de vacaciones
Holiday plans

In this unit you will learn
- *How to talk about the future*
- *How to express intentions*
- *How to describe places*
- *How to talk about the weather*

1 Vamos a ir en tren *We're going by train*

🔊 **CD1, TR 7, 00:18**

Elisa and Antonio, from Chile, talk about their holiday plans.
Note the following future forms in this dialogue: **ya saldrás de
vacaciones** *you will soon go on holiday*, **podrás descansar** *you will
be able to rest*, **iré** *I will go*, **tomaré** *I will take*. Note also forms like
pensamos *we are thinking of*, **piensas** *you are thinking of*, **voy /
vamos a ...** *I am/we are going to ...*

Elisa	Hola, ¿qué tal?
Antonio	Hola, ¿cómo te va?
Elisa	No muy bien. Estoy muy cansada. ¡Tengo mucho trabajo!

Antonio	Bueno, ya saldrás de vacaciones y podrás descansar. ¿Tienes algún plan para este verano?
Elisa	Bueno sí, iré con Alfonso al sur por un par de semanas. Pensamos llegar hasta Chiloé. Es la primera vez que voy. Yo no conozco nada del sur.
Antonio	Te va a gustar mucho. Chiloé es precioso. ¿Van en auto?
Elisa	No, vamos a ir en tren y pensamos volver en bus. Y tú, ¿qué piensas hacer?
Antonio	Bueno, yo tomaré mis vacaciones en febrero. Voy a ir a México y Ecuador.
Elisa	¡Estupendo! ¿Vas solo?
Antonio	No, voy con dos amigos de la oficina.
Elisa	¿Y por cuánto tiempo van?
Antonio	Bueno, es un tour, vamos a estar ocho días en México y cuatro días en Quito.
Elisa	¡Te felicito! Dicen que México es un país muy lindo. Espero que lo pases muy bien.
Antonio	Gracias. Tú también.
Elisa	Adiós.
Antonio	Chao.

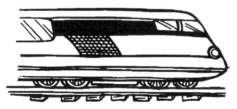

Vamos a ir en tren y pensamos volver en bus

Insight

The future tense is not the only form used for talking about the future in Spanish. There are others which are used equally or even more frequent than the future. One of them is the construction with '**ir**' ('*to go*') followed by the preposition 'a' and an infinitive: '**Te va a gustar**' '*You are going to like it*', '**Voy a ir a México**' '*I'm going (to go) to Mexico*'. (See Grammar, paras 1 and 2.)

cansado/a *tired*
llegar hasta *to go all the way to*
la primera vez *first time*
no conozco nada del sur *I don't know the south at all*
solo/a *on my/your own*
¿por cuánto tiempo ...? *How long ... for?*
¡te felicito! *congratulations!*
espero que lo pases muy bien *I hope you have a very good time*

Means of transport

Some of the words associated with transport vary within Latin America. While the more general words for a local bus, **el bus** or **el autobús** will probably be understood almost everywhere, other words are used alongside or instead of this: **el camión**, in Mexico and Central America, **el colectivo**, in Argentina and Venezuela, **la combi** in Peru, **el ómnibus** in Uruguay, **el micro** (short for 'el microbús') in some countries, **la micro**, in Chile, **la guagua**, in the Caribbean. A long-distance bus is normally known as **el bus** but in some places, for example, Bolivia, it is referred to as **la flota**.

The words **el coche** and **el automóvil**, for a car, will be familiar to most Latin Americans, but some regions will use other terms: **el carro** is the standard word in a number of places, but not in the Southern Cone countries (Argentina, Uruguay, Chile), where the most commonly used term is **el auto**.

Saying goodbye

¡**Adiós!** *goodbye*, and **hasta luego**, *see you (later)*, are standard terms and are used in all Latin American countries. ¡**Chao!**, or ¡**Chau!** in some places, is strictly familiar and is common in many Latin American countries. Diminutives of these expressions, like **adiosito, hasta lueguito, chaíto**, are more colloquial.

los meses	the months
enero *January*	**julio** *July*
febrero *February*	**agosto** *August*
marzo *March*	**septiembre/setiembre** *September*
abril *April*	**octubre** *October*
mayo *May*	**noviembre** *November*
junio *June*	**diciembre** *December*

Insight

Note that in Spanish, months are written with small letters. The Spanish for *in January*, *in February*, etc. is **en enero**, **en febrero**, while dates such as *on 15th April*, on *30th May*, are expressed as **el quince de abril**, **el treinta de mayo**.

las estaciones	the seasons
el otoño *autumn*	**la primavera** *spring*
el invierno *winter*	**el verano** *summer*

Say it in Spanish

Ricardo, a Spanish-speaking friend, asks you about your holiday plans. Use the guidelines to answer his questions.

Ricardo	¿Tienes algún plan para este verano?
Ud.	*Say you will go to Cuba with a friend.*
Ricardo	Te va a gustar mucho Cuba. Es un país muy interesante. ¿Y por cuánto tiempo van?
Ud.	*Say you are going to be four days in Havana and three days in Santiago de Cuba. Ask your friend what he is thinking of doing.*
Ricardo	Voy a ir a Guatemala.
Ud.	*Say it is a very nice country and add that you hope he has a very good time.*
Ricardo	Gracias. Tú también.

2 No hace frío *It isn't cold*

Alfonso tells Elisa about the weather in Chiloé. First, try learning these expressions: **¿Qué tal el tiempo?** *What's the weather like?* **(No) hace frío** *It is (not) cold,* **Llueve mucho** *It rains a lot.*

Elisa	¿Qué tal el tiempo en Chiloé ¿Crees que hará frío?
Alfonso	No, en esta época del año no hace frío, pero sí puede llover. En el sur llueve mucho, especialmente en Chiloé.
Elisa	Tendremos que llevar algo para la lluvia, por si acaso.
Alfonso	Sí, creo que sí.

Insight

Many of the expressions used for talking about the weather use the verb '**hacer**' '*to do, make*': '**¿Crees que hará frío?**' '*Do you think it will be cold?*' (For more phrases of this kind. See Key phrases and Grammar, para 5.)

la época *time*
tendremos que *we will have to*
llevar *to take, carry*
algo *something*
la lluvia *rain*
por si acaso *just in case*
creo que sí *I think so*

Now answer these questions in English:

a Does Alfonso think it may be cold in Chiloé?
b What does Elisa propose to take with them?

Key phrases

Talking about the future

Iré / iremos a ...	*I / we will go to ...*
Tomaré / tomaremos mis / nuestras vacaciones.	*I / we will take my / our holidays.*
Voy / vamos a ir / estar ...	*I am / we are going to go / be ...*

Expressing intentions

Pienso / pensamos ir a ...	*I am / we are thinking of going to ...*
¿Qué piensas hacer?	*What are you thinking of doing?*

Describing places

Es un país / una ciudad muy lindo(a) / bonito(a).	*It's a very beautiful country / city.*
Es precioso(a).	*It's gorgeous / lovely.*

Talking about the weather

¿Qué tal el tiempo?	*What's the weather like?*
Hace frío / calor.	*It is cold / hot.*
Llueve (mucho).	*It rains (a lot).*

Grammar

1 *Talking about the future and expressing intentions*

To refer to the future you can use:

a The future tense:

Iré con Alfonso al sur.	*I am going to the south with Alfonso.*
¿Hará frío?	*Will it be cold?*

b The construction **ir a** with an infinitive:

Voy a ir a México.	*I am going to Mexico.*
Vamos a estar diez días en México.	*We are going to be in Mexico for ten days.*

c The present tense, particularly with verbs which indicate movement:

¿Van en auto?	*Are you going by car?*
¿Por cuánto tiempo van?	*How long are you going for?*
Llegan mañana a las 10.00.	*They are arriving tomorrow at 10.00.*

d The verb **pensar** *to think, to intend, to plan,* followed by the infinitive, another common way of expressing intentions.

¿Qué piensas hacer este verano?	*What are you planning to do this summer?*
Pienso ir a Costa Rica.	*I'm thinking of going to Costa Rica.*

Of these four ways of referring to the future, the future tense is the least common, particularly in Latin America, where **ir a +** the infinitive is far more frequently used, especially in colloquial speech. However, you will hear the future tense in some contexts and with certain verbs, for instance when there is an implication of inevitability, e.g. **Tendremos que llevar algo para la lluvia** *We'll* *have to take something for the rain*, or when there is uncertainty, e.g. **¿Crees que hará frío?** *Do you think it will be cold?*, or simply for reasons of economy, e.g. **iré con él** instead of **voy a ir con él**. In formal spoken language, the future tense is more frequent (e.g. a tourist guide outlining plans for an excursion: **Saldremos del hotel a las 7:00** *We'll leave the hotel at 7.00*). In the press, the future tense is the standard form used to refer to future events.

Insight

If you are uncertain about which of the above constructions to use, or if you have difficulty remembering the forms of the future tense, don't hesitate to use the construction with **ir + a** + infinitive, especially if you are talking about your future plans. It's easier to remember and you will certainly be understood.

2 The future tense

To form the future tense, you use the infinitive followed by the appropriate ending, which is the same for the three conjugations (-**ar**, -**ir**, and -**er**). Here is an example of a fully conjugated regular verb. Note that all forms, except the **nosotros** one have a written accent.

tomar	to take
tomar**é**	*I will take*
tomar**ás**	*you will take* (fam, sing)
tomar**á**	*you will take* (pol, sing), *he, she, it will take*
tomar**emos**	*we will take*
tomar**án**	*you will take* (pl), *they will take*

Here are some more examples of the use of the future tense:

Tomaremos una semana de vacaciones.	*We will take a week's holiday*
Veremos qué podemos hacer.	*We'll see what we can do.*
¿Adónde irás este verano?	*Where will you go this summer?*

Irregular future forms

Some verbs have an irregular stem in the future tense but the endings are the same as for regular verbs. Here is a list of the most important.

decir *to say, to tell*	diré, dirás, dirá, diremos, dirán
hacer *to do, to make*	haré, harás, hará, haremos, harán
poder *can, to be able to*	podré, podrás, podrá, podremos, podrán
poner *to put*	pondré, pondrás, pondrá, pondremos, pondrán
querer *to want*	querré, querrás, querrá, querremos, querrán
saber *to know*	sabré, sabrás, sabrá, sabremos, sabrán
salir *to go out*	saldré, saldrás, saldrá, saldremos, saldrán
tener *to have*	tendré, tendrás, tendrá, tendremos, tendrán
venir *to come*	vendré, vendrás, vendrá, vendremos, vendrán

Here are some examples of the future tense with irregular verbs:

El avión saldrá a las 7:00 de la mañana.	*The plane will leave at 7.00 in the morning.*
Tendrán que estar en el aeropuerto dos horas antes.	*You'll have to be at the airport two hours earlier.*
El autobús vendrá a las 4:30.	*The bus will come at 4.30.*

Insight

Verbs derived from those above form the future in a similar way. '**contradecir**' '*to contradict*', '**predecir**' '*to predict*', '**deshacer**' '*to undo*', '**rehacer**' '*to do again*', '*redo*', '**detener**' '*to detain*', '**contener**' '*to contain*', '**prevenir**' '*to prevent*', etc.

3 *Time expressions associated with the future*

The following expressions of time are normally associated with the future.

mañana *tomorrow*
pasado mañana *the day after tomorrow*
la próxima semana, la semana próxima *next week*
el próximo mes / año, el mes/año próximo *next month / year*
la semana / el mes / año que viene *next / the coming week / month / year*
dentro de dos días / una semana *within two days /a week*

4 Describing places: ser to be and tener to have

To describe places, Spanish normally uses **ser** *to be* or **tener** *to have*. To say where a place is, use **estar** *to be* (see Unit 2). To say what you can find in a place use **hay** *there is / are*.

Es un lugar/ sitio muy lindo / bonito.	It is a very beautiful place.
Tiene playas muy buenas.	It has very good beaches.
Está en el sur/norte.	It is in the south/north.
Hay museos excelentes.	There are excellent museums.

Insight

In description, '**ser**' is normally associated with characteristics ('**es una ciudad grande**' '*it is a large city*'), while '**tener**' can refer to facilities or amenities ('**tiene buenos teatros**' '*it has good theatres*'). '**Estar**' can also be used to describe something but only in relation to a particular point in time ('**la habitación no está limpia**' '*the room is not clean*'), that is, a state or condition rather than a general characteristic.

5 Describing the weather

To describe the weather, Spanish normally uses the verb **hacer** *to do, make*.

Hace / hará (mucho) frío/calor.	*It is/will be (very) cold / hot*
Hace / hará sol/viento.	*It is/will be sunny/windy.*
Hace / hará buen/mal tiempo.	*The weather is / will be good / bad.*

Other weather expressions require different verbs:

Llueve.	*It rains. It is raining.*
Está lloviendo.	*It is raining.*
Nieva.	*It snows.*
Está nevando.	*It is snowing.*
Está nublado / despejado.	*It is overcast / clear.*

6 Conocer and saber to know

In dialogue 1 above you encountered the verb **conocer** *to know* or *to be acquainted with something, a person or a place*. **Saber**, above, also translates into English as *to know*, but it is used to refer to knowledge of a fact or the ability to do something. Like **conocer**, the first person singular of **saber** in the present tense is irregular: **sé** *I know*. Compare the following:

Conozco México.	*I know Mexico.*
Conozco a Isabel.	*I know Isabel.*
No sé dónde está Quito.	*I don't know where Quito is.*
No sé manejar.	*I don't know how to drive.*

Insight

Note the use of personal 'a' before '**Isabel**'. Remember that if the direct object, in this case 'Isabel', is a person Spanish uses 'a' before the name. See also: '**Visitaré a mi madre**' '*I'll visit my mother*', '**Invitaremos a Raúl y Mónica**' '*We'll invite Raúl and Mónica*'. (See Unit 4, Grammar, para 7.)

Practice

1 You have been posted by your company to Chile, and during your first holiday there you decide to visit other parts of Latin America with a local friend. The following holiday advertisement in a Chilean

newspaper catches your attention, and one of the destinations –
Quito, Mexico – seems to be what you want. The following day in
your office you talk about it with a Chilean colleague.

MEXICO–CANCUN
RIO–ACAPULCO

ESPECTACULARES TOURS

MEXICO-RIO
(14 días, 2 personas)
$999 CU

CANCUN-MEXICO-RIO
(12 días, 2 personas)
$1.290 CU

MEXICO-TAXCO
ACAPULCO-QUITO
(12 días, 2 personas)
$1.089 CU

MIAMI-MEXICO
(13 días, 2 personas)
$1.199 CU

MEXICO-QUITO
(12 días, 2 personas)
$949 CU

MIAMI-ORLANDO
(8 días, auto, 4 personas)
$849 CU

CUBA
(7 días, 2 personas, media pensión)
$990 CU

PRECIOS INCLUYEN:
• Pasaje Aéreo • Hotelería • Excursiones • Traslados

Avda. Providence 1941
Fonos: 2334428/29 2331774
2316676 • 2318608 • Fax: 2334428

Economy
Tour

Colega	¿Qué piensas hacer este verano?
Ud.	*Say you are thinking of going to Mexico and Quito.*
Colega	¡Qué interesante! México es un país muy lindo y Quito también me gusta mucho. ¿Vas por mucho tiempo?
Ud.	*No, you are going to be there 12 days in all* (en total).
Colega	¿Es un tour?
Ud.	*Yes, it is a tour and it's not very expensive. It costs* 1500 *dollars.*
Colega	No está caro. ¿Incluye el pasaje aéreo?

(Contd)

Ud.	*Yes, it includes the flight, 4-star hotels, excursions and transfers.*
Colega	Me parece muy barato. ¿Vas a ir solo/a?
Ud.	*No, you are going to travel with a friend. Ask your colleague what he is going to do in the summer.*
Colega	Voy a ir a la playa con mi familia. Pensamos ir a Viña del Mar.

QV

el pasaje aéreo *plane ticket, flight*
la estrella *star*
el traslado *transfer*
c/u (cada uno) *each one*

Insight

Because of great distances, travelling between different countries in Latin America is normally done by plane. It can take many hours to fly between two countries or even within a single country. Flying time between Buenos Aires or Santiago de Chile and Mexico is nine hours, while if you were to fly non-top between the Chilean northern border to the southern city of Punta Arenas it would take you about five hours (there are no direct flights though).

2 You decide to go on the tour advertised above, but before you travel you e-mail a Mexican acquaintance to tell him of your visit to Mexico. In his reply, your Mexican friend suggests some places to visit together during your stay in Mexico City. Read what he says, then check your understanding by answering the questions which follow. First study these key words and phrases.

QUICK VOCAB

me alegro mucho de *I am glad …*
que vengas … *you are coming*
aunque *although*
estoy seguro *I am sure*
como tendrás *as you will have*
el lugar *place*

el barrio *district*
así que *so*
juntos *together*
si te interesa *if it interests you*

> Me alegro mucho de que vengas a México. Aunque la ciudad es enorme, estoy seguro de que te gustará. Como tendrás algunos días libres, te llevaré en el coche a conocer algunos de los lugares más interesantes de la ciudad. Podremos ir a Coyoacán, que es un barrio típico, con buenos restaurantes y algunos monumentos importantes. Allí está el Museo de Frida Khalo. Yo no lo conozco, así que lo visitaremos juntos.
>
> Si te interesa, podremos ir a Cuernavaca y Taxco, dos ciudades coloniales que no están muy lejos de México …

The word **México** in the passage refers to Mexico City. That is the word most Mexicans use to refer to the capital city.

Insight

Frida Kahlo (1907–1954) was a Mexican painter whose fame extended well beyond her native country. Her paintings, many of them colourful self-portraits and still life, show the influence of Mexican folk art and the main European art tendencies of her time. Some of her work reflects the great suffering she experienced after a serious illness and later on an accident which left her confined to bed for a long time. She was married twice to the Mexican muralist Diego Rivera.

Answer these questions in English:

  a What is Coyoacán?
  b What museum will you be able to visit there?
  c What cities will your friend take you to?
  d Are they far from Mexico City?

3 In his reply, your Mexican acquaintance also gives you information about the weather in Mexico City. Read it through, then check your understanding by answering the questions below.

En general, el clima es bastante agradable, aunque en invierno a veces hace un poco de frío, especialmente entre diciembre y enero, que es cuando tú vendrás. Pero en esta época del año no llueve mucho. El invierno este año ha sido muy suave, con mucho sol y algunos días de bastante calor. En todo caso, tendrás que traer un suéter para las mañanas y para la noche…

Answer these questions in English:

    a What is the weather generally like in Mexico City?
    b Is it cold in winter?
    c Does it rain in December and January?
    d What does your acquaintance suggest you bring?

4 In Mexico you are going to stay at the Hotel Ana Luisa, a 4-star hotel. In this description of the hotel, all the verbs are missing. Complete the passage with the appropriate verb, then check your answers in the Key to the activities.

El hotel Ana Luisa es un hotel de 4 estrellas que ___ situado frente al Monumento de la Revolución, a pocos pasos del Paseo de la Reforma. Este elegante hotel ___ 250 habitaciones, todas con baño privado, TV a color, teléfono y mini-bar. En el hotel Ana Luisa ___ dos restaurantes de comida internacional, dos bares y una cafetería. Para su confort durante los meses de verano, el hotel ___ aire acondicionado.

a pocos pasos de *a few steps away from*
el baño privado *en suite bathroom*
los meses de verano *summer months*
el aire acondicionado *air conditioning*

Insight

The preposition '**de**', one of the most common in Spanish, comes up several times in the previous text. Note its uses in: '**un hotel de 4 estrella**s' '*a four-star hotel*', '**Monumento de la Revolución**' '*Monument to the Revolution*', '**a pocos pasos de …**' '*a few steps away from …*', '**restaurantes de comida internacional**' '*international cuisine restaurants*', '**los meses de verano**' '*the summer months*'.

....

◀️ **CD1, TR 7, 03:04**

5 While in Mexico, you might have a chance to visit Veracruz. A friend back home went on holiday there and he liked it very much. He has recommended somewhere to stay: **Motel Miraflores**. Listen to this advertisement from Mexican radio, and pay special attention to the facilities they announce at **Motel Miraflores**. Then make a list of them in English. The vocabulary which follows includes some new words you will hear in the advertisement. You should be able to guess the meanings of other new words.

el paraíso *paradise*
para que usted disfrute *so that you may enjoy*
cómodamente *comfortably*
la estancia *stay*
antena parabólica *satellite dish*
la cama *bed*
la alberca *swimming pool (Mex)*
siempre deseará volver *you will always want to come back*
sin número *without number*

◀️ **CD1, TR 7, 03:51**

6 In Quito, Ecuador, you will stay at the Hotel Quito. Listen to how someone from Quito describes the hotel, then answer the questions below. First study these new words and phrases:

la piscina *swimming pool*
en la parte trasera *at the back*
el espacio verde *green area*
bien grandes *very large*
Techo del Mundo *roof of the world*
los salones *room, hall*
se hacen *are held*
las convenciones *conferences*
aparte *besides*

Answer these questions in English:

- **a** How many rooms has the hotel got?
- **b** How many restaurants does it have?
- **c** What other facilities does it have?

7 It is your last day in the office before your departure for Mexico and you are very busy. A colleague is trying to set up an urgent meeting with you. Answer his questions by looking at the diary notes below.

VIERNES 31	
10:00	*Entrevista con el Sr. Valdés*
11:00	*Ir al banco.*
12:00	*12:30 – Reunión con el director de producción.*
13:00	*Almuerzo con el gerente.*
14:00	*--*
15:00	*Llamar a la agencia de viaje para reconfirmar hora del vuelo.*

Answer these quesions in Spanish:

- **a** ¿Qué vas a hacer a las 11:00?
- **b** ¿Y a las 12:30?
- **c** ¿Vas a almorzar solo/a?
- **d** ¿Estarás libre en la tarde? ¿A qué hora?

8 You are already thinking about your next holiday, which may be in Panama or Peru. They sound like good places to escape to in winter. Listen first to what Elizabeth from Panama City says about the weather in her country. Then listen to Karina Tomas, a Peruvian, describing Lima, the capital of Peru. First, look at the new vocabulary, then check your comprehension by answering the questions.

el clima *climate*
la temperatura promedio *average temperature*
todo el año *the whole year*
netamente *essentially*
lluviosa *rainy*
seca *dry*

QUICK VOCAB

Are these questions true or false (**verdadero o falso**)?

   a La temperatura promedio en Panamá es de dieciocho grados centígrados.
   b En invierno llueve mucho.
   c En verano no llueve.

aún *still*
se conservan *they are retained*
la época colonial *colonial times*
el zoológico *zoo*
en cuanto a *as regards*
cálido *warm*
las lluvias *rains*

QUICK VOCAB

Answer these questions in English:

   d How does Karina describe Lima?
   e What does Lima have to offer, according to her?
   f What is the weather like?

9 The people you will meet in Mexico and Ecuador will probably ask you about your own city. How would you answer the following questions:

  a ¿Cómo es la ciudad?
  b ¿Cuántos habitantes tiene?
  c ¿Cómo es el clima?

10 On the seat next to you on the plane you find a newspaper giving information on the weather in different capital cities, including Mexico, your destination. Study the table below and then answer these questions in Spanish:

  a ¿Hace sol en México?
  b ¿Cómo está el tiempo en Londres?
  c ¿Está lloviendo en París?
  d ¿Cómo está el tiempo en Madrid?
  e ¿Cuál será la temperatura mínima en Madrid? ¿Y la máxima?

El tiempo en el mundo			
Ciudades	**Mín**	**Máx**	**Estado**
Amsterdam	9	25	despejado
Atenas	17	25	despejado
Berlín	13	18	nublado
Bruselas	18	27	despejado
Buenos Aires	12	20	lluvioso
Caracas	18	28	despejado
Lima	17	23	variable
Londres	16	23	despejado
Los Ángeles	16	26	nublado
Madrid	12	22	lluvioso
México	12	26	nublado
Miami	22	29	despejado
Moscú	12	15	nublado
Nueva York	17	25	nublado
París	12	25	despejado
Río de Janeiro	20	26	despejado
Roma	11	23	despejado
Tokio	18	22	nublado

Test yourself

1 Put the verbs in brackets in the correct form of the future tense.

    a Mis hijos (salir) de vacaciones con sus amigos, pero nosotros (quedarse) en casa.

    b ¿Qué (hacer) tú este verano? Yo no (poder) salir, (tener) que trabajar.

    c (Yo) le (enviar) un email a Alfonso y lo (invitar) a mi fiesta.

    d Mis padres (llegar) el lunes que viene. (Ellos) (estar) aquí una semana.

    e Mi marido (vender) el auto/carro y (comprar) otro.

2 Give the Spanish for each of the following.

    a What are you planning to do this Saturday? (fam.)

    b Pablo and Sara are going to spend a few days with us.

    c They are arriving next Friday.

    d We are thinking of travelling to Ecuador.

    e How long are you going to stay? (pl.)

Test 1 focuses on the future tense while Test 2 assesses your ability to ask and make statements about future plans. Both are important but the constructions in Test 2 are the ones you are more likely to hear in everyday spoken language. If you are happy with your performance go on to the next unit in which you will learn the essential language needed to ask for travel information and make a hotel booking.

8

De viaje
Travelling

In this unit you will learn
- *How to ask and give travel information*
- *How to book in at a hotel*
- *How to say how long you have been doing something*

---

1 Sale a las dieciocho treinta *It leaves at 6.30 p.m.*

Elisa and her husband Alfonso are travelling to Puerto Montt, in southern Chile, and from there to the island of Chiloé. Elisa is buying train tickets. Key words and phrases here are **el tren** *train*, **sale** *it leaves*, **llega** *it arrives*, **el boleto** *ticket*, **de ida** *single*, **de ida y vuelta** *return*.

Elisa	Buenos días. ¿A qué hora hay trenes a Puerto Montt?
Empleado	Tiene el rápido, que sale a las dieciocho treinta, y el expreso, que sale a las veintiuna treinta.
Elisa	¿A qué hora llega el rápido?
Empleado	A las catorce horas del día siguiente.
Elisa	¿Y el expreso?
Empleado	El expreso llega a las diecinueve diez del día siguiente. El rápido demora diecinueve horas y media y el expreso veintiuna horas con cuarenta minutos.
Elisa	Bueno, en ese caso prefiero el rápido. Lleva coche dormitorio, ¿verdad?
Empleado	Sí, lleva departamentos sencillos, para dos personas, y departamentos grandes, para cuatro.
Elisa	¿Cuánto cuesta el departamento sencillo?
Empleado	El sencillo vale cuarenta y cinco mil pesos ida y vuelta.
Elisa	Quiero de ida solamente.
Empleado	De ida le sale a veinticinco mil pesos.
Elisa	¿Por persona?
Empleado	No, ése es el precio del departamento.
Elisa	Muy bien, deme dos boletos para el sábado 15 de febrero.
Empleado	Aquí tiene. Son veinticinco mil pesos.
Elisa	Gracias.

Insight

In many parts of Latin America trains have been replaced by long-distance buses. Insufficient investment on rail modernization on the part of governments has led to a deterioration of services, with the result that most people prefer to use faster and more efficient buses and planes. Since this dialogue was written the train service between the Chilean capital Santiago and Puerto Montt, 630 miles south of Santiago, has been discontinued.

rápido *fast*
el día siguiente *following day*
demora *it takes*
llevar *to carry, to have*
el coche-dormitorio / cama *sleeping car*
el departamento / compartimento / compartimiento *compartment*
sencillo *single*
le sale a ... pesos *it will cost you/ comes to ... pesos*
solamente / solo *only*

....
Insight
'**Salir**' means '*to work out*' or '*to cost*' in sentences like the following: '**Sale a cinco mil pesos**' '*It works out at/costs five thousand pesos*', '**En autobús sale más barato**' '*By bus it works out cheaper*'. '**De ida le sale ...**' translates literally as '*A single (ticket) will cost you ...*'.
....

Ask in Spanish

You are buying train tickets for a long distance journey in a South American country.

a Ask what time the train leaves.
b Ask what time it arrives.
c Ask how much a return ticket costs.
d Ask whether they have tickets for Friday 12th. You want two.

_____

2 Una habitación para dos *A room for two*

Alfonso is booking a hotel room for him and Elisa. First, try learning these key phrases: **¿tiene una habitación?** *have you got a room?*, **con / sin desayuno** *with/without breakfast*, **nos vamos** *we are leaving*, **¿cómo se escribe?** *how do you spell it?*

Alfonso	Buenas tardes.
Recepcionista	Buenas tardes.
Alfonso	¿Tiene una habitación para dos personas?
Recepcionista	Sí, sí tenemos.
Alfonso	¿Cuánto cuesta?
Recepcionista	Dieciocho mil pesos.
Alfonso	¿Con desayuno?
Recepcionista	No, sin desayuno. El desayuno es aparte.
Alfonso	Bueno, está bien.
Recepcionista	¿Cuántos días van a quedarse?
Alfonso	Dos días solamente. Nos vamos el martes.
Recepcionista	De acuerdo. Me da su nombre, por favor.
Alfonso	Alfonso Abucadís.
Recepcionista	¿Cómo se escribe el apellido?
Alfonso	A-b-u-c-a-d-i-s. Abucadís.
Recepcionista	¿Y la dirección?
Alfonso	Calle Las Acacias 731, departamento D, Santiago.
Recepcionista	Bien, aquí tienen la llave. Es la pieza veinticuatro, en el segundo piso, al final del pasillo. Allí está la escalera.
Alfonso	Gracias.

Insight

There is more than one word for *room* in Spanish. The standard one, which will be understood everywhere, is '**la habitación**', but, in some countries, the words '**el cuarto**' or '**la pieza**' are used. '**Una habitación individual**' es '**una habitación sencilla**' in some countries.

aparte *separate*
quedarse *to stay*
de acuerdo *fine*
¿me da su nombre? *will you give me your name?*
la llave *key*
el pasillo *corridor*
la escalera *stairs*

QUICK VOCAB

How was the following expressed in the dialogue?

a Breakfast is not included.
b How many days are you going to stay?
c Two days only.
d We are leaving on Tuesday.

Some key survival phrases

¿Cómo se escribe su apellido?	*How do you spell your surname?*
¿Puede deletrearlo, por favor?	*Can you spell it, please?*
¿Cómo se pronuncia su nombre?	*How do you pronounce your name?*
¿Cómo se dice (breakfast) en español?	*How do you say (breakfast) in Spanish?*
¿Cómo dice?	*Pardon me?/Sorry?*
¿Puede repetir, por favor?	*Can you repeat, please?*
¿Puede hablar más despacio, por favor?	*Can you speak more slowly, please?*
Perdone, no entiendo.	*I'm sorry, I don't understand.*
Perdone, no hablo muy bien español.	*I'm sorry, I don't speak Spanish very well.*
¿Qué significa ...?	*What does ... mean/it mean?*
¿Habla usted inglés?	*Do you speak English?*

Insight

The use of **se** in some of the previous sentences is impersonal, somewhat equivalent to English *one* or *you*, as in *What can one/you do?* In Spanish, the verb which follows **se** must be in the third person, singular or plural.

3 ¿Tiene agua caliente? *Does it have hot water?*

A tourist from Venezuela arrives at a hotel in Puerto Montt. Note the word she uses for *room*, **un cuarto**. Note also the following key phrases: **con baño** *with a bathroom*, **con baño compartido** *with a* *shared bathroom*, **¿sirven desayuno?** *do you serve breakfast?*, **se paga aparte** *it's paid separately.*

🔊 CD2, TR 1, 05:40

Turista	Buenos días.
Recepcionista	Buenos días.
Turista	¿Tiene un cuarto individual?
Recepcionista	Sí, sí tenemos.
Turista	¿Cuánto vale?
Recepcionista	Doce mil pesos.
Turista	¿Tiene baño?
Recepcionista	No, es con baño compartido, pero también hay una habitación con baño. Esa cuesta quince mil pesos.
Turista	¿Sabe?, yo prefiero una con baño. ¿Tiene agua caliente?
Recepcionista	Sí, sí, tiene agua caliente, sí.
Turista	¿Y ustedes sirven desayuno?
Recepcionista	No, no señora. El desayuno se paga aparte.
Turista	Bueno, bueno.
Recepcionista	Bien, por favor, ¿puede escribir su nombre y dirección aquí? Y su firma también.
Turista	De acuerdo.

¿puede escribir …? *can you write …?*
la firma *signature*

QV

Ask in Spanish

You arrive in a hotel in a Latin American country.

a Ask whether they have a single room (use the word **habitación**)
b Ask whether the room has a bathroom.
c Ask whether it has hot water.
d Ask whether they serve breakfast.

4 ¿Cuánto tiempo llevan aquí? *How long have you been here?*

Elisa meets a colleague of hers in Puerto Montt. Two key phrases here are **¿cuánto tiempo hace que están aquí?** and **¿cuánto tiempo llevan aquí?**, which are two alternative ways of saying *how long have you been here?* Note also the words for *why?* **¿por qué?** and *because* **porque**.

📶 CD2, TR 1, 06:27

Elisa	Andrés, ¡qué sorpresa! ¿Qué haces aquí?
Andrés	Estoy aquí de vacaciones con mi señora y los niños. Ellos están en el hotel ahora.
Elisa	Te presento a Alfonso, mi marido. (*addressing Alfonso*) Éste es Andrés, un compañero de trabajo.
Alfonso	Mucho gusto.
Andrés	Hola, encantado.
Elisa	¿Cuánto tiempo hace que están aquí?
Andrés	Hace una semana, pero nos vamos pasado mañana.
Elisa	¿Por qué se van tan pronto?
Andrés	Porque Carmen tiene que volver al trabajo.
Elisa	¡Qué lástima!
Andrés	Y ustedes, ¿cuánto tiempo llevan aquí?
Elisa	Llevamos dos días solamente, pero pensamos estar dos semanas. Vamos a ir a Chiloé.

Insight

Exclamations in Spanish have two exclamation marks, an inverted one at the beginning and one at the end of the sentence. Note that Spanish does not use the equivalent of English 'a' in '**¡Qué sorpresa!**' *'What a surprise!'*, '**¡Qué lástima!**' *'What a pity!'*. As you listen to the recording of the previous dialogue note also the stress on '**qué**' in '**¿por qué?**' *'why?'*, and the stress in '**por**' in '**porque ...**' *'because ...'*.

mi marido (or esposo) *my husband*
mi señora (or esposa / mujer) *my wife*
compañero/a de trabajo *colleague*
pasado mañana *the day after tomorrow*
tan pronto *so soon*

Say it in Spanish

What expressions were used in the dialogue to say the following?

a What are you doing here?
b I'm here on holiday.
c We are leaving the day after tomorrow.
d We've been here two days only.

Key phrases

Asking and giving travel information

¿A qué hora hay trenes / autobuses a ...?	*What time are there trains / buses to...?*
¿A qué hora sale / llega?	*What time does it leave / arrive?*
Llega / sale a las ...	*It leaves / arrives at ...*

Booking in at a hotel

¿Tiene una habitación individual (or sencilla) / doble?	*Have you got a single / double room?*
¿Tiene una habitación para dos / tres?	*Have you got a room for two / three?*
Quiero / prefiero / quisiera una habitación con baño.	*I want / prefer / would like a room with a bathroom.*
¿Tiene agua caliente?	*Does it have hot water?*
¿Sirven desayuno?	*Do you serve breakfast?*
con / sin desayuno	*with/without breakfast*

Saying how long you have been doing something

¿Cuánto tiempo hace que estás / vives aquí?	*How long have you been / lived here?*
Hace un año que estoy / vivo aquí.	*I've been / lived here for a year.*
¿Cuánto tiempo llevas trabajando / esperando?	*How long have you been working / waiting?*
Llevo una semana trabajando / esperando.	*I've been working / waiting for a week.*

Grammar

1 *Impersonal sentences*

Notice the use of **se** in impersonal sentences such as the following, in which 'se' translates '*you*'.

¿Cómo se escribe?	*How do you spell it?*
¿Cómo se pronuncia?	*How do you pronounce it?*
¿Cómo se dice?	*How do you say it?*

2 *Saying how long you have been doing something*

a Hace + time phrase + que + present tense
To refer to an action or a state which began in the past and is still in progress, use this construction with the present tense.

¿Cuánto tiempo hace que estás aquí?	*How long have you been here?*
Hace dos semanas que estoy aquí.	*I've been here for two weeks.*
¿Cuánto tiempo hace que trabajas en Chile?	*How long have you been working in Chile?*
Hace un año que trabajo en Chile.	*I've been working in Chile for a year.*

b Present tense + desde hace + time phrase

An alternative to the construction above, with exactly the same meaning, is this one in which the verb is highlighted by being placed in initial position.

Estoy aquí desde hace dos semanas.
Trabajo en Chile desde hace un año.

c Llevar + time phrase (+ gerund)

Another way of referring to an action or state which began in the past and is still in progress, is to use this construction with llevar in the present tense.

¿Cuánto tiempo llevan aquí?	*How long have you been here?*
Llevamos (aquí) dos días solamente.	*We've been here for two days only.*
¿Cuánto tiempo llevas con Rodrigo?	*How long have you been with Rodrigo?*
Llevo un año con él.	*I've been with him for a year.*

All the previous sentences refer to a state rather than an action. If an action is involved use '**llevar**' with a time phrase and a verb. The form of the verb must be that of the Spanish equivalent of '-*ing*' in English, which is known as gerund: '**-ando**' for '**-ar**' verbs (**trabajando, hablando**), and '**-iendo**' for verbs ending in '**-er**' and '**-ir**' (**bebiendo, viviendo**).

Llevo un año viviendo en Bogotá.	*I've been living in Bogotá for a year.*
Lleva seis meses saliendo con Laura.	*He's been going out with Laura for six months.*
Llevan mucho rato bebiendo.	*They've been drinking for a long while.*

Insight

If the verb is understood, as with '**vivir**' and '**trabajar**', this can be left out: '**Llevo un año (viviendo) en Bogotá**' '*I've been (living) in Bogotá for a year*', '**Llevo tres años (trabajando) en esta empresa**' '*I've been (working) in this company for a year*'.

3 Para / por

Observe the uses of **para** and **por** in the following examples:

Para el sábado 15 de febrero.	*For Saturday, 15th February.*
Una pieza para dos.	*A room for two.*
Cinco mil pesos por persona.	*Five thousand pesos per person.*

Practice

1 On a visit to Chile you and your travelling companion decide to go by bus from Santiago to Valparaíso, on the coast. Use the guidelines below to fill in your part in the following conversation with the ticket office employee.

Usted	*Good morning. What time does the next bus for Valparaíso leave?*
Empleado	A las nueve cuarenta.
Usted	*How much is the return ticket?*
Empleado	Seis mil quinientos pesos.
Usted	*I want two return tickets.*
Empleado	Son trece mil pesos.
Usted	*(Paying for your tickets) What time does the bus arrive in Valparaíso?*
Empleado	A las once quince.

2 Your next trip in Chile will be to the city of Concepción, about 300 miles south of Santiago. You are telling a Chilean friend about your planned journey.

Ud.	*Say you are going to travel to Concepción.*
Amigo	¿Cuándo piensas viajar?
Ud.	*Say you are leaving on November 20th.*
Amigo	¡Qué bien! Concepción es una ciudad muy bonita. Te va a gustar. Hace mucho tiempo que no voy allí. ¿Vas en bus?
Ud.	*You are going to travel by train and bus.*

¡qué bien! *great!*
demora bastante *it takes a long time*

QV

3 Someone has recommended the Hotel Arauco in Concepción to you, and you decide to get a room there. Write the conversation you might have with the hotel receptionist, using dialogue 2 as a model and some of the words and phrases listed under **Key phrases**. In the **Key to the activities** you will find another model dialogue to compare with your own version.

dos noches *two nights*
cinco días *five days*
una semana *a week*
¿cuánto cuesta / vale? *how much does it cost?*
¿está incluido el desayuno? *is breakfast included?*

QUICK VOCAB

4 While reading a newspaper in Concepción you spot an adventure holiday advertisement offering excursions to the spectacular rapids of the river Futaleufú in Chilean Patagonia. This is the sort of holiday that might interest one of your friends back home. Read the advertisement to see what they are offering and then answer the questions below.

el descenso *descent*
la balsa *raft*
disfrutar *to enjoy*
la aventura *adventure*
la salida *departure*
el vuelo *flight*
el traslado *transfer*
el alojamiento *accommodation*
el equipo *equipment*

QUICK VOCAB

EXCURSIONES PATAGONIA

DESCENSO EN BALSA POR EL RIO FUTALEUFÚ

Disfrute cinco días de excitante aventura en los rápidos más espectaculares del mundo en Futaleufú, al norte de la Patagonia chilena.

Salidas semanales desde el 1 de diciembre hasta el 15 de abril.

El programa incluye:

Vuelos Puerto Montt-Chaitén-Puerto Montt
Traslados en autobús Chaitén-Futaleufú-Chaitén
Alojamiento cuatro noches en hotel Futaleufú, categoría superior
Todas las comidas
Equipo de rafting y guías bilingües español-inglés
(No incluye traslados hasta Puerto Montt)
Consulte precios y horarios de salidas. Descuentos para grupos.

EXCURSIONES PATAGONIA
Teléf. (56 2) 569 39 08

a How frequent are the departures?
b How do you travel from Puerto Montt to Chaitén?
c How do you travel from Chaitén to Futaleufú?
d How many nights' accommodation does the excursion include?
e What else does the excursion include?

Insight
Patagonia is a region at the southern end of South America. On the west is the **Patagonia chilena** and across the Andes, on the east, is the **Patagonia argentina**.

5 One of your new acquaintances in Chile is Soledad, who has recently moved from northern Chile to Santiago. How would you ask her how long she has been doing each of the following and how would she reply? Use full sentences.

   a estar en Santiago – un año (use 'llevar')
   b vivir en esta casa – seis meses (use 'hacer')
   c practicar yoga – un año y medio (use 'hacer')
   d estudiar inglés – tres años (use 'llevar')
   e conocer a Mario – cuatro años (use 'hacer')
   f trabajar en esta empresa – ocho meses (use 'llevar')

◄» **CD2, TR 1, 07:55**

6 Guillermo, someone you met in Santiago, would like to go to Mendoza in Argentina, across the Andes from Chile. He is not sure how best to travel there, so he asks advice from his friend Carlos. Listen to their conversation, then answer the questions below. These key words will help you:

me gustaría *I would like*
si en bus o… *whether by bus or …*
mira *look*
muchísimo más *very much more*
veces *times*
el pasaje *fare*
te puedo recomendar *I can recommend to you*
te los puedo dar *I can give them to you*

QUICK VOCAB

Are these statements true or false (**verdadero o falso**)?

   a Carlos recomienda el bus porque el viaje es más barato.
   b El bus demora dieciséis horas.
   c El pasaje en bus no es caro.
   d El hotel Plaza está en la calle principal.

7 The passage which follows deals with long-distance transport in Latin America. Study the key words before you read the text, then answer the questions opposite.

los países de habla hispana *Spanish-speaking countries*
varía *it varies*
suele ser *it usually is*
soler (o > ue) *(verb to express often)*
por ferrocarril *by railway*
la red ferroviaria *rail network*
la razón *reason*
los viajes de larga distancia *long-distance journeys*
llevan *they have*
el tiempo de vacaciones *holiday season*
por lo que *so*
con antelación / por adelantado *in advance*
llamado/a *called*

América es un gran continente, y el transporte en los países de habla hispana varía entre lo más primitivo y lo más moderno y sofisticado. En general, predomina el transporte por carretera, que suele ser más rápido y más eficiente que el transporte por ferrocarril. La mayoría de los países hispanoamericanos no tiene una red ferroviaria importante. Argentina es una excepción. En otros países, en México y Chile por ejemplo, la red ferroviaria es mucho más reducida y presenta grandes deficiencias. Por esta razón, en los viajes de larga distancia, la mayoría de la gente prefiere utilizar el autobús o el avión.

En algunos países, entre ellos México, Chile, Argentina, existe un excelente servicio de autobuses de larga distancia, a precios bastante económicos. En México, por ejemplo, hay un servicio de autobuses (llamados también **camiones**) de primera clase que llevan aire acondicionado y baño (llamado también **lavabo** o **sanitario**). Este servicio, con asientos reservados, es mucho más cómodo que el servicio de segunda clase. En tiempo de vacaciones, mucha gente viaja en autobús, por lo que es necesario reservar los asientos con antelación.

Answer these questions in English:

  a How do most people travel in Latin America?
  b What does the text say about first-class long-distance buses in Mexico?
  c What do you need to do during holiday time if you want to travel by bus? Why?

Test yourself

Fill in the blanks with a suitable word.

  a ¿A qué hora ____ el próximo autobús para Mendoza?
  b ¿Y a qué hora ____ a Mendoza?
  c Deme dos ____ de ____ y vuelta.
  d Quiero reservar una habitación ____ dos personas ____ el 15 de abril.
  e '¿Cómo se ____ su apellido?' – 'B-r-o-w-n'.
  f ¿ ____ repetir, por favor? No ____ muy bien español.
  g Cristóbal está en México ____ hace tres años.
  h Hace sólo un año ____ estudio español.
  i ¿Cuánto tiempo ____ (tú) viviendo con María?
  j (Yo) ____ seis meses trabajando en los Estados Unidos.

This test assesses a number of key points, two of which are constructions used for saying how long you or others have been doing something. Did you get them right? If so, congratulations! These, like the rest of the words needed for completing the test, will be very useful for you in conversations with Spanish speakers or as a traveller.

9

Un recado
A message

In this unit you will learn
- *How to talk about the past*
- *How to say how long ago something happened*
- *How to use the phone*

---

1 ¿Cuándo hizo la reserva? *When did you make the reservation?*

Dennis Clerk arrives in a hotel in Santiago, Chile, where a room has been booked for him. Note how the following is expressed: **tengo una habitación reservada** *I have a room booked*, **una amiga reservó la habitación** *a friend booked the room*, **hace una semana** *a week ago*.

◉ CD2, TR 2, 00:10

Dennis Clerk	Buenas tardes. Mi nombre es Dennis Clerk. Tengo una habitación reservada.
Recepcionista	Perdone, ¿puede repetir su nombre, por favor?
Dennis Clerk	Dennis Clerk. C-l-e-r-k. Clerk.
Recepcionista	Un momentito, por favor. ¿Cuándo hizo la reserva?
Dennis Clerk	Bueno, no la hice yo. Una amiga, la señorita Barbara Butler, reservó la habitación por teléfono, hace una semana más o menos.

Insight

Forms like '**hizo**' '*you (he/she) made*', '**hice**' '*I made*', '**reservó**'
'*she (he/you) booked*', correspond to the simple past or preterite
tense, which is treated in para 1 of the Grammar section. Note
also the word '**reservada**' '*reserved, booked*', which refers to '**la
habitación**', a feminine word, and therefore ends in **-a**.

por teléfono *over the telephone*
más o menos *more or less*
¿Podría llenar ...? *Could you fill in ...?*
la ficha *registration form*
si es tan amable *if you would be so kind*
llenar / rellenar *to fill in*
cómo no *certainly*

QUICK VOCAB

Say it in Spanish

How is the following expressed in the dialogue?

a Can you repeat your name?
b When did you make the reservation?
c I didn't do it myself.

---

2 ¿Quiere dejar algún recado? *Would you like to leave a message?*

Dennis Clerk telephones señora Patricia Miranda, a Chilean
businesswoman, to make an appointment to see her. Note how the
following is expressed: **quisiera hablar con ...** *I'd like to speak to ...*,
dígale que llamó ... *tell her/him that ... called*, **salió** *he / she went out*,
llegué ayer *I arrived yesterday*.

Recepcionista	Seguros Ibero-américa, buenos días.
Dennis Clerk	Buenos días. Quiero el anexo dos cinco cero, por favor.
Recepcionista	Un momentito. *(The receptionist puts him through to extension 250.)*
Secretaria	¿Aló?
Dennis Clerk	Buenos días, quisiera hablar con la señora Patricia Miranda, por favor.
Secretaria	La señora Miranda salió a almorzar con un cliente. Va a volver a las cuatro. ¿Quiere dejar algún recado?
Dennis Clerk	Sí, por favor dígale que llamó Dennis Clerk. Llegué ayer a Santiago y estoy en el hotel Santiago Park Plaza. La voy a llamar a las cuatro y media.
Secretaria	Muy bien, señor Clerk. Le daré su recado.

Insight

'**Salió**' (from '**salir**') '*she (he/you) went out*', '**llamó**' (from '**llamar**') '*he (she/you) called*', and '**llegué**' (from '**llegar**') '*I arrived*' are all forms of the preterite tense or simple past (see Grammar, para 1). '**Daré**' (from '**dar**') '*I will give*' is a future tense form (see Unit 7, Grammar, para 2).

el seguro *insurance*
el anexo (Chile) / la extensión *extension*
almorzar *to have lunch*
llamar *to call*
dígale *tell her / him*
le daré *I'll give her / him*
¿quiere dejar ...? *do you want to leave ...?*
el recado *message*

Answer these questions in English:

a What word in Spanish does the secretary use on the phone to say *hello?*

b Where is señora Miranda?

c What message does Dennis Clerk leave for her?

Insight

Telephone numbers in Spanish are read out as pairs of figures or as single figures, for example: **extensión** (or **anexo**, in Chile) **dos-cincuenta** or **dos-cinco-cero** (250), **teléfono seis-tres-nueve-seis-cinco-cero-siete** or **seis-treinta y nueve-sesenta y cinco-cero-siete** (639 6507).

---

3 Ya volvió *She has come back already*

Dennis Clerk telephones señora Miranda again. Note how the following is expressed: **¿podría decirme ...?** *could you tell me ...?*, **¿de parte de quién?** *who is calling?*, **volvió** *she/he came/has come back*.

Secretaria	¿Aló?
Dennis Clerk	Buenas tardes. ¿Podría decirme si volvió la señora Miranda?
Secretaria	Sí, ya volvió. ¿De parte de quién?
Dennis Clerk	De parte de Dennis Clerk.
Secretaria	Ah sí, un momentito señor Clerk.

Insight

'**Volvió**' (from '**volver**') '*she (he/you) came back*' is a form of the preterite or simple past. Note also '**¿Podría decirme si ...?**' '*Could you tell me if/whether ...?*' **Podría** (from '**poder**' '*can, to be able to*') is often used in polite requests as an alternative to '**¿puede ...?**' '*can you ...?*'.

si *if* **de parte de ...** *this is ..., from ...*
ya *already*

Say it in Spanish

You have been trying to get your friend Alfonso on the phone.
Use the guidelines below to complete your part of the conversation
with señora Díaz, his mother.

Señora Díaz	¿Aló?
Ud.	*Say good evening and ask whether Alfonso has come back.*
Señora Díaz	Sí, volvió hace un momento. ¿De parte de quién?
Ud.	*Say who is calling.*
Señora Díaz	Un momentito, por favor.

4 Fue muy agradable *It was very pleasant*

Dennis Clerk meets señora Miranda and they talk about his journey.
Note the following past tense forms: **llegó** *you arrived,* **llegué**
I arrived, **fue** *it was,* **estuve aquí** *I was here,* **me gustó** *I liked it.*

Señora Miranda	Encantada de conocerlo, señor Clerk. Bienvenido a Chile.
Dennis Clerk	Muchas gracias.
Señora Miranda	¿Cuándo llegó?
Dennis Clerk	Llegué el miércoles en la noche.
Señora Miranda	¿Y qué tal el viaje?
Dennis Clerk	Fue muy agradable, aunque un poco largo.
Señora Miranda	¿Es la primera vez que viene a Santiago?
Dennis Clerk	No, estuve aquí hace cinco años y me gustó mucho.
Señora Miranda	Me alegro.

¿y qué tal el viaje? *and how was the journey?*
hace cinco años *five years ago*
agradable *pleasant*
aunque *although*
largo/a *long*
la primera vez *the first time*
me alegro (alegrarse) *I'm glad (to be glad)*

Say it in Spanish

On a visit to Santiago you talk about your journey with a Chilean. Use the guidelines below to complete your part of the conversation.

Chileno	¿Es la primera vez que visita Santiago?
Ud.	*Say you were in Santiago two years ago. Say you liked it very much.*
Chileno	Me alegro mucho. ¿Y cuándo llegó?
Ud.	*Say you arrived on Saturday morning.*
Chileno	¿Y qué tal el viaje?
Ud.	*Say it was a bit long.*

Insight

Note the following formal greeting in Dialogue 4, in which a woman greets a man: '**Encantada de conocerlo**' '*Pleased to meet you*'. A man would say '**encantado**', and if the person you are meeting is a woman '**lo**' changes into '**la**': '**Encantado de conocerla**'. A simpler introduction is '**mucho gusto**' '*pleased to meet you*', formal and informal, which is invariable (see Key phrases, Unit 1). Younger people often use the informal '**hola**' '*hello*'.

Key phrases

Talking about the past

¿Cuándo hizo la reserva / llegó?	*When did you make the reservation / arrive?*
Volvió / llegó / salió.	*He/she came back / arrived / went out.*
Me gustó (mucho).	*I liked it (very much).*

Saying how long ago something happened

Reservó la habitación hace una semana.	*He / she booked the room a week ago.*
Estuve aquí hace cinco años.	*I was here five years ago.*

Using the phone (see also Unit 11)

¿Aló? ¿Sí? (South Am), ¿Bueno? (México), ¿Holá? (River Plate)	*Hello?*
Quiero la extensión / el anexo (Chile) / el interno (River Plate) ...	*I want extension ...*
Quisiera hablar con ...	*I'd like to speak to ...*
¿Podría hablar con ...?	*Could I speak to ...?*
¿De parte de quién?	*Who is speaking? / Who shall I say?*
De parte de ...	*This/it is (name).*
¿Quiere dejar un recado	*Would you like to leave a message?*
Dígale que ...	*Tell him / her that ...*

Grammar

1 *Looking back: the preterite tense*

Usage

To refer to events which happened and were completed in the past, as in *She went out for lunch*, English uses the simple past, which

162

corresponds to the preterite tense in Spanish, **Salió a almorzar.**
Here are some further examples:

Una amiga reservó la habitación.	*A friend booked the room.*
Llegué el lunes.	*I arrived on Monday.*
Fue muy difícil.	*It was very difficult.*
Estuvo aquí el año pasado.	*He / she was here last year.*
¿Qué hiciste ayer?	*What did you do yesterday?*
Salí con Antonia.	*I went out with Antonia.*

Events which happened in the recent past are normally expressed by Latin Americans with the preterite tense.

Ya almorcé.	*I've already had lunch.*
Hoy trabajamos mucho.	*We worked a lot today.*
Esta mañana vi a Isabel.	*I saw Isabel this morning.*

An alternative way of referring to recent past events is to use the perfect tense (see Unit 12), which is generally infrequent in Latin America in such contexts.

Ya he almorzado.	*I've already had lunch.*
Hoy hemos trabajado mucho.	*We've worked a lot today.*
Esta mañana he visto a Isabel.	*I've seen Isabel this morning.*

Formation
There are two sets of endings for the preterite tense, one for -**ar** verbs and another one for verbs in -**er** and -**ir**.

reservar	*to book*
reserv**é**	*I booked*
reserv**aste**	*you booked* (fam, sing)
reserv**ó**	*you booked* (pol, sing), *he, she booked*
reserv**amos**	*we booked*
reserv**aron**	*you booked* (pl), *they booked*

Note that the first person plural, **reservamos** *we booked*, is the same as for the present tense (see Unit 3).

volver	*to return*
volv**í**	*I returned*
volv**iste**	*you returned* (fam, sing)
volv**ió**	*you returned* (pol, sing), *he, she returned*
volv**imos**	*we returned*
volv**ieron**	*you returned* (pl), *they returned*

Here are some further examples of the use of the preterite tense with regular verbs.

¿Hablaste con él?	*Did you speak to him?*
Hablé con él el sábado.	*I spoke to him on Saturday.*
Nos quedamos una semana allí.	*We stayed there for a week.*
Bebió demasiado.	*He / she drank too much.*
No entendí nada.	*I didn't understand anything.*
Vivieron aquí muchos años.	*They lived here for many years.*
Subió a su habitación.	*He / she went up to his / her room.*

Irregular forms
Some verbs form the preterite tense in an irregular way. Here is a list of the main ones. Note the similarity among some of the forms.

andar *to walk*	anduve, anduviste, anduvo, anduvimos, anduvieron
estar *to be*	estuve, estuviste, estuvo, estuvimos, estuvieron
tener *to have*	tuve, tuviste, tuvo, tuvimos, tuvieron
poder *to be able, can*	pude, pudiste, pudo, pudimos, pudieron
poner *to put*	puse, pusiste, puso, pusimos, pusieron
saber *to know* '	supe, supiste, supo, supimos, supieron
hacer *to do, make*	hice, hiciste, hizo, hicimos, hicieron
querer *to want, love*	quise, quisiste, quiso, quisimos, quisieron
venir *to come*	vine, viniste, vino, vinimos, vinieron
decir *to say*	dije, dijiste, dijo, dijimos, dijeron
traer *to bring*	traje, trajiste, trajo, trajimos, trajeron

dar *to give*	di, diste, dio, dimos, dieron
oír *to hear*	oí, oíste, oyó, oímos, oyeron
ver *to see*	vi, viste, vio, vimos, vieron
ir *to go*	fui, fuiste, fue, fuimos, fueron
ser *to be*	fui, fuiste, fue, fuimos, fueron

Here are some examples of the use of the preterite with irregular verbs.

¿Hizo usted la reserva?	*Did you make the reservation?*
No pude hacerla.	*I couldn't do it.*
No quiso venir con nosotros, vinimos solos.	*He / she didn't want to come with us, we came on our own.*
Fui a la fiesta de María, que estuvo muy buena.	*I went to María's party, which was very good.*
Fue el sábado.	*It was on Saturday.*
Le dije que lo necesitaba, pero no lo trajo.	*I told him / her that I needed it, but he / she didn't bring it.*

For other irregular preterite forms, see the Irregular verbs section.

Insight

It is important that you learn irregular preterite forms at this stage as most of them correspond to verbs which are very common. Note that verbs which derive from those above are irregular in the same way: '**detener**' *'to detain'*, '**componer**' *'to compose'*, '**rehacer**' *'to do again'*, *'to redo'*, '**predecir**' *'to predict'*, etc.

2 Time phrases associated with the past

To talk about the past, use time phrases like the following:

ayer	*yesterday*
ayer en la mañana / tarde / noche	*yesterday morning / afternoon / evening*
anteayer / antes de ayer / antier (México, Colombia, etc.)	*the day before yesterday*

la semana pasada	*last week*
el mes / año pasado	*last month/ year*
el lunes / martes pasado	*last Monday / Tuesday*
anoche	*last night*
en 1999	*in 1999*
hace mucho / poco tiempo	*a long/short time ago*

3 Saying how long ago something happened

Hace + time phrase + preterite tense
To say how long ago something happened, use **hace** in this construction with a time phrase and a verb in the preterite tense.

¿Cuánto tiempo hace que llegó?	*How long ago did you / he / she arrive?*
Llegué hace una semana.	*I arrived a week ago.*
Hace un año que llegó.	*He / she arrived a year ago.*

Insight

Compare the construction above with the one you learnt in Unit 8, in which '**hace**' is used with a present tense verb to refer to an action which began in the past and is still in progress: '**¿Cuánto tiempo hace que vive usted aquí?**' *'How long have you been living here?'*, '**Vivo aquí desde hace un mes**' or '**Hace un mes que vivo aquí**' *'I've been living here for a month'*.

Practice

1 Write a dialogue based on this situation, using dialogue 1 as a model.

- You arrive in a hotel in a Latin American country. At the reception desk you identify yourself and say that you have a reservation.

- The receptionist asks you to repeat your name. You do so and spell your surname for him.

- He wants to know when you made the reservation. Explain that this was not made by yourself, but by your secretary who phoned directly from your home town (give the name of the town) about five days ago.

- The receptionist finally finds the reservation. He's given you room 50 on the fifth floor. Before giving you the key, he asks you to fill in the registration form.

mi secretaria *my secretary*
directamente *directly*
desde *from*
más o menos *about, more or less*

2 What would you say, in Spanish, in these situations?
  a You are in a hotel in Santiago, Chile, and the telephone rings in your room. You lift up the receiver and say …?
  b You telephone Viña San Sebastián in Chile, a company you are doing business with, and ask for **extension 2552**.
  c The secretary on extension 2552 answers the phone. Ask to speak to señor Juan Miguel García.
  d The secretary asks who is speaking. Identify yourself.
  e You meet señor Juan Miguel García for the first time. Say how pleased you are to meet him.
  f Back at your hotel, you telephone señorita Elena Alonso, an acquaintance of yours. She is not at home at the moment, and the person who answers the phone asks if you want to leave a message. Ask them to tell señorita Alonso that you phoned and to inform her that you arrived in Santiago two days ago. Say which hotel you are staying at (**Hotel Plaza**) and give the room number (**habitación 50**).

3 At the office of señor Solís, a businessman from Santiago, Chile, the receptionist has taken two messages for him. The first is from señora Carmen Puig, from Venezuela and the second from señorita Marilú Pérez, a Chilean. Listen to the two messages then note down each message in English. First, look at these key words:

el mensaje *message*   **urgentemente** *urgently*
el recado *message*   **vino** *he / she came*
la reunión *meeting*

4 Back in his country, Dennis Clerk receives a postcard from someone he met in Chile. Unfortunately, it got a bit smudged. Here are the words you need to fill in. Put them in the right order in the gaps below.

    a estuvimos   **e** gustó
    b levanté   **f** fue
    c fui   **g** tomé
    d senté   **h** entramos

Querido Dennis:

Me alegro mucho de haberte conocido y espero que vuelvas a Chile el año próximo, como me prometiste. Tengo recuerdos muy bonitos de tu estadía en Chile. Para mí _____ muy especial.

Ayer en la tarde _____ con Mónica al café donde nos conocimos. Allí _____ hasta las cinco de la tarde. Después Mónica y yo _____ a un cine a ver una película inglesa que nos _____ mucho. Hoy me _____ muy tarde, _____ un café y después me _____ frente a mi escritorio a escribirte esta tarjeta.

Te abraza
María Soledad

querido/a *dear*
de haberte conocido *to have met you*
espero que vuelvas *I hope you come back*
prometiste *you promised*
los recuerdos *memories*
la estadía *stay (in Spain, la estancia)*
nos conocimos *we met*
la película *film*
después *afterwards*
el escritorio *desk*
la (tarjeta) postal *postcard*
te abraza (abrazar) *love (to embrace)*

QUICK VOCAB

5 What questions would you need to ask to get the following replies?

   a Llegué ayer en la tarde.
   b El viaje fue bastante tranquilo.
   c Sí, la señorita Alonso ya volvió.
   d No, no es la primera vez que vengo. Estuve en Santiago hace un año y medio.
   e Sí, me gustó mucho Chile.
   f Sí, ya cené.

◄» **CD2, TR 2, 07:35**

6 Marilú, a Chilean, was asked about her last holiday. Listen to what she says, then answer the questions below. First, look at this new vocabulary:

QUICK VOCAB

la costa *coast*
disfrutamos *we enjoyed it*
ya que *as*
maravillosas *wonderful*
el aire *air*
tan puro *so clean (pure)*
harto *a lot*
nadar *to swim*
llenos de energía *full of energy*
deportes *sports*

Insight

The use of '**harto**' meaning '*a lot*' or '*very much*' is characteristic of Chilean Spanish. In other countries it is either unheard of or used very infrequently. This word is normally found in the expression '**estar harto/a de**' '*to be fed up with (someone)*' ('**Estoy harto/a de él**' '*I'm fed up with him*') or '*to be fed up of (doing something)*' ('**Estoy harto de trabajar tanto**' '*I'm fed up of working so much*').

Answer these questions in English:

    a Where did Marilú go during the holidays?
    b Where did they stay?
    c How does she describe the place?
    d How does she express the following: *we went out a lot, we sunbathed, we swam, we played some sports*?

7 A Latin American friend asks you about your last holiday. Answer his questions using real or imaginary information.
    a ¿Dónde fuiste de vacaciones?
    b ¿Fuiste solo/a o acompañado/a?
    c ¿Dónde te quedaste?
    d ¿Cuánto tiempo estuviste allí?
    e ¿Qué hiciste durante tus vacaciones?
    f ¿Cuánto tiempo hace que volviste?

Test yourself

Fill in the blanks in each sentence with the correct preterite forms of the verb in brackets.

    a Carlos ____ anteayer/antier, Martín y Sofía ____ anoche, y yo ____ esta mañana. (llegar)
    b Victoria y yo ____ nuestras vacaciones en Ecuador. Laura y José las ____ en Cuba. (pasar)
    c Durante la fiesta (yo) no ____ nada, pero Enrique ____ demasiado. (beber)
    d ¿Qué ____ (tú) el fin de semana? Yo no ____ nada especial. (hacer)
    e (Yo) ____ dos semanas de vacaciones, pero María sólo ____ una semana. (tener)
    f El domingo Teresa y yo ____ al cine, pero Alfonso y Pablo ____ al fútbol. ¿Adónde ____ ustedes? (ir)

g Ustedes ____ en el autobús, ¿verdad? Yo ____ en el auto/carro. (venir)

h Maruja e Isabel no ____ venir a la reunión. Víctor tampoco ____ venir. (querer)

i (Nosotros) le ____ la verdad a Julio, pero él no ____ absolutamente nada. (decir)

j Ayer ____ la última película de Almodóvar. ¿La ____ tú? (ver)

This test focuses on the use of the preterite tense, one of the most frequent tenses in Latin American Spanish. If you are uncertain about your answers check them in the **Key to the activities** and go back to those verbs that you got wrong, especially irregular and spelling changing ones. Once you feel confident that you know all their forms go on to Unit 10 in which you will learn another form of the past.

10

Vivía en España
I used to live in Spain

In this unit you will learn
- *How to say what you used to do or were doing*
- *How to describe places and people you knew*
- *How to say what you are doing now*

---

1 ¿Qué hacías en Barcelona? *What were you doing in Barcelona?*

Marta and José Luis, both Argentinian, talk about Barcelona, where Marta used to live. Key words and phrases here are **vivía/s** *I/you used to live,* **hacías** *you used to do,* **trabajaba** *I used to work,* **estoy buscando ...** *I'm looking for ...* Note also the use of **vos** instead of **tú**, and the change in the accentuation of verbs in the second person singular of the present tense, a feature which is characteristic of Argentinian Spanish.

José Luis	Hola, ¿cómo te llamás?
Marta	Me llamo Marta, ¿y vos?
José Luis	Yo me llamo José Luis. ¿Sos de Buenos Aires?
Marta	Sí, soy de acá, pero recién volví. Vivía en España. Estuve allá varios años.
José Luis	¡No me digas! Yo estuve en España hace un par de años y me gustó mucho. ¿Dónde vivías vos?
	(Contd)

☏ CD2, TR 3, 00:19

Marta	En Barcelona. ¿Conocés Barcelona?
José Luis	Sí, pasé una semana allá. Es una ciudad muy linda. Y vos, ¿qué hacías en Barcelona?
Marta	Trabajaba con un colega argentino. Yo soy psicóloga. ¿Y vos, qué hacés?
José Luis	Recién terminé mis estudios en la universidad. Estudié arquitectura y ahora estoy buscando trabajo.
Marta	¡Qué tengas suerte!
José Luis	Gracias.

Insight

Forms like '**vivía**' (*I/he/she used to live …*), '**hacías**' ('*you used to do …*') refer to actions which were habitual in the past. Such forms correspond to the imperfect tense, which is the main focus of this unit. (See Grammar, para 1.)

QUICK VOCAB

sos *you are* (fam., Argentina)
acá / allá *here / there*
recién volví / terminé *I have just returned / finished*
varios/as *several*
¡no me digas! *you don't say!*
pasé (pasar) *I spent (to spend)*
¡que tengas suerte! *good luck!*

Insight

The use of '**vos**' instead of '**tú**' is the norm in Argentina and Uruguay for familiar address. Other countries use it as well, but not as the standard form. In some places, for example Chile, it is prevalent only in uneducated speech. As a non-native speaker you do not need to learn this form, but you should be aware of it if you are travelling to the River Plate area or have contact with people from that region of South America.

Match each question with an appropriate answer

a	¿Qué hacías?	**1**	Medicina.
b	¿Qué estudiabas?	**2**	En un apartamento / departamento
c	¿Dónde trabajabas?	**3**	Estudiaba en la universidad.
d	¿Dónde vivías?	**4**	En un banco

---

2 Estaba frente a la playa *It was opposite the beach*

Marta describes the place where she used to live. Key words here are **era** *it was*, **estaba** *it was* (position), **tenía** *it had*. Note also how she says what she used to do: **viajaba** *I used to travel*, **compartía** *I used to share*, **pasaba** *I used to spend* (time).

CD2, TR 3, 01:50

José Luis	¿En qué parte de Barcelona vivías?
Marta	Bueno, yo no vivía en la ciudad misma. Vivía en Sitges, un lugar muy lindo que está a media hora de Barcelona. Viajaba a Barcelona en tren los días de semana. Los fines de semana los pasaba en Sitges. Compartía un departamento con una amiga catalana. Era una chica bastante joven, y era muy simpática. Nos llevábamos muy bien.
José Luis	¿No extrañás todo eso?
Marta	Bueno, la verdad es que estoy contenta de estar otra vez en Buenos Aires, pero sí, a veces extraño la vida allá. Teníamos un departamento muy agradable. No era muy grande, pero estaba frente a la playa y tenía una vista maravillosa.
José Luis	Y ahora, ¿dónde vivís?
Marta	Estoy viviendo en la casa de mis padres en Villa Devoto, pero pienso alquilar un departamento más cerca del centro.
José Luis	¡Ojalá que tengas suerte!
Marta	Gracias.

QUICK VOCAB

mismo/a *itself*
los días de semana *weekdays*
catalán / catalana *Catalan, Catalonian*
nos llevábamos muy bien *we got on very well*
extrañar *to miss*
la verdad es que ... *the truth is that ...*
otra vez *again*
teníamos *we had*
maravilloso/a *wonderful*
alquilar *to rent, hire*
ojalá que ... *let's hope that ...*

Fill in the blanks

In an e-mail to a friend Ricardo described the house where he used to live, and the friends he used to share it with. Fill in the blanks below with a suitable verb from the list: **tenía, trabajaba, era, estudiaba, estaba, compartía.**

La casa en que vivía _____ muy linda y _____ a pocos minutos del centro de la ciudad. No _____ muy grande, pero _____ bastante cómoda, y _____ tres habitaciones. Yo _____ la casa con Javier y Ana. Javier _____ arquitectura y _____ un excelente amigo. Ana _____ en un hospital. Ella _____ enfermera *(nurse)*.

Key phrases

Saying what you used to do or were doing

¿Qué hacías?	*What did you do / were you doing ...?*
(Yo) vivía / compartía / trabajaba ...	*I used to live / share / work ...*

Describing places and people you knew

Era grande / bonito(a).	*It was big / pretty.*
Estaba frente a la playa / cerca del centro de la ciudad.	*It was opposite the beach / near the city centre.*
Tenía tres habitaciones / una vista maravillosa.	*It had three rooms / a wonderful view.*
Era joven / simpático(a).	*He / she was young / nice.*
Era alto(a) / delgado(a).	*He / she was tall / slim.*
Tenía cabello largo y ojos oscuros.	*He / she had long hair and dark eyes*

Saying what you are doing now

Estoy buscando trabajo / viviendo con mis padres.	*I'm looking for work / living with my parents.*

Grammar

1 *The imperfect tense*

Usage
The imperfect tense is used to say what you used to do or were doing and to describe people, places and things you knew in the past.

Unlike the preterite tense, which you studied in Unit 9, it denotes actions which were incomplete or whose beginning or end is not specified. Compare for instance:

(preterite tense)
    Viví allí durante un año.   *I lived there for a year.*
(imperfect tense)
    En 1992 yo **vivía** allí.   *In 1992 I was living there.*

The first sentence refers to an event which lasted over a definite period of time and ended in the past, therefore the preterite tense is used. The second sentence focuses on the action itself, *I was living*. We don't know when the action was completed, therefore the imperfect tense is used.

In descriptive language in general, for instance *she was nice, the apartment was pleasant*, there is no concern for time (except to show that a past experience is being referred to, e.g. **era simpática** as opposed to **es simpática**), so the imperfect tense is used.

Note, however, that this difference between the two tenses in Spanish is not always expressed in English, as English often uses the simple past where Spanish would use the imperfect tense, for example:

Yo trabajaba con un colega.   *I worked / used to work / was working with a colleague.*

El apartamento era agradable.   *The apartment was nice.*

Formation

There are two sets of endings for the imperfect tense, one for **-ar** verbs and another for **-er** and **-ir** verbs.

trabajar	to work
trabaj**aba**	*I worked / used to work / was working*
trabaj**abas**	*you worked / used to work / were working* (fam, sing)
trabaj**aba**	*you worked / used to work / were working* (pol, sing) *he, she worked / used to work / was working*
trabaj**ábamos**	*we worked / used to work / were working*
trabaj**aban**	*you worked / used to work / were working* (pl) *they worked / used to work / were working*

Note that the first and third person singular share the same endings.

tener	to have
ten**ía**	*I had / used to have*
ten**ías**	*you had / used to have* (fam, sing)
ten**ía**	*you had / used to have* (pol, sing) *he, she had / used to have*
ten**íamos**	*we had / used to have*
ten**ían**	*you had / used to have* (pl) *they had / used to have*

Note again that the first and third person singular share the same form. Here is another example demonstrating the use of the imperfect tense:

Vivíamos en un departamento muy agradable que **estaba** frente al mar. Los fines de semana **nos levantábamos** muy tarde, **desayunábamos** y después **bajábamos** a la playa. En la playa **había** siempre mucha gente que **venía** de Barcelona a pasar el fin de semana, especialmente durante el verano. A partir de octubre, Sitges **era** un lugar muy tranquilo.

bajar *to go down*
había *there were*
la gente *people*

a partir de *starting in*
tranquilo *quiet*

Irregular imperfect forms
There are only three irregular verbs in the imperfect tense:

ir *to go*   iba, ibas, iba, íbamos, iban
ser *to be*   era, eras, era, éramos, eran
ver *to see* veía, veías, veía, veíamos, veían

Here is an example demonstrating the use of the imperfect tense with irregular verbs:

Yo **veía** a Carmen todos los días. Carmen **era** alta, delgada, de pelo muy negro y ojos cafés. Carmen y yo **íbamos** a la playa a tomar el sol y nadar. Carmen **era** muy linda e inteligente.

tomar el sol *to sunbathe*   **nadar** *to swim*

Notice that before an i, y changes to e: e inteligente.

2 Estar + gerund

To refer to events which are taking place at the moment of speaking, you can use the simple present tense, e.g. **¿Qué haces?** *What are you doing?* or the present continuous, which is formed with the verb **estar** followed by a gerund (words like **buscando** *looking for* and **viviendo** *living*).

Estoy buscando trabajo.   *I am looking for work.*
Estoy viviendo en la casa de mis *I am living in my parents' house.*
  padres.

There are two endings for the gerund in Spanish, one for -**ar** verbs and one for -**er** and -**ir** verbs.

-ar verbs form the gerund with -ando:
    (trabajar)   Estoy trabajando.   *I am working.*

-er and -ir verbs form the gerund with -iendo:
    (comer)   Estamos comiendo.   *We are eating.*
    (escribir)   Ellos están escribiendo.   *They are writing.*

Insight

Actions in progress at the moment of speaking can sometimes be expressed with the present tense. '**¿Qué haces?**' *'What are you doing?'*, '**¿Quién llama?**' *'Who's calling?'*, '**¿Con quién hablo?**' *'Who am I speaking to?'* (on the phone).

3 The use of vos for tú

In certain regions of Latin America, **tú** is replaced by **vos**. This is the standard form in the River Plate area (Argentina, Uruguay). Verb endings corresponding to **vos** are generally the same as for **tú**, except in the present tense, the present subjunctive (Unit 13) and the imperative (Units 12 and 13). The following examples illustrate the use of **vos** with present tense verbs:

Standard	**Argentinian**
¿Cómo te llamas (tú)?	**¿Cómo te llamás (vos)?**
	What's your name?
¿Qué haces (tú)?	**¿Qué hacés (vos)?**
	What do you do?
¿Dónde vives (tú)?	**¿Dónde vivís (vos)?**
	Where do you live?

Note that stem-changes do not apply to **vos**:

¿Cuándo vuelves (tú)?	**¿Cuándo volvés (vos)?**
	When are you coming back?
¿Qué dices (tú)?	**¿Qué decís (vos)?**
	What are you saying?
¿Qué quieres (tú)?	**¿Qué querés (vos)?**
	What do you want?

Eres, from **ser to be**, changes in Argentina to **sos**:

¿(Tú) eres de aquí?
¿(Vos) sos de aquí?   *Are you from here?*

> **Insight**
> **Vos** for **tú** you (familiar) is also used in a few other regions and countries in Latin America, including many parts of Central America and the Andean region, but its use is not as extensive as it is in the River Plate area.

4 Recién (just) + preterite tense

To refer to an action which has just taken place, use the word recién *just*, followed by a verb in the past:

Recién terminé.   *I have just finished.*
Recién volví.   *I have just returned.*
Recién salió.   *He / she has just gone out.*

This usage is Latin American. In Spain, **recién** is only used before past participles, e.g. **El pan está recién hecho** *The bread has just been made*. Peninsular Spanish normally uses a construction with **acabar de** followed by the infinitive, e.g. **Acaba de llegar** *He/she has just arrived*. This construction is also used by Latin Americans, though perhaps less frequently (see Unit 13)

Practice

1 In the passage below, which is based on dialogues 1 and 2, all the verbs are missing. Try to complete it with the verbs from the list, without looking at the dialogues.

a pasaba	**g** se llamaba
b estaba	**h** tenía
c compartía	**i** era
d vivían	**j** vivía
e trabajaba	**k** gustaba
f había	**l** viajaba

En 1990, Marta _____ en Sitges y _____ con un colega argentino en Barcelona. Marta _____ a Barcelona en tren los días de semana. Los fines de semana los _____ en Sitges donde _____ un departamento con una amiga catalana. Su amiga _____ Montserrat. El departamento donde ellas _____ no _____ muy grande, pero_____ una vista maravillosa, ya que _____ frente a la playa. A Marta le _____ mucho Sitges, especialmente a partir de octubre, cuando _____ poca gente en el lugar.

2 Below is an extract from an e-mail written by María Inés, an Argentinian, to a correspondent. María Inés writes about her life in Bariloche, in southern Argentina, before she came to live in Buenos Aires. Read it through, then check your understanding by answering the questions below. Here are some key words:

preguntar *to ask*
acerca de *about*
la vida *life*
antes de *before*
te conté (contar) *I told you (to tell)*
el lago *lake*
ganaba (ganar) *I used to earn (to earn)*
la temporada *season*
a pesar de que *although*
así fue como … *this was how …*
hice mis valijas *I packed my suitcases*
el paisaje *landscape*
el aire puro *pure air*

Querido Paul:

En tu última carta me preguntás acerca de mi vida antes de venir a Buenos Aires. Bueno, ya te conté que llegué aquí hace cinco años. Antes vivía en Bariloche, una ciudad muy linda que está a unos 1.700 kilómetros de Buenos Aires.

Bariloche es un lugar de mucho turismo y yo trabajaba como guía en una agencia de viajes. Vivía en un departamento muy agradable, frente al lago. Durante el verano estaba siempre muy ocupada y ganaba bastante plata, pero a partir de marzo, cuando terminaba la temporada de vacaciones, la vida era muy tranquila y a veces un poco monótona.

Mi familia vivía en Buenos Aires y los extrañaba, a pesar de que en Bariloche tenía algunos amigos. Así fue como un día hice mis valijas y decidí volver a la capital. Estoy contenta de estar aquí otra vez, aunque a veces extraño el paisaje y el aire puro de Bariloche ...

Insight

In narrative contexts, such as that above, the imperfect often occurs in conjunction with the preterite tense, with the imperfect serving as a kind of descriptive framework for the actions that took place, which are expressed with the preterite: '**Salí de casa temprano esa mañana.** *Hacía* **frío y caminé rápidamente hacia la estación.** *Eran* **las ocho ...**'
'*I left the house early that morning. It was cold and I walked quickly towards the station. It was eight o'clock ...*'

QV

me preguntás (Arg.) *you ask me*
la valija (Arg.) *suitcase*

Answer these questions in Spanish:

    a ¿Dónde vivía María Inés?
    b ¿En qué trabajaba?
    c ¿Cómo era su departamento?
    d ¿Dónde estaba su departamento?

e ¿Cómo era la vida a partir de marzo?
f ¿Por qué decidió volver a Buenos Aires?

3 Look at this plan of the flat where María Inés used to live and then answer the questions which follow.

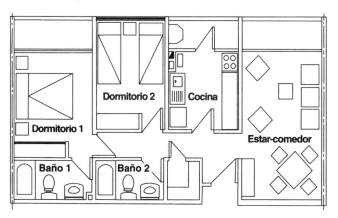

a ¿Cuántos dormitorios tenía el departamento?
b ¿Cuántos baños tenía?
c ¿Dónde estaba la cocina?
d ¿Cuántas camas había en el dormitorio uno?

Insight

Note the use of 'habïa' in '¿Cuántas camas había ...?' 'How many beds were there?'. The use of 'habïan' instead of the singular 'habïa' is not uncommon in Latin America when this is followed by a noun in the plural. This usage is incorrect and should be avoided.

el estar *sitting room*   **la cocina** *kitchen*

🔊 **CD2, TR 3, 03:18**

4 Now listen to Carlos García, an Argentinian who used to live in São Paulo, Brazil. He talks about his life in that city. Look at the key words, then answer the questions.

¿Siempre has vivido …? *Have you always lived …?*
daba clases de pintura *I used to teach painting*
el barrio *district, area*
arborizados *with many trees*
la vegetación *vegetation*
los vecinos *neighbours*
¿Qué tal eran? *What were they like?*
como todos los brasileros *like all Brazilians*
todavía *still*

Insight

Carlos, from Argentina, uses the word **brasileiros** to refer to *Brazilians*. An alternative word is **brasileño**. The ending **-eño** to denote nationality or place of origin is also found in a few other words, including **panameño** *Panamanian*, **hondureño** *from Honduras*, **caraqueño** *from Caracas* (Venezuela).

Are these statements true or false (**verdadero o falso**)?

a Carlos era profesor de pintura.
b El barrio de Vila Mariana tenía poca vegetación.
c El departamento de Carlos era grande.
d Carlos tenía buenos vecinos.
e Carlos volvió a Buenos Aires porque no le gustaba San Pablo.

5 Imagine you are asked by a Latin American friend about your life five or ten years ago. Answer these questions giving real or imaginary information.

a ¿Dónde vivías tú hace cinco / diez años?
b ¿Estabas soltero/a o casado/a?
c ¿Con quién vivías?
d ¿Qué hacías? ¿Estudiabas / trabajabas?
e ¿Dónde estudiabas / trabajabas?
f ¿Te gustaba tu trabajo?
g ¿Cómo era tu casa?

6 At a party you meet Pedro, an Ecuadorean who now lives in your country. Follow the guidelines below to ask him questions, using the familiar form.

    a Ask where he lived before.
    b Ask in what part of Ecuador he lived.
    c Ask what he used to do there.
    d Ask what he is doing here.

◆》 **CD2, TR 3, 04:20**

7 Carlos García, from Argentina, describes his native Buenos Aires. Listen to the description, then answer the questions below. First, look at these key words:

¿Cómo describirías …? *How would you describe …?*
los rincones *corners*
la unidad común *common unity*
el movimiento cultural *cultural life (movement)*
el alma *soul*
la vida nocturna *nightlife*
expresarse *to express oneself*
la tendencia *tendency*
los porteños *name given to the inhabitants of Buenos Aires*
entristecer *to become sad*
la melancholia *melancholy*

QUICK VOCAB

Insight

Note that **el alma** *soul* is a feminine word, but because the word begins with an accentuated '**a**', **la** *the* (fem.) changes into **el** (masc.). The plural, however, is **las almas** *souls*. The same rule applies in **el agua – las aguas** *water(s)*, **el arte – las artes** *art(s)*, **el haba – las habas** *broad beans(s)*, etc.

Now answer these questions in English:

    a How does Carlos describe Buenos Aires?
    b What does he like most about the city?
    c What doesn't he like about the city?

8 During a holiday in a Latin American country, you meet someone you like very much. When you get back home that evening you describe that person to your Spanish-speaking friend.

Use this description as a guideline, and add further information if you wish.

▶ He / she was very good-looking, dark, tall and slim.
▶ He / she had black hair and green eyes.
▶ He / she was about your age.
▶ He / she was very nice.

9 Write a brief passage recounting a period in your life, including information about a place and someone you used to know. Try using some of the words and phrases from earlier parts of the unit and, with a help of a dictionary, add others of your own.

Test yourself

    1 Choose the correct form of the verb in the following sentences.
      a Esta mañana (vi/veía) a Manuel. (Estuvo/Estaba) en un café con una chica.
      b (Fue/Era) una chica alta y muy guapa. (Tuvo/Tenía) unos veinticinco años.
      c (Conocí/Conocía) a Manuel hace un mes en casa de Julia. Ella me lo (presentó/presentaba).
      d Un día Manuel me (llamó/llamaba) por teléfono y me (invitó/invitaba) a salir.
      e Yo (estuve/estaba) muy ocupada aquel día y no (pude/podía) aceptar su invitación.

2 How would you say the following in Spanish?

    a She used to call me everyday. I liked her a lot.

    b She was living with a friend not far from my house. They had a nice apartment.

    c Her friend was working in a hospital. He was a doctor.

    d I used to visit them from time to time.

    e She's living in Paris now. She is studying French.

The contrast between the preterite and the imperfect is a very important one and not always easy to understand, so if most of your answers were correct, congratulations! You have covered all the most essential tenses in your Spanish course. If you feel you still need some further revision before you carry on, check para 1 of the **Grammar** section again or study paras 10 and 11 of the **Grammar summary** at the back of the book.

11

Me gustaría alquilar un coche
I would like to hire a car

In this unit you will learn
- *How to hire a car*
- *How to offer to do something*
- *How to make requests*
- *How to make a telephone call*

1 Allá alquilan coches *There they rent cars*

Gonzalo, an Argentinian, asks his friend Lucía to recommend a car rental agency. First, try learning these key phrases: **Me gustaría alquilar un coche** *I'd like to hire a car,* **¿Me podrías recomendar alguna agencia?** *Could you recommend an agency?*

CD2, TR 4, 00:05

Gonzalo	Hola Lucía, buen día.
Lucía	Buen día, Gonzalo.
Gonzalo	¿Qué vas a hacer hoy?
Lucía	Voy a ir a nadar. ¿Querés venir conmigo?
Gonzalo	No, gracias. Me gustaría alquilar un coche para salir con Silvia y los chicos. ¿Me podrías recomendar alguna agencia?
Lucía	Sí, sí, a media cuadra del Centro Cívico está la agencia Nahuelhuapi. Allá alquilan coches.
Gonzalo	¿Cerca del Centro Cívico dijiste?
Lucía	Sí, dos cuadras más abajo, a la derecha.

buen día (Arg.) *good morning*
hoy *today*
alquilar / arrendar *to hire, rent*
conmigo *with me*
los chicos / niños *children*
a media cuadra *half a block away*
¿... dijiste? *...did you say? (fam)*
más abajo *further down*

QUICK VOCAB

Say it in Spanish

How would you express the following in Spanish?

a We'd like to hire a car.
b Could you (formal) recommend us an agency?
c It's half a block from here.
d It's four blocks further down, on the left.

---

2 Alquilando un coche *Hiring a car*

Gonzalo hires a car. First, try learning these key phrases: **¿Qué me recomienda?** *What do you recommend?*, **Le recomiendo ...** *I recommend ...*, **¿Cuánto cuesta el alquiler?** *How much is the rental?*

Empleada	Buen día. ¿Qué desea?
Gonzalo	Buen día. Quisiera alquilar un coche ¿Qué me recomienda?
Empleada	Bueno, tenemos varios modelos. ¿Quiere un coche chico?
Gonzalo	No demasiado chico. Somos cuatro personas.
Empleada	Bueno, en ese caso le recomiendo el Ford Fiesta, que tiene capacidad para cuatro personas. Es un coche bastante cómodo y económico.
Gonzalo	¿Cuánto cuesta el alquiler?
Empleada	Si es por uno o dos días, cuesta noventa dólares diarios, con kilometraje ilimitado. Por semana, vale cuatrocientos dólares. El impuesto y el seguro están incluidos.
Gonzalo	Bueno, lo quiero por dos días solamente, sábado y domingo.
Empleada	Muy bien. ¿Quiere reservarlo ahora?
Gonzalo	Sí, prefiero reservarlo ahora mismo.
Empleada	Pase por aquí, por favor.

Insight

In '**¿qué me recomienda?**' and '**le recomiendo …**' the only possible position for '**me**' and '**le**' is before the verb (see previous Insight). Note also the different meanings of '**por**' in '**por uno o dos días**' *'for one or two days*', '**por semana**' *'per week*', '**por aquí**' *'this way*'.

QUICK VOCAB

chico/a *small*
la capacidad *room*
cómodo/a *comfortable*
el kilometraje ilimitado *unlimited mileage*
ahora mismo *right now*
pase por aquí *come this way*
el impuesto *tax*
el seguro *insurance*

Answer these questions in English

a How does the employee describe the car she recommends?
b How much is the rental per day?
c What does the rental price include?
d How long does Gonzalo want the car for?

---

3 En la estación de servicio *At the petrol station*

Gonzalo stops at a petrol station (**estación de servicio**) to fill up.
Practise saying these key sentences first: **¿Se lo lleno?** *Shall I fill it up for you?*, **Llénelo** *Fill it up*, **¿Me revisa la presión de las ruedas?** *Will you check the tyre pressure for me?*, **¿Le miro el aceite?** *Shall I look at the oil for you?*

Empleado	¿Se lo lleno?	
Gonzalo	Sí, llénelo. Y me revisa la presión de las ruedas también.	
Empleado	¿Le miro el aceite?	
Gonzalo	No, el aceite está bien.	
Empleado	Listo señor.	
Gonzalo	¿Cuánto es?	
Empleado	Son quince pesos.	
Gonzalo	Gracias. ¿Me podría decir si falta mucho para llegar a Esquel?	
Empleado	Veinte kilómetros más o menos.	
Gonzalo	Gracias.	

CD2, TR 4, 02:48

Insight

In '**¿se lo lleno?**' '*shall I fill it up for you?*' (literally, '*to you it I fill up?*'), '**se**' stands for '**le**' '*to you*'. '**Le**' and '**lo**' cannot go together, so '**le**' changes into '**se**'. But note '**¿le lleno el estanque?**' '*shall I fill up the tank for you?*'

llenar *to fill up*
reviser *to check*
la rueda *wheel*
el aceite *oil*
la gasolina *petrol*
listo/a *ready*

....
Insight

'**Faltar**' is normally used in the third person singular or plural in sentences like the following: '**¿falta mucho?**' *'is it far to go?'*, '**faltan 20 km para llegar a (Buenos Aires)**' *'it's another 20 km before we reach (Buenos Aires)'*, '**falta media hora para la salida**' *'the departure will be in half an hour'*.
....

Answer these questions in English:

a What services does Gonzalo request at the service station?
b What expression does he use to say *Could you tell me …?*

---

4 Una rueda pinchada *A puncture*

Gonzalo has a puncture, and he drives to the nearest garage to have the tyre repaired. Note the use of the word **la goma**, Argentinian Spanish for *tyre*, known as **la llanta or el neumático** in other Latin American countries.

Gonzalo	Buenas tardes. ¿Podrían repararme esta goma?
Mecánico	¿Para cuándo la quiere?
Gonzalo	Para esta misma tarde. Tenemos que volver a Bariloche.
Mecánico	A las tres y media se la puedo tener lista.
Gonzalo	Sí, está bien. Vuelvo a esa hora.

pinchada *punctured*
reparar *to repair*
a esa hora *at that time*

Say it in Spanish

What expressions are used in the dialogue to say the following?

a Could you repair ... for me?
b When do you want it for?
c I can have it ready for you.

5 Una llamada telefónica *A telephone call*

Back at his hotel, Gonzalo makes an international telephone call through the hotel switchboard. First, try learning these key sentences: **Quiero llamar a Londres** *I want to call London*, **Es una**

llamada de persona a persona *It's a personal call*, **¿Hay mucha demora?** *Is there a long delay?*

CD2, TR 4, 04:16

Telefonista	¿Hola?
Gonzalo	Hola, telefonista. Llamo desde la habitación trescientos diez. ¿Sería posible hacer una llamada internacional desde mi habitación? Quiero llamar a Londres.
Telefonista	Sí, sí se puede. ¿A qué número de Londres desea llamar?
Gonzalo	Al 81–601 1326.
Telefonista	81–601 1326.
Gonzalo	Es una llamada de persona a persona.
Telefonista	¿Su nombre, por favor?
Gonzalo	Gonzalo Lira.
Telefonista	¿Y el nombre de la persona con quien desea hablar?
Gonzalo	Robert Major. M-a-j-o-r, Major. ¿Hay mucha demora?
Telefonista	No, en este momento no. Cuelgue por favor. Yo lo llamaré.
Gonzalo	Gracias.

Insight

Since the above dialogue was written London telephone numbers have changed – (0) 81 is now (0) 208. Note also '**se puede**', an impersonal sentence, in which '**se**' translates '*you*' or '*one*': '**Sí, sí, se puede**' 'Yes, you can'. The repetition of 'sí' or 'no', for emphasis, is common in Spanish: '**sí, sí, sí, claro**' '*yes, sure*', '**no, no, claro que no**' '*no, of course not*'.

QV

llamo (llamar) desde *I am calling (to call) from*
¿sería posible ...? *would it be possible ...?*
la llamada *telephone call*
cuelgue (colgar) *hang up (to hang up)*

Say it in Spanish

While travelling in a Latin American country you telephone your family back home.

Use the guidelines below to talk to the operator at your hotel.

a Say you are calling from room twenty-five.
b Ask if it would be possible to phone (name the country) from your room.
c Say it is a personal call, and give the telephone number and the name of the person you want to call.

Key phrases

Hiring a car

Me gustaría / Quisiera alquilar / arrendar un coche / carro.	*I would like to hire a car.*
¿Cuánto cuesta / vale el alquiler?	*How much is the rental?*
Cuesta ... diarios / por día / semana.	*It costs ... per day / week.*
Quiero un coche / carro chico (or pequeño) / grande / mediano.	*I want a small / big / medium sized car.*
Lo quiero por dos días / una semana.	*I want it for two days / a week.*
¿Está incluido el impuesto / iva / seguro?	*Is tax / VAT / insurance included?*

Offering to do something

¿Se lo lleno?	*Shall I fill it up?*
¿Le reviso/miro ...?	*Shall I check / have a look at ...?*

Making requests

¿Me revisa la presión de las ruedas / el aceite?	*Will you check the air pressure in the wheels / the oil?*
¿Podría(n) repararme el coche / carro / este neumático?	*Could you repair my car / this tyre?*
Lo / la quiero para hoy / esta tarde.	*I want it for today / this afternoon.*

Making a telephone call (see also Unit 9)

Quiero / quisiera llamar a Londres / Nueva York.	*I want / would like to call London / New York.*
¿Sería posible hacer una llamada internacional / de larga distancia / de persona a persona?	*Would it be possible to make an international / long distance / personal call?*
Quiero hacer una llamada con cobro revertido / por cobrar.	*I want to reverse the charges.*
¿Hay mucha demora?	*Is there a long delay?*

Grammar

1 *The conditional tense*

To say what you would like, as in *I would like to hire a car*, and to ask whether something is possible, e.g. *Could you repair this tyre?* or *Would it be possible to make an international phone call from my room?*, you can use the conditional tense.

Formation
Like the future tense (see Unit 8), the conditional is formed with the infinitive, to which the appropriate ending is added. The endings are the same for -**ar**, -**er** and -**ir** verbs. Here is the conditional tense of a regular verb:

ser	to be
ser**ía**	*I would be*
ser**ías**	*you would be* (fam, sing)
ser**ía**	*you would be* (pol, sing)
	he, she, it would be
ser**íamos**	*we would be*
ser**ían**	*you would be* (pl)
	they would be

Notice that the first and third person singular are the same and that all forms carry an accent. The '**-ía**' ending is the same as that of the imperfect tense of '**-er**' and '**-ir**' verbs (**saber: sabía, sabías, sabía,** etc.).

Here are some examples of the use of the conditional tense with regular verbs:

Me gustaría ir a la Argentina.	*I would like to go to Argentina.*
¿Qué te gustaría hacer?	*What would you like to do?*
Preferiría un coche chico.	*I would prefer a small car.*
¿Cuándo irían a Sudamérica?	*When would you / they go to South America?*

Remember that **gustar**, *to like*, takes the third person of the verb (see Unit 6): **me gustaría** *I would like*, **te gustaría** *you would like* (fam), **le gustaría** *you* (pol) / *he* / *she would like*, **nos gustaría** *we would like*, **les gustaría** *you* / *they would like*.

Irregular conditional forms
Verbs with irregular stems in the future tense (see Unit 8) also have them in the conditional. The endings are the same as those of regular verbs. Here are some of the most common:

decir	*to say, to tell*	diría, dirías, diría, diríamos, dirían
hacer	*to do, to make*	haría, harías, haría, haríamos, harían
poder	*can, to be able*	podría, podrías, podría, podríamos, podrían

(Contd)

salir	*to go out, to leave*	saldría, saldrías, saldría, saldríamos, saldrían
tener	*to have*	tendría, tendrías, tendría, tendríamos, tendrían
venir	*to come*	vendría, vendrías, vendría, vendríamos, vendrían

¿Qué diría él?	*What would he say?*
Yo no lo haría.	*I wouldn't do it.*
¿Podrían repararlo?	*Could you repair it?*

For other irregular conditional forms, see the Irregular verbs section.

2 Conmigo, contigo ... with me, with you ...

With me translates into Spanish as **conmigo**. *With you* (fam) becomes **contigo**.

¿Quieres venir conmigo?	*Do you want to come with me?*
No puedo ir contigo.	*I can't go with you. (fam)*

With other persons, use **usted** (pol), **él, ella, nosotros, nosotras, ustedes, ellos, ellas**

Iré con usted.	*I will go with you. (pol)*
Iremos con él.	*We will go with him.*

Remember that, in the first and second person singular, other prepositions (words like *for*, *without*, *to*) are followed by mí and ti (see Unit 5, Grammar, para 5).

Para mí un café.	*Coffee for me.*
¿Y para ti?	*And for you?*

3 Offering to do something: the present tense

Spanish speakers normally use the present tense when offering to do something, usually preceded by one or two object pronouns (see Grammar, Unit 5).

¿Le limpio el coche / carro?	*Shall I clean the car for you? (pol)*
¿Se lo limpio / reviso?	*Shall I clean it / check it for you? (pol)*
¿Le hago la habitación?	*Shall I make the room for you? (pol)*
¿Te ayudo?	*Shall I help you? (fam)*

Insight

To express offers, as in the previous sentences, English normally uses 'shall', '*Shall I open the window (for you)?*' whereas Spanish uses the present tense, with '**te**' (fam, sing), '**le**' (pol, sing) or '**les**' (fam or pol, pl), '*for you*', preceding the verb: '**¿(Te) abro la ventana?**', literally '*(For you) I open the window?*'

---

4 *Making requests*

a The present tense

To make simple requests Spanish speakers normally use a construction with the present tense, usually preceded by one or two object pronouns, as above.

¿Me permite usar su teléfono?	*Will you let me use your telephone?*
¿Me lo llena, por favor?	*Will you fill it up for me?*

Insight

As with offers above, requests usually start with a pronoun indicating the person who is making the request, which may be '**me**' (for '**yo**' '*I*') or '**nos**' (for '**nosotros**' '*we*'): '**¿Me/Nos puede ayudar?**' '*Can you help me/us?*'

---

b ¿Podría...? Could you...?

To make more polite requests, use **poder** in the conditional tense.

Por favor, ¿podría ayudarme?	*Could you help me, please?*
¿Me podrías recomendar algo?	*Could you recommend something (to me)?*
¿Podría repararmelo/la?	*Could you repair it for me?*

c Other forms of making requests

As in English, there are a number of other expressions used for making polite requests:

¿Le importaría ayudarme?	*Would you mind helping me?*
¿Sería tan amable de bajarme la maleta?	*Would you so kind as to get my suitcase down for me?*
¿Me haría el favor de escribírmelo?	*Would you please write it down for me?*

Requests can also be made with the imperative or command form (see Unit 12)

Llénemelo, por favor.	*Fill it up, please.*
Por favor, ayúdenos.	*Please, help us.*

Practice

1 You are in a Latin-American city, staying at a hotel in calle **Mac Iver** (marked on the map). You would like to hire a car and you ask the hotel receptionist to recommend a car rental firm. He recommends one, which is on **calle Agustinas,** opposite **cerro** (*hill*) **Santa Lucía,** two blocks down **calle Moneda,** then left at **Santa Lucía** and left again at **calle Agustinas,** as shown on the map. Use dialogue 1 as a model to write the conversation between you and the hotel receptionist. You can then compare your own version of the dialogue with the one in the **Key to the activities.**

2 At the car rental agency you speak to the person in charge

```
......................................................
:                        TARIFAS                      :
:                                                      :
:          MODELO              DÍA          SEMANA     :
: A        Económico          $ 27.300      $ 175.000  :
: B        Mediano            $ 34.300      $ 224.000  :
: C        Todo Equipado      $ 45.500      $ 294.000  :
: F        Lujo               $ 66.500      $ 413.000  :
: D        Van                $ 77.000      $ 455.000  :
: E        Doble cabina 4 x 4 $ 77.000      $ 455.000  :
......................................................
```

Empleado	Buenos días. ¿Qué desea?
Ud.	*Say you would like to hire a car. Ask him what he recommends.*
Empleado	Bueno, tenemos varios modelos. ¿Qué tipo de auto busca usted?
Ud.	*Say you want a small car, not too expensive.*
Empleado	El más económico que tenemos es éste. Es un coche pequeño y muy bueno.
Ud.	*Ask what the rental is per day.*
Empleado	Por día cuesta veintisiete mil trescientos pesos. Es un precio bastante conveniente.
Ud.	*And per week?*
Empleado	Ciento setenta y cinco mil pesos.
Ud.	*Ask if that is with unlimited mileage.*
Empleado	Sí, no hay recargo por kilómetro.
Ud.	*Ask if VAT and insurance are included.*
Empleado	Sí, están incluidos en el precio.
Ud.	*Say that is fine. You'll take it.*
Empleado	¿Tiene su licencia de conducir al día?
Ud.	*Yes, here it is.*
Empleado	Gracias.
Ud.	*Ask if it would be possible to leave the car in another city. You want to travel south and leave the car there. You prefer to come back by train.*
Empleado	No, no se puede. Tendría que devolver el coche aquí mismo.

el recargo *surcharge*
la licencia de conducir *driving licence*
al día *valid, up to date*
devolver *to return (something)*

Insight

La licencia de conducir *driving licence* will be understood in all countries, in some Latin American regions you will hear alternative forms such as **la licencia** (or **el permiso** or **el carnet**) **de manejar**.

3 You may have difficulties with your car, so be prepared! What would you say in Spanish in these situations? If necessary, revise dialogue 3 and **Key phrases.**

    a Your car is running out of petrol. You stop a passer-by and ask if there is a service station nearby.

    b At the service station you ask the attendant to fill it up for you.

    c You need the oil and the tyre pressure checked.

    d The windscreen is dirty (**el parabrisas está sucio**), so you ask the attendant to clean it for you.

    e Fifty miles down the road you have a puncture. You change the wheel, then stop at a garage where you ask the mechanic to mend the tyre for you.

    f Before continuing your journey, you ask the mechanic if Santa Isabel is a long way off.

4 While on holiday, you telephone your manager Andrew Bronson at your office back home. It is company business, so you decide to reverse the charges. Use Dialogue 5 as a model, and the relevant expressions under **Key phrases,** to write a conversation between you and the hotel operator. You can then compare your own version of the dialogue with the model in the **Key to the activities.**

◄》 **CD2, TR 4, 05:55**

5 Carlos García, from Buenos Aires, Argentina, was asked where he would like to spend his next holiday. Listen to what he says, then answer the questions. First, look at these key words:

pasar *to spend*
próximo/a *next*
la imagen *image*
quedó profundamente grabada *remained deeply imprinted*

Now answer these questions in English:

a Why would Carlos like to spend his next holiday in Bariloche?
b Who would he go with and for how long?

◄》 **CD2, TR 4, 06:42**

6 Carlos García was then asked what sort of car he would like to have. Listen to his reply, then complete the sentences below. First, look at these key words:

Complete these sentences:

a Carlos preferiría un coche ———— . (*size*)
b Él preferiría un coche ———— . (*type*)
c Él compraría un coche ———— . (*colour*)
d Él usaría el coche para ———— y ———— . (*use*).

7 How would you say the following in Spanish?
    a I'd like to call David in New York. You have his number. Will you give it to me? (familiar)
    b Operator, I'd like to make an international call from my room. Would that be possible?

c I want to reverse the charges.

d Shall I give you the name and telephone number? (polite)

e Will you please tell him that I am Nora Vargas and that I'm calling him from Mexico?

f Could you tell me how much the call came to?

Test yourself

a Give the Spanish for '*We would like to hire a car*'

b Give the Spanish for '*How much is the rental?*'

c Give the English for '*El impuesto y el seguro están incluidos*'.

d Give the English for '*Faltan dos kilómetros para llegar a la ciudad*'.

e Give the English for '*¿Se lo lleno?*'

f Choose the correct reply for the question above: **(1)** '*Sí, lléneme*', **(2)** '*Sí, llénemelo*', **(3)** '*Sí, lléneselo*'.

g Give the Spanish for the phrases in italics: '*¿Quieres venir with me?* 'Sí, iré *with you*' (fam./sing)

h Give an alternative word order for the following: '*¿Podría reservármelo para mañana?*

i Give the conditional for the verb in brackets: '*¿Me (hacer) usted el favor de ayudarme con el equipaje?*

j Give the conditional for the verb in brackets: '*¿(Ser) usted tan amable de llamarme un taxi?*

Car hire, requests and offers are the main focus of this test. Among those related to car hire there are some fixed expressions which you just need to memorize. If you are interested in the the subject and still need some further study, go back to Dialogues 1 and 2 and the **Key phrases**. The questions related to requests and offers assess your ability to handle some key grammatical constructions. Make sure you got them right before you go on to the next unit.

12

¿Ha estado en Cusco?
Have you been to Cusco?

In this unit you will learn
- *How to talk about what you have done*
- *How to express obligation and need*
- *How to give instructions and commands*

---

1 Tengo que estar a las siete en el aeropuerto
I have to be at the airport at seven

Roberto, from Argentina, is in Lima, Peru. At a party, Roberto talks to Pilar, a Peruvian. Key phrases here are **He estado** *I have been*, **¿Ha ido alguna vez ...?** *Have you ever been ...?*, **No he tenido ...** *I haven't had ...*, **Me han dicho** *I've been told*, **Ya he tomado demasiado** *I've had too much to drink*.

♪ CD2, TR 5, 00:06

Pilar	¿Es la primera vez que viene a Lima?
Roberto	No, he estado aquí varias veces. Vengo aquí por negocios y, además, el Perú me gusta mucho. ¿Usted es de Lima?
Pilar	No, yo soy de Arequipa, pero vengo mucho a Lima. Tengo parientes aquí. ¿Ha ido alguna vez a Arequipa?
Roberto	No, no he estado nunca allá. No he tenido tiempo. Me han dicho que es una ciudad muy linda. Me gustaría mucho ir.

Pilar	Sí, no deje de ir. Le va a gustar. Es muy diferente a Lima. Si va a Arequipa, llámeme. Le daré mi número de teléfono. Yo misma le enseñaré la ciudad.
Roberto	Muchas gracias.
Pilar	¿Se sirve otro pisco sour?
Roberto	No, gracias. Ya he tomado demasiado y tengo que irme pronto. Mañana tengo que estar a las siete en el aeropuerto.

Insight

Forms like '**he estado …**' '*I have been …*', '**¿ha ido alguna vez a …**' '*have you ever been to …?*' (literally, '*… gone to*'), '**Me han dicho que …**' '*I have been told that …*' (literally, '*they have told me that …*'), etc. correspond to the perfect tense, which is normally used to relate events that have some connection with the present, or which have taken place in the recent past. (See Grammar, paragraph 1.)

la primera vez *first time*
varias veces *several times*
el negocio *business*
además *besides*
los parientes *relatives*
no deje de ir *don't fail to go*
llámeme *call me*
yo mismo/a *I myself*
enseñar / mostrar *to show*
¿se sirve …? *will you have …? (food or drink)*

Insight

'**Pisco**', '*a clear spirit*' made from grapes, comes from Peru and Chile, and is usually mixed with lemon and egg-white to make a drink known as '*pisco sour*'.

True or false? (¿**Verdadero o falso?**)

a Roberto no ha estado en Lima antes.
b Está en Lima de vacaciones.
c No conoce Arequipa.

---

2 Lléveme al Hotel Continental *Take me to the Hotel Continental*

Roberto takes a taxi to his hotel.

CD2, TR 5, 02:18

Roberto	¡Taxi!
	(*The taxi stops and Roberto gets in.*)
Taxista	Buenas noches, señor.
Roberto	Buenas noches, lléveme al Hotel Continental en la calle Puno, por favor.
Taxista	Muy bien, señor.

Insight

'**Lléveme**' '*take me*', from '**llevar**', and '**llámeme**' '*call me*', from '**llamar**' (see previous dialogue), are polite imperative or command forms. Note the position of the '**me**' '*me*' after the verb. (See Grammar, paragraph 3.)

 taxista *taxi driver*

Say it in Spanish

How would you say the following in Spanish?

a Take me to the airport, please.
b Take us to calle San Martín, please.

---

3 Deme la cuenta *Give me the bill*

Roberto asks the hotel receptionist to prepare the bill for him and to wake him up in the morning. Note the following key words and phrases: **deme** *give me*, **¿me despierta?** *will you wake me up?*, **envíemelo** *send it to me*.

Roberto	Buenas noches.
Recepcionista	Buenas noches, señor.
Roberto	Por favor, deme la cuenta de la habitación doscientos treinta. Me voy mañana temprano.
Recepcionista	Sí, señor. Se la daré enseguida.
Roberto	Ah, y me despierta a las seis de la mañana, por favor. Tengo que salir del hotel a las seis y media.
Recepcionista	¿Quiere tomar el desayuno en la habitación o prefiere bajar al comedor?
Roberto	Envíemelo a la habitación, por favor.
Recepcionista	Muy bien, señor.
Roberto	Gracias.

CD2, TR 5, 02:40

Insight

'**Deme**' and '**envíemelo**' are both polite *imperative* or command forms. The first derives from '**dar**' '*to give*', the second from '**enviar**' '*to send*', both '**-ar**' verbs. The '**a**' of '**-ar**', then, has changed into '**-e**' to form the imperative.

me voy (irse) *I am leaving (to leave)*
temprano *early*
se la daré *I will give it to you*
enseguida / en seguida *right away*
despertar *to wake up*
bajar *to go down*

Say it in Spanish

Use the guidelines below to express the following:

a Ask the hotel receptionist for the bill for room 150. Say you are leaving tomorrow morning.

b Ask to be woken up at 7.30. You've got to be at the airport at 9.00.

4 En el aeropuerto *At the airport*

Roberto goes to the airline desk and hands in his ticket. Key phrases here are **¿Me da ...?** *Will you give me ...?*, **Tiene que pagar / embarcar ...** *You have to pay / board*, **Pase por ...** *Go through ...*

Empleada	Me da su pasaporte, por favor. *(Roberto hands in his passport.)* Gracias. ¿Cuál es su equipaje?
Roberto	Tengo esta valija solamente.
Empleada	¿Tiene equipaje de mano?
Roberto	Este bolso.
Empleada	Bien. ¿Fumador o no fumador?
Roberto	No fumador. Y prefiero un asiento junto al pasillo, por favor.
Empleada	Sí, cómo no ... Aquí está su pasaje, su pasaporte y su tarjeta de embarque. Primero tiene que pagar su impuesto de aeropuerto y después pase por policía internacional. Tiene que embarcar a las nueve y media por la puerta número seis.
Roberto	¿Está retrasado el vuelo?
Empleada	Sí, hay media hora de retraso.

Insight

Look at the following phrases in this and the previous dialogues, which express some kind of obligation or need: '**tiene que pagar/embarcar**' '*you have to pay/board*', '**tengo que salir**' '*I have to leave*' (Dialogue 3), '**tengo que irme**' '*I have to leave*'. (See Grammar, para. 2.) Note that since this dialogue was written Latin American airlines, like all airlines, do not allow smoking on board.

el equipaje de mano *hand luggage*
la valija *(River Plate)* **/ maleta** *suitcase*
el bolso *bag*
(no) fumador *(non) smoker*
junto al pasillo *on the aisle*
el pasaje *ticket (for transport)*
la tarjeta de embarque *boarding card*
retrasado/a *delayed*
el retraso *delay*

QUICK VOCAB

Say it in Spanish

You are at a small airport in a Latin American country, where you need to communicate in Spanish. Use the guidelines in English to fill in your part of the conversation:

Key phrases

Talking about what you have done

¿Ha estado alguna vez en / ido alguna vez a Sudamérica?	*Have you ever been to South America?*
No he estado / ido nunca allá.	*I have never been there.*
He estado aquí una vez / dos veces / varias veces.	*I have been here once / twice / several times.*

Expressing obligation and need

Tengo que estar allá / salir a las seis y media.	*I have to be there / leave at half past six.*
Tiene que embarcar / pagar su impuesto.	*You have to board / to pay your tax.*

Giving instructions and commands

Deme la cuenta.	*Give me the bill.*
Lléveme/nos al aeropuerto / a la terminal.	*Take me / us to the airport/ terminal.*
Envíemelo/la a la habitación.	*Send it to my room.*

Grammar

1 The perfect tense

Usage

The perfect tense is used to say what you or others have done. It is much less frequent in Latin America than in Spain. To refer to recent past events, e.g. *I have worked too much today*, Latin Americans will normally use the preterite tense, **Hoy trabajé demasiado,** while most Spaniards will use the perfect tense, **Hoy he trabajado demasiado.** However, with certain phrases, such as **alguna vez** *ever*, **una vez / dos veces** *once / twice*, **varias veces** *several times*, **nunca** *never* and **todavía** *still*, which bear some relationship with the present tense (the idea of *so far, up till now*), the perfect tense is fairly frequently used in Latin America. Look at the following examples.

He estado aquí varias veces.	*I have been here several times.*
¿Ha ido alguna vez a Arequipa?	*Have you ever been to Arequipa?*
No he ido nunca.	*I have never been.*
He hablado con ella sólo una vez.	*I have spoken to her only once.*
Todavía no han llegado.	*They still haven't arrived.*

Formation

To form the perfect tense, you need to use the present tense of **haber** (auxiliary verb *to have*) followed by a past participle (the Spanish equivalent of forms like *drunk, gone*), which is invariable. To form the past participle of **-ar** verbs, add **-ado** to the stem, e.g. **estar** *to be* – **estado** *been*; to form the past participle of **-er** and **-ir** verbs, add **-ido** to the stem: **tener** *to have* – **tenido** *had*, **ir** *to go* – **ido** *gone*. Here are two examples, one showing an **-ar** verb, the other showing an **-er** verb.

estar	to be
he estado	*I have been*
has estado	*you have been* (fam, sing)
ha estado	*you have been* (pol, sing) / *he, she, it has been*
hemos estado	*we have been*
han estado	*you have been* (pl)
	they have been

tener	to have
he tenido	*I have had*
has tenido	*you have had* (fam, sing)
ha tenido	*you have had* (pol, sing), *he, she, it has had*
hemos tenido	*we have had*
han tenido	*you have had* (pl)
	they have had

Here are some examples of the use of the perfect tense:

Todavía / Aún no hemos terminado.	*We haven't finished yet.*
Nunca he viajado a Sudamérica.	*I have never travelled to South America.*
He ido muchas veces al Perú.	*I have been to Peru many times.*

Insight

The past participle remains the same for all persons, with no change for masculine or feminine or singular or plural, unless this is being used as an adjective: '**un hombre educado/ una mujer educada**' '*a well brought up man/woman*' (but, '**Ellos han educado bien a sus hijos**' '*They have brought up their children well*'). With '**estar**', when denoting the result of an action, the past participle must show gender and number agreement: '**el trabajo está terminado**' '*the job is finished*', '**están bien alimentados**' '*they are well fed*'.

Irregular past participles
Some verbs form the past participle in an irregular way. Here are the most common:

abrir *to open*   **abierto** *opened*
decir *to say, to tell*   **dicho** *said, told*
escribir *to write*   **escrito** *written*
hacer *to do, to make*   **hecho** *done, made*
ver *to see*   **visto** *seen*
volver *to come back*   **vuelto** *come back*

Me han dicho que es una ciudad muy bonita.   *I have been told it's a very nice city.*
Aún / Todavía no le he escrito.   *I still haven't written to him/her.*
Los he visto varias veces.   *I have seen them several times.*

For other irregular past participles, see Irregular verbs in the back of the book.

Insight
'He', 'has', 'ha', etc. and the past participle cannot be split up, and any pronouns used with them must precede the form of 'haber': '**Se lo he dicho varias veces**' *'I've told him/her several times'*, '**Me lo ha dado Antonia**' *'Antonia has given it to me'*.

2 Expressing obligation and need

a Tener que + infinitive
Obligation and need are usually expressed with the construction tener que *to have to*, followed by the infinitive.

¿Qué tienes que hacer?   *What do you have to do?*
Tengo que trabajar / estudiar.   *I have to work / study.*
Tenemos que volver pronto.   *We have to come back soon.*
Tuvimos que hacerlo.   *We had to do it.*

b Haber que + infinitive

Obligation and need is also expressed with the impersonal form
haber que followed by the infinitive. In the present, use **hay que**
one has to, you / we have to; in the past, use **había** or **hubo que**
one had to, you / we had to; for future reference **habrá que** *one will
have to, you / we will have to*; and to say *one would have to, you/
we would* have to use habría. This construction is very common in
the spoken language.

Hay que tener visa.	*You need to have a visa.*
Hay que reservar una habitación.	*You need to book a room.*
Había/hubo que decírselo.	*We had to tell him/her/them.*
Habría que tener cuidado.	*One would have to be careful.*

c Deber + infinitive

A less frequent alternative is the construction with **deber** *must*
followed by the infinitive. This is normally used to express stronger
obligation or need.

No debes hacerlo.	*You mustn't do it.*
Debes traerlo.	*You must bring it.*

Deber is often used in the conditional with the meaning of should:

No deberíamos gastar tanto.	*We shouldn't spend so much.*
Deberías estar preparado.	*You should be prepared.*

3 The imperative or command form

Usage

To give instructions and commands, and to make suggestions,
for example *call me, please take me to the hotel*, you can use the
imperative form, which is normally followed or preceded by the
phrase **por favor** to soften the command:

Si va a Arequipa, llámeme.	*If you go to Arequipa, call me.*
Lléveme al hotel Continental,	*Please take me to the Continental*
por favor.	*Hotel.*

Formation
a Formal or polite imperative
In Spanish there are different imperative forms depending on
who you are talking to (formal or informal) and whether you are
speaking to one or more than one person (singular or plural). To
form the imperative for 'usted' you need the stem of the first person
singular of the present tense followed by the appropriate ending:
'-e' for verbs in '-ar' and '-a' for those in '-er' and '-ir'. For the
'ustedes' form add '-n'.

Infinitive	Present (1st person)	Imperative (usted/ustedes)
hablar to speak	hablo	hable(n)
comer to eat	como	coma(n)
subir to go up	subo	suba(n)

Hable con ella. *Speak to her.*
Coma un poco más. *Eat some more.*
Suban por aquí. *Go up this way.*

The negative imperative is formed by placing no before the verb:
'no hable(n)', 'no coma(n)', 'no suba(n)'.

Irregular formal imperatives
As the imperative is formed from the first person singular of the
present tense, verbs which are irregular or stem-changing in the
first person singular of the present tense are also irregular (though
not always in the same way) or stem-changing in the imperative.
Here are some examples:

Infinitive	Present (1st person)	Imperative (sing./pl.)
decir to say	digo	diga(n)
hacer to do, to make	hago	haga(n)
oír to hear, to listen	oigo	oiga(n)
traer to bring	traigo	traiga(n)
venir to come	vengo	venga(n)

Haga el favor de venir.	*Please come.*
¿Diga?	*Can I help you? (lit. Say?)*
Traiga un café, por favor.	*Bring a coffee, please.*

A few verbs form the formal imperative or command in a different way:

Infinitive	Formal imperative
dar to give	dé(n)
estar to be	esté(n)
ir to go	vaya(n)
saber to know	sepa(n)
ser to be	sea(n)

Vaya lentamente.	*Go slowly.*
Sean prudentes.	*Be cautious.*

b Positive informal imperative

The imperative for '**tú**' has different positive and negative forms. To form the positive command for '**tú**' use the second person singular of the present tense but without the final '**-s**'.

Present tense	Positive informal imperative
tú hablas	habla
tú comes	come
tú subes	sube

Habla con Raúl.	*Speak to Raúl.*
Come con nosotros.	*Eat with us.*
Sube esa escalera.	*Go up those stairs.*

Verbs which change their stem in the present tense make a similar change in the positive (and negative) informal form: '**jugar**' – '**juegas**' *'you play'* – '**juega**' *'play'*; '**pensar**' – '**piensas**' *'you think'* – '**piensa**' *'think'*, etc.

c Negative informal imperative

To form the negative imperative for 'tú' use the same form as for 'usted' (see a above) and add an '-s' : 'hable' – 'no hables', 'coma' – 'no comas', 'suba'- 'no subas', 'salga – no salgas', 'vaya' –'no vayas', etc.

Irregular informal imperatives

A few verbs have irregular *positive* 'tú' forms, while negative ones follow the normal pattern: 'di' (from 'decir'), 'haz' (from 'hacer'), 've' (from 'ver'), 'pon' (from 'poner'), 'sal' (from 'salir'), 'sé' (from 'ser'), 'ten' (from 'tener'), 'ven' (from 'venir'). But 'no digas', 'no hagas', 'no salgas', etc.

Hazlo hoy.	*Do it today.*
Ponlo aquí.	*Put it here.*
Ven conmigo.	*Come with me.*

Pronouns with imperatives

Pronouns go at the end of a positive form but before a negative one. Positive imperatives which carry a pronoun may need an accent. Here are some examples:

Llámeme.	*Call me.*
No me llame.	*Don't call me.*
Envíemelo a la habitación.	*Send it to my room. (lit. Send it to me to the room.)*
No me lo envíe a la habitación.	*Don't send it to my room.*
Hazlo.	*Do it.*
No lo hagas.	*Don't do it.*
Díselo.	*Tell him/her.*
No se lo digas.	*Don't tell him/her.*

4 The present tense as a substitute for the imperative

The present tense is often used in place of the imperative to soften the command, instruction or suggestion. Consider the following examples:

Por favor, ¿me **lleva** al aeropuerto?	*Will you take me to the airport, please?*
Lléveme al aeropuerto, por favor.	*Take me to the airport, please.*
¿Me **llama** a las seis?	*Will you call me at six?*
Llámeme a las seis.	*Call me at six.*

(See Making requests, Unit 11.)

Practice

1 You are visiting Peru, and at a party given by some Peruvian friends you meet someone. Use the guidelines in English to complete the conversation.

Conocido/a	¿Es la primera vez que viene al Perú?
Ud.	*Yes, it is the first time. You like it very much. It is a nice country, although you haven't seen very much yet.*
Conocido/a	¿Ha estado en Cusco?
Ud.	*No, you haven't been to Cusco yet, but you hope to go next week. You are going to visit Machu Picchu too. You've been told it is very interesting. Now, ask if he / she has ever been to Europe.*
Conocido/a	No, no he estado nunca en Europa, pero me encantaría ir. Tengo parientes en España y me han invitado. ¿Usted conoce España?
Ud.	*Yes, you have been there several times. You like Spain a lot, especially the south.*
Conocido/a	Usted habla muy bien español. ¿Dónde lo aprendió?
Ud.	*Thank him / her and say you studied Spanish at school. Ask if he / she speaks English.*
Conocido/a	He estudiado inglés varios años, pero todavía no lo hablo muy bien. Lo encuentro muy difícil. Prefiero que hablemos español.
Ud.	*Say that's all right.*
Conocido/a	¿Se sirve otro pisco sour?

| Ud. | Say no, thank you. You've already had two. It is enough. And, besides, tomorrow you have to get up early so you must go back to your hotel soon. |
| Conocido/a | No se preocupe usted, yo lo / la llevaré en mi carro. |

aunque *although*
me encantaría *I would love*
aprender *to learn*
suficiente *enough*
además *besides*
así que ... *so* ...
pronto *soon*

QUICK VOCAB

2 Your Peruvian acquaintances do not seem to realize you have only been in the country a few days. They keep asking you what places you have visited. Look at the examples, then answer their questions below.

- ¿Ha visto la catedral?
- Sí, ya la vi.
- ¿Ha ido al Museo Nacional de Arte?
- No, todavía no he ido.

a ¿Ha estado en el Museo de Cultura Peruana? (sí)
b ¿Ha visitado el Palacio de Gobierno? (no)
c ¿Ha visto el Museo del Oro? (sí)
d ¿Ha conocido el barrio de Miraflores? (no)

el Palacio de Gobierno *Government Palace*
el Museo del Oro *Gold Museum*

QV

◀» **CD2, TR 5, 04:35**

3 Karina Tomas from Peru was asked whether she had ever been to Cusco. Listen to her answer and to what she says about travelling to this old Inca city and the ancient Inca ruins of Machu Picchu. The key words which follow will help you to understand and the questions that follow will help you to check your comprehension.

conserva *it retains*
la cultura incaica *Inca culture*
mediante *by*
no sé a cuánto tiempo está *I don't know how long it takes*
la única forma *the only way*

Answer these questions in English:

   a When was Karina in Cusco?
   b What does she say about the city?
   c How can you travel from Lima to Cusco?
   d How can you travel from Cusco to Machu Picchu?

Insight

Karina is mistaken when she says that there is a train from
Lima to Cusco as the only railway line from Lima goes to
Huancayo in the Peruvian Central Andes. It is possible to
travel to Cusco by train starting at either Arequipa in the
south of Peru or Juliaca or Puno in the Altiplano.
Karina is right that there is a train from Cusco to Machu
Picchu, but the ruins can be reached on foot via the Inca trail
starting at Ollantaytambo in the Sacred Valley. There is a
daily limit of 500 walkers on this four-day trek, and one needs
to register with one of the many tour agencies in Cusco.

4 Use an appropriate verb from the list to express polite instructions
and commands with the polite form of the imperative.

hacer, subir, darme, llamarme, escribir, cerrar, decirnos

   a _____ la cuenta, por favor.
   b _____ su nombre aquí, por favor.
   c _____ el favor de llamarme a las 8.00.
   d _____ dónde está.
   e Si va a Buenos Aires, _____ por teléfono.
   f _____ este equipaje a la habitación número 510, por favor.
   g Por favor, _____ la puerta.

5 Match each question on the left with the corresponding answer on the right.

a	¿Dónde está el mostrador de Aerolatina?	**1**	Esta mochila y una maleta.
b	¿Pasillo?	**2**	No, hay una hora y media de retraso.
c	¿Cuál es su equipaje?	**3**	No, ventanilla.
d	¿Tiene equipaje de mano?	**4**	Número doce.
e	¿Va a salir a la hora el avión?	**5**	Este bolso solamente.
f	¿Cuál es la puerta de embarque?	**6**	Al fondo del pasillo, frente al mostrador de Aeroperú.

el mostrador counter   **a la hora** on time

6 At a tourist office in a Latin American country you are given a leaflet giving advice on what to do and what not to do whilst visiting the country. Read it through and see how much you can understand, then translate the leaflet for a travelling companion who does not understand Spanish.

Recomendaciones para los turistas

Para su propia seguridad, el Servicio Nacional de Turismo de nuestro país le hace las siguientes sugerencias:

♦ Cambie su dinero y cheques de viaje sólo en los bancos o casas de cambio autorizadas.
♦ No cambie dinero en las calles.
♦ Deje sus objetos de valor en la caja de seguridad de su hotel.
♦ No salga con grandes sumas de dinero.
♦ Al tomar un taxi, observe lo que marca el taxímetro, esa es la cantidad que deberá pagar. En nuestro país no hay recargos adicionales.
♦ En lo posible, utilice los servicios de taxi de su propio hotel.

QUICK VOCAB

autorizados/as *authorized*
los objetos de valor *valuables*
la caja de seguridad *safe deposit box*
la suma *sum*
marcar *to indicate, to show*
el taxímetro *taxi meter*
la cantidad *amount*
el recargo *surcharge*

7 Information of the kind above is often given in the familiar form when addressing younger people. Imagine that this is the case and make all appropriate changes to verbs and other words using the 'tú' form.

Test yourself

Complete the following sentences with the appropriate form of the verbs in brackets, making other necessary changes.

a Hoy he (ver) a Isabel, pero no hemos (tener) tiempo de hablar.
b '¿Qué has (hacer) hoy?' – 'He (estar) con mis padres, que han (venir) a verme'.
c Elena y Oscar han (volver) de sus vacaciones. Lo han (pasar) muy bien.
d '¿Le has (decir) a Blanca que la reunión es a las tres?' – 'Sí, le he (escribir) un email'.
e Hola, Ana, ¿cómo está usted? Por favor, (darme) el teléfono del señor Valdés. (Tener) que hablar con él.
f Por favor, (enviarnos) dos desayunos a la habitación 220.

g Este es un secreto entre tú y yo. No (decírselo) a Pedro. Y no (contárselo) a Graciela tampoco.

h Lo siento, señor, el director está ocupado. Por favor, (llamarlo) después de las 3:00.

i '¿Quiere dejarle algún recado?' – 'Sí, por favor (decirle) que me llame al número 641 8976'.

j (Tú) (tener) que venir a mi casa. (Darme) tu email y te enviaré la dirección.

Questions a–d assess your knowledge of the perfect tense, while the remaining questions focus mainly on imperative forms. If you still uncertain about these two key points, go back to paras 1 and 3 of the Grammar section, otherwise you can do the last unit of your course.

....

Siga derecho
Go straight on

In this unit you will learn
- *How to express hope*
- *How to express certainty, uncertainty and possibility*
- *How to make complaints*
- *How to ask for and give directions*
- *How to describe minor ailments*

_____

1 Mi maleta no ha llegado *My suitcase hasn't arrived*

Diana Ray is reporting her luggage loss to an airline employee at the airport in Lima. First, try learning these key phrases: **Estoy seguro/a de que aparecerá** *I'm sure it will appear,* **Espero que la encuentren** *I hope you find it,* **cuando aparezca** *when it appears,* **Es muy posible que llegue ...** *It's very likely that it may arrive ...*

Diana	Buenos días.
Empleada	Buenos días. ¿Qué desea?
Diana	Acabo de llegar en el vuelo 435 de Aerolatina que venía de Londres, pero mi maleta no ha llegado.

CD2, TR 6, 00:18

Empleada	Perdone, ¿en qué vuelo dice que venía?
Diana	En el vuelo 435 de Aerolatina.
Empleada	Y usted tomó el avión en Londres, ¿verdad?
Diana	Sí, en Londres.
Empleada	¿Cuál es su nombre?
Diana	Diana Ray, r-a-y, Ray.
Empleada	¿Tiene usted el ticket de su equipaje?
Diana	Sí, aquí está.
Empleada	Este vuelo hizo escala en París, y posiblemente, por error, su maleta fue enviada a París. No se preocupe usted. Estoy segura de que aparecerá.
Diana	Espero que la encuentren. Tengo toda mi ropa en la maleta. Es una maleta grande, de color verde oscuro. Tiene una etiqueta con mi nombre.
Empleada	Deme la dirección y el teléfono del hotel donde se quedará para llamarla cuando aparezca. Mañana hay otro vuelo de Aerolatina que viene de París. Es muy posible que llegue en ese vuelo. Yo misma me encargaré de buscarla.
Diana	Muchas gracias.

Insight

'**Acabar de**' followed by the infinitive is used for saying what you have just done: '**acabo de llegar**' '*I have just arrived*'. Consider also the following verbs in the key sentences above: '**encuentren**', '**aparezca**', '**llegue**'. These have exactly the same form as the command form for '**usted**' that you learnt in Unit 12, but here they have been used to refer to actions which are *unreal* or which have not yet taken place.
(See Grammar, paras 1 and 2.)

fue enviado/a *it was sent*
aparecer *to appear*
esperar *to hope*
encontrar *to find*
verde oscuro/a *dark green*

QUICK VOCAB

la etiqueta *label*
encargarse *to see to, to take care of*
buscar *to look for*

Say it in Spanish

Can you find the Spanish for the following expressions in the dialogue?

a It stopped over in Paris.
b by mistake
c I'll take care of (looking for) it myself.

___

2 Una habitación ruidosa *A noisy room*

Diana's room at the hotel is rather noisy, so she complained to the hotel receptionist about it. First, try learning these key sentences:
No pude dormir *I could not sleep,* **debido a la bulla del tráfico** *due to the traffic noise,* **La habitación es demasiado ruidosa** *The room is too noisy.*

CD2, TR 6, 02:44

Diana	Buenos días.
Recepcionista	Buenos días. ¿En qué puedo servirle?
Diana	Yo estoy en la habitación número 315 y anoche no pude dormir debido a la bulla del tráfico. La habitación es demasiado ruidosa. ¿No tendría una más tranquila?
Recepcionista	Un momentito, por favor. Veré qué habitación puedo darle.
	(The receptionist comes back to the desk.)
	Sí, puedo darle una habitación interior si no le importa. Es un poco oscura, pero muy tranquila.
Diana	No me importa. Prefiero cambiarme ahora mismo.

| Recepcionista | Muy bien, señora. La habitación 420, en el cuarto piso, estará lista dentro de un momento. Acaba de irse la persona que estaba allí. |
| Diana | Muchas gracias. |

Insight

'**Si no le importa**' '*If you don't mind*', '**No me importa**' '*I don't mind*'. In this construction the verb '**importar**' 'to mind' is used in the third person singular, preceded by '**me**', '**te**', '**le**', '**nos**', or '**les**' (as for '**gustar**', unit 6): '**¿Les importa esperar un momento?**' '*Do you mind waiting a moment?*', '**No nos importa**' '*We don't mind*'.

QUICK VOCAB

anoche *last night*
dormir *to sleep*
interior *at the back*
oscuro/a *dark*
dentro de un momento *in a moment*

Say it in Spanish

What expressions are used in the dialogue to say the following?

a Can I help you?
b Wouldn't you have a quieter room?
c I'll see what room I can give you.
d Right now.
e The person who was there has just left.

3 Doble a la izquierda *Turn left*

Diana's suitcase has appeared, so she is now ready to tour the city. She asks the hotel receptionist how to get to the museum. Note how she asks whether this is very far: **¿Podría decirme si está muy**

lejos ...? As you read or listen to the dialogue, make a note of the directions given by the receptionist. Try guessing their meaning before you look at the vocabulary.

Diana	Perdone, ¿podría decirme si está muy lejos el Museo Nacional de Arte?
Recepcionista	No, no está lejos. Está a unas siete u ocho cuadras de aquí, en el Paseo Colón. Al salir del hotel doble a la izquierda y siga derecho por la avenida Garcilaso de la Vega hasta el Paseo Colón. Allí tuerza a la izquierda otra vez y continúe por esa calle. El museo está en la segunda cuadra, a la derecha.
Diana	Muchas gracias.
Recepcionista	De nada.

Insight

'**Doble**' (from '**doblar**') '*turn*', '**siga**' (from '**seguir**') '*go on*', '**tuerza**' (from '**torcer**') '*turn*', '**continúe**' (from '**continuar**') '*continue*', '*go on*' are all formal imperative forms, the form of the verb that you learnt in Unit 12. Forms such as these are common when giving directions to strangers.

QUICK VOCAB

u *or (before a word beginning with o or ho)*
al salir *as you leave*
siga derecho *go straight on*
hasta *as far as*
otra vez *again*

What do these directions mean?

It is your first day in a Latin American town and you are trying to find your way around. Can you give the English for these directions?

a Está a unas tres o cuatro cuadras de la catedral, a la izquierda.
b Siga derecho hasta el parque, y después doble a la derecha.

c En la esquina, tuerza a la izquierda, y continúe por esa calle hasta el final.

d Al llegar a la plaza verá un edificio grande de color amarillo. Ese es el museo.

---

4 Un dolor de estómago *A stomach ache*

Diana is at the chemist's buying something for a stomach ache. First, try learning these key sentences: **Me cayó mal** *It didn't agree with me*, **¿Tiene fiebre?** *Have you got a fever?*, **Me duele el estómago** *I have a stomach ache*, **Tengo náuseas** *I feel sick.*

Empleada	Buenas tardes. ¿Qué desea?
Diana	Quisiera algo para el dolor de estómago. Anoche comí algo que me cayó mal. No dormí en toda la noche.
Empleada	¿Tiene fiebre?
Diana	No, fiebre no tengo, pero no me siento bien. Todavía me duele un poco el estómago y tengo náuseas.
Empleada	No creo que sea nada serio. Posiblemente se trata de una infección muy leve. Le daré estas pastillas que son muy buenas. Tome una cada cuatro horas con un poco de agua hasta que se sienta mejor. Y trate de comer sólo comidas livianas. Nada de frituras.
Diana	Muchas gracias. ¿Cuánto es?
Empleada	Son cuatro soles.

🎧 CD2, TR 6, 05:52

Insight

'**Tome**' (from '**tomar**') '*take*' and '**trate**' (from '**tratar**') '*try*' are both formal imperative forms (see Unit 12). Note also '*sea*' in '**no creo que sea ...**' '*I don't think it is ...*', and '**sienta**' in '**hasta que se sienta ...**' '*until you feel ...*'. These two verbs are exactly the same in form as the imperative for '**usted**' but they have been used differently. (See Grammar, paras. 1 and 2.)

sentirse (e > ie) *to feel*
doler (o > ue) *to ache*
se trata de (tratarse de) *it is (to be, to have to do with)*
leve *slight*
la pastilla *tablet, pill*
cada *every, each*
trate de (tratar de) *try to (to try to)*
la comida liviana *light meal*
la fritura *fried food*

How is the following expressed in the dialogue?

a Anoche no pude dormir.
b No tengo fiebre.
c Me siento mal.
d Creo que no es nada serio.

Key phrases

Expressing hope

Espero que la encuentren / aparezca.	*I hope you find it / it appears.*
Espero que sí / no.	*I hope so / not.*

Expressing certainty, uncertainty and possibility

Estoy seguro/a de que aparecerá / la encontraremos.	*I'm sure it will appear / we'll find it.*
Es muy posible que llegue / la encontremos.	*It's very likely that it will arrive / we'll find it.*
No creo que sea nada serio.	*I don't think it's anything serious.*
Posiblemente se trata de una infección.	*It's probably an infection.*

Making complaints

Mi maleta/equipaje no ha llegado.	*My suitcase/luggage hasn't arrived.*
Mi habitación es demasiado ruidosa.	*My room is too noisy.*
El aire acondicionado/La calefacción no funciona.	*The air conditioning/heating doesn't work.*
Faltan toallas/frazadas.	*There aren't enough towels/ blankets.*
No hay jabón/papel higiénico.	*There's no soap/toilet paper.*
La habitación está sucia.	*The room is dirty.*
La bañera/El lavamanos está atascada/o.	*The bath tub/washbasin is blocked.*

Insight

Vocabulary in this area is not the same in all Latin American countries. In some countries 'a blanket' is '**una cobija**', while 'a washbasin' is '**el lavatorio**' or '**el lavabo**'. Don't be discouraged by these differences in usage, as hotel staff are normally aware of them. At this stage it may be enough for you to learn a single form.

Asking for and giving directions

¿Podría decirme si está muy lejos / dónde está?	*Could you tell me if it's very far / where it is?*
Siga derecho.	*Go straight on.*
Doble / tuerza a la derecha / izquierda.	*Turn right / left.*
Continúe/siga por esa calle.	*Go on along that street.*

Describing minor ailments

No me siento/encuentro bien.	*I don't feel well.*
Me duele el estómago / la cabeza.	*I have a stomach / head ache.*
Tengo dolor de estómago / cabeza	
Tengo fiebre/gripe/náuseas.	*I have a fever / cold / feel sick.*
La comida me cayó mal.	*The food didn't agree with me.*

Grammar

1 *The subjunctive*

Alongside *indicative* tenses, all the ones you have learnt in this book, with the exception of the *imperative*, a form of the verb used for giving commands, Spanish uses a small range of other tenses, corresponding to what is known as the *subjunctive*.

The indicative is used for statements of fact.

Viven en Costa Rica   *They live in Costa Rica.*

(*present indicative*)

Trabajaba conmigo   *He / she used to work with me.*

(*imperfect indicative*)

The subjunctive is used in sentences expressing unreality, uncertainty, possibility and probability, and some kind of emotion, such as hope.

Espero que **sea** cierto.   *I hope it's true.*
Es posible que **vuelvan**.   *They may come back.*
Es probable que **llueva**.   *It may rain.*
No creo que **estén** en casa.   *I don't think they are at home.*

Note that positive sentences with **creer** require an indicative verb.

Creo que **están** en casa.   *I think they are at home.*

The subjunctive is little used in English nowadays, except in sentences such as *If I were you..., I wish you were here!* In Spanish, however, the subjunctive is quite common, in the spoken language as well as in writing. Read the notes below to find out how to use this so called *mood* of the verb.

Using the subjunctive

a Look at this sentence: *I hope (that) she arrives soon.*

It has two clauses: a main clause, *I hope*, and a subordinate clause, *(that) she arrives soon.* The verb in the main clause and the one in the subordinate clause are both in the same tense: the present tense. In Spanish, however, certain verbs, such as those expressing hope (e.g. **esperar** *to hope*), some kind of wish (e.g. **querer** *to want*), doubt or possibility (e.g. **dudar** *to doubt*), require the use of the subjunctive in the subordinate clause.

Espero que ella **llegue** pronto.	*I hope (that) she arrives soon.*
Queremos que nos **acompañes.**	*We want you to accompany us.*
Dudo que me **llamen.**	*I doubt (that) they will call me.*
Es muy posible que **llegue** en ese vuelo.	*It's very likely (that) it will come on that flight.*
No creo que **tenga** suficiente dinero.	*I don't think he / she has enough money.*

In these sentences, the verbs which follow the clause introduced by que are all in the subjunctive, in this case the *present subjunctive.* The word *that* is optional in these English sentences, whereas **que** cannot be omitted. Note also that in all the examples above the subject of the main verb is different from that of the verb in the subordinate clause. If this is not the case, use the infinitive and not the subjunctive.

Espero **llegar** pronto.	*I hope to arrive soon.*
Queremos **acompañarte.**	*We want to accompany you.*

b The subjunctive is also used after certain conjunctions, such as those indicating purpose (e.g. **para que** *in order that*) and time (e.g. **cuando** *when,* **hasta que** *until*), but only when these refer to the future.

Lo traeré **para que lo veas.**	*I'll bring it so that you can see it.*
La llamaré **cuando aparezca.**	*I'll call you when it appears.*
Trabajaré **hasta que termine.**	*I'll work until I finish.*

The verbs following these conjunctions are in the present subjunctive. This is the most frequently used subjunctive tense, and it is the only one covered in this book. If you wish to study the remaining subjunctive tenses, the *imperfect,* the *perfect* or the *pluperfect,* refer to one of the reference grammar books in the **Taking it further** section.

Insight

Note that conjunctions which indicate time, such as '**cuando**', '**hasta que**', etc., are used with the indicative when the action referred to by the verb is a fact. Compare the following pairs of sentences: '**Cuando termino, siempre me voy a casa**' '*When I finish, I always go home*' (a fact, therefore indicative), but '**Cuando termine, me iré a casa**' '*When I finish, I'll go home*' (not yet a reality, therefore subjunctive).

2 The present subjunctive

The *present subjunctive* normally occurs in sentences with the verb in the main clause in the present indicative, the future, the perfect or the imperative.

No **creo** que **esté** en casa.	*I don't think he / she is at home.*
Le **diré** que **venga**.	*I'll tell him / her to come.*
Me **han pedido** que vaya.	*They have asked me to go.*
Dile que me **llame**.	*Tell him / her to call me.*

Formation of the present subjunctive

Like the imperative, which you learnt in Unit 12, the present subjunctive is formed from the first person singular of the present tense, e.g. **viajo** *I travel,* **como** *I eat,* **subo** *I go up.* Drop the -o and add the appropriate ending: there is one set of endings for -**ar** verbs and another for -**er** and -**ir** verbs. The first and third person singular of the present subjunctive have the same form as the polite imperative that you learnt in Unit 12. Here are three examples:

viajar (*to travel*)	viaj**e**, viaj**es**, viaj**e**, viaj**emos**, viaj**en**
comer (*to eat*)	com**a**, com**as**, com**a**, com**amos**, com**an**
subir (*to go up*)	sub**a**, sub**as**, sub**a**, sub**amos**, sub**an**

Here are some further examples demonstrating the use of the present subjunctive:

Es probable que ellos **escriban**.   *They may write. (possibility)*
Espero que él **viaje** a Venezuela. *I hope he travels to Venezuela.*
                                       (hope)
No creo que él **llame**.   *I don't think he will call.* (doubt)

Irregular forms of the present subjunctive
As with imperatives, verbs which are irregular or stem-changing in the first person of the present tense, e.g. **tener** *to have*, and **encontrar** *to find*, are also irregular or stem-changing in the present subjunctive. Here is an example:

Present tense: **tengo** (*I have*)

Present subjunctive: tenga, tengas, tenga, tengamos, tengan

No creo que él **tenga** dinero.   *I don't think he has money.*
Espero que **tengamos** tiempo.   *I hope we have time.*

For other examples of irregular forms look at irregular imperatives in Unit 12 and the list of irregular verbs at the back of the book.

Some verbs are irregular in a different way:

dar	*to give*	dé, des, dé, demos, den
estar	*to be*	esté, estés, esté, estemos, estén
haber	*to have*	haya, hayas, haya, hayamos, hayan
ir	*to go*	vaya, vayas, vaya, vayamos, vayan
ser	*to be*	sea, seas, sea, seamos, sean

Espero que esta habitación **sea** mejor.   *I hope this room is better.*
No creo que él **esté** allí.   *I don't think he is there.*
Cuando **vayas** a Lima llámalo.   *When you go to Lima,*
                                             call him.

For other irregular present subjunctive forms, see the table of irregular verbs starting at the back of the book.

Insight

The subjunctive can be a bit tricky for English speakers and in the early stages you may find it difficult to decide whether you need the subjunctive or not. Don't be discouraged by this. Even if you make mistakes in this area you will still be understood. Accuracy will come with time and lots of practice.

3 Giving directions: present tense or imperative

Directions are normally given using the present tense (see Unit 3) or the imperative form (see Unit 12). Both forms are equally frequent in this context, and it may be easier for you to use the present tense, but you will need to understand the imperative form when native speakers use it.

Present tense	Imperative
(Usted) **dobla** a la derecha.	**Doble** a la derecha. *Turn right.*
(Usted) **tuerce** a la izquierda.	**Tuerza** a la izquierda. *Turn left.*
(Usted) **sigue** por esa calle.	**Siga** por esa calle. *Go on along that street.*

Note that the polite imperative has the same form as the first and third person singular of the present subjunctive.

4 Al + infinitive

This construction with **al** followed by the infinitive is fairly frequent in Spanish and translates into English in more than one way.

Al salir del hotel...	*When you leave / On leaving the hotel ...*
Al llegar al parque tuerza a la izquierda.	*When you reach the park turn left.*
Al volver entramos en un café.	*When we were coming back /On our way back we went into a café.*

5 Acabar de + infinitive to have just...

To talk about actions or events which have just taken place, as in
I have just arrived, use the present tense of **acabar** (lit. *to finish*)
followed by the preposition **de** and the infinitive.

Acabo de llegar.	*I have just arrived.*
Acaba de irse.	*He / she has just left.*
Acabamos de almorzar.	*We have just had lunch.*

An alternative to this is the construction with **recién** followed by
a verb in the preterite tense, which corresponds to Latin American
usage (see Unit 10).

Recién llamó.	*He / she has just called.*
Recién lo vimos.	*We have just seen him.*

Practice

1 You have just arrived in a Latin American country.
Unfortunately, your luggage is missing, so you decide to go to the
airline desk to complain.

Empleada	¿Qué desea?
Ud.	*Say you have just arrived on flight 310 of Hispanair which was coming from ..., but unfortunately your luggage has not arrived.*
Empleada	¿Qué equipaje traía usted?
Ud.	*You had two suitcases, one large one and one small one. Say you have the luggage receipts. Both suitcases have labels with your name (say your name).*
Empleada	Lo siento mucho. Estas situaciones ocurren a veces, pero normalmente el equipaje aparece uno o dos días después. Seguramente no lo enviaron, o lo enviaron a otra ciudad. El vuelo hizo escala en Amsterdam y Madrid.
	(Contd)

una maleta grande y una pequeña

lo siento mucho *I am very sorry*
ocurrir *to happen*
traer *to bring*
el nombre completo *full name*

Insight

In '**no se preocupe (usted)**' '*don't worry*', the verb '**preocuparse**' '*to worry*' is in the imperative form (formal, sing). The familiar singular form is '**no te preocupes**'. In '**cuando aparezcan**' '*when they appear*', '**aparecer**' '*to appear*' is in the present subjunctive. '**Aparecer**' is conjugated like '**conocer**', whose present subjunctive forms are '**conozca, conozcas, conozca...**', etc.

2 Put the infinitives in brackets in the appropriate form of the present subjunctive.

   a Cuando (nosotros, ir) a Perú, visitaremos Machu Picchu.
   b Posiblemente (ellos, pasar) sus vacaciones en Chile.
   c Llamaré a la recepción para que (ellos, enviar) el desayuno.
   d Esperaremos aquí hasta que el avión (llegar).

e Espero que mañana no (hacer) mucho calor. Quiero salir de compras.

f No creo que Carmen (venir) hoy. Está muy ocupada.

g Te traje un regalo. Espero que te (gustar).

h Está muy nublado. Es posible que (llover).

3 Your first night at a hotel was a nightmare (**una pesadilla**). Several things went wrong, so you want to complain to the hotel management. Here is what you want to say. How would you express it in Spanish? Use from the words and phrases below.

a The air conditioning didn't work.

b There was no hot water.

c The washbasin was blocked.

d There were no towels in the bathroom.

e The room is too noisy. You couldn't sleep last night.

f You want to move into a quieter room.

el aire acondicionado *air conditioning*
atascado *blocked*
funcionar *to work*
el agua caliente *hot water*
el lavamanos/lavatorio *washbasin*
la toalla *towel*

QUICK VOCAB

◄) **CD2, TR 6, 07:09**

4 Some people are never happy! Listen to these complaints, then say in English what each person is complaining about. The first complaint takes place in an aeroplane and both speakers are Chilean. The second and third take place in a restaurant and the people complaining are first a Venezuelan and then a Chilean. First, look at these new words:

el asiento *seat*
¡lo siento tanto! *I am so sorry!*
No es culpa nuestra. *It is not our fault.*
cambiar *to change*

QV

¡epa muchacho! *Lit. come on boy! (Venezuela, very informal)*
¿vale? *OK? (very common in Venezuela)*
pedí *I ordered*
la sopa de mariscos *seafood soup*
pasar *to happen*
tan ocupados *so busy*
hoy día *today*
tantos clients *so many customers*

5 Your hotel is at the corner of **avenida Abancay** and **calle Miró Quesada,** number 2 on the map opposite. Today you want to visit the Cathedral, number 1 on the map. How would you get there from your hotel? Choose the correct directions, **a, b** or **c.**

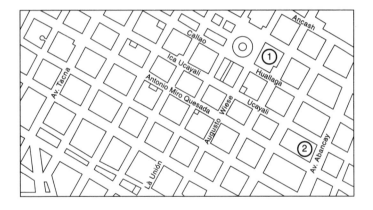

a Siga derecho por Miró Quesada hasta la calle Augusto Wiese. Allí doble a la izquierda y camine tres cuadras hasta llegar a la Catedral.

b Al salir del hotel, doble a la derecha y camine tres cuadras hasta la calle Augusto Wiese. En Augusto Wiese doble a la derecha. La Catedral está a dos cuadras de allí, a la derecha, en la esquina de la calle Huallaga.

c Cuando salga del hotel, siga por la calle Miró Quesada y continúe hasta la calle La Unión que está pasado Augusto Wiese. Doble a la derecha y siga por esa calle hasta que encuentre la Catedral, que está en la esquina de las calles Callao y La Unión.

6 While you are waiting to ask for information in the tourist office in Lima, you hear another tourist asking for directions. Listen to the conversation and complete the transcript below with the missing words. If you do not have the recording, try guessing what those words are.

Turista	Buenas tardes. Para _____ al Teatro Segura, por favor.
Recepcionista	Sí, cómo no. Al _____ de aquí, _____ por la calle Ucayali, camine de frente hacia Abancay. Ahí _____ a la _____ izquierda, camine dos _____ y media, y ahí está el Teatro Segura.
Turista	Gracias.
Recepcionista	_____.

≈ CD2, TR 6, 08:20

camine de frente *walk straight on*
hacia *towards*
ahí *there*

QV

7 You are not feeling very well and decide to see a doctor. It probably has something to do with some food you had last night. Use the guidelines to complete this conversation with the doctor.

Doctor	¿Qué le pasa?
Ud.	*Say you are feeling unwell. You have a stomach ache and diarrhoea.*
Doctor	¿Desde cuándo se siente así?
Ud.	*It started last night. You went out for a meal with some friends and you had fish and fried potatoes. Surely that was it. Later when you got back to your hotel you started to feel unwell.*
Doctor	¿Ha tenido vómitos?
Ud.	*Yes, you have vomited and you seem to have a fever too. (The doctor examines you and gives you a prescription, **una receta**.)*
	(Contd)

Doctor	No creo que sea nada grave. Se trata simplemente de una infección estomacal. Con esta receta vaya a la farmacia y compre estas pastillas que son muy buenas. Tome dos cada seis horas. Estoy seguro de que se sentirá mejor.
Ud.	*Say you hope so.*

Insight

Note the present subjunctive in '**No creo que sea nada grave**' '*I don't think it's anything serious*'. If the sentence was positive, the verb would be in the indicative: '**Creo que es grave**' '*I think it's serious*'. '**Vaya**', '**compre**' and '**tome**' are the formal, singular imperative forms for '**ir**', '**comprar**' and '**tomar**'.

¿qué le pasa? *what's the matter?*
empezar *to start*
grave *serious*
la diarrea *diarrhoea*
la infección estomacal *stomach infection*

◄) **CD2, TR 6, 09:01**

8 You might not like the idea of visiting a doctor who needs to advertise on the radio to get patients, but if you had to, here is one from Veracruz, in Mexico! Listen to the advertisement, then answer the questions that follow. First, look at these key words:

la fractura *fracture*
la luxación *dislocation*
la cirugía *surgery*
la traumatología *orthopaedic surgery*
la ortopedia *orthopaedics*
las consultas *surgery hours*

Complete these sentences:

a Las horas de consulta del doctor Manuel Loyo de Valdés son de
_____ a _____ y de _____ a _____ .
b El doctor atiende en González Pajés número _____ .
c El número de teléfono del doctor es el _____ .

◀) **CD2, TR 6, 09:42**

9 A patient arrives at a doctor's surgery in Peru. Listen to his
conversation with the receptionist and note down the days and
times when the surgery is open. First look at these key words:

pedir hora *to ask for an appointment (with doctor or dentist)*
atender *to be available*

10 How would you express the following in Spanish?
a I hope we can find a room.
b I don't think it's important.
c I'm sure they'll come.
d It may rain.
e I think he's in the office.
f We'll invite her so that you see her.
g We'll stay here until we finish.
h When Sara arrives, please tell her that I want to speak to
her. (fam)

Test yourself

1 Choose the correct verb to complete the following sentences.
a María acaba de (salido/salir).
b Estoy seguro de que (encuentre/encontrará) su maleta.
c Espero que el hotel (es/sea) bueno.
d Te llamaré cuando (llegue/llego) a Lima.
e Llamaré a Santiago para que me (reservan/reserven) una
habitación.

2 Choose the right word from the list to complete the following sentences.

llegar tengo doble duele siga siento

a ____ derecho/de frente hasta la plaza San Martín.
b En la próxima esquina ____ a la izquierda.
c Al ____ a la calle Rosal tuerza a la derecha.
d No me ____ bien. Me ____ el estómago.
e ____ dolor de cabeza.

This is the final test in your course. Question 1 assesses the correct use of the subjunctive, while question 2 focuses on directions and expressions related to minor ailments. If you are happy with your performance, don't stop here. Go through some of the key points in your book again or else get yourself a good grammar book, if you haven't got one, and do some further study. Keep up your Spanish! *¡Sigue con tu español!*

Congratulations on finishing *Complete Latin American Spanish!*

We hope you have enjoyed working your way through the course. We are always keen to receive feedback from people who have used our courses, so why not contact us and let us know your reactions? We'll be particularly pleased to receive your praise, but we should also like to know if things could be improved. We always welcome comments and suggestions, and we do our best to incorporate constructive suggestions into later editions. You can contact us at: Teach Yourself Books, Hodder Headline Ltd, 338 Euston Road, London NW1 3BH, UK.

We hope you will want to build on your knowledge of Spanish and have made a few suggestions to help you do this in the section entitled **Taking it further**.

¡Buena suerte!

Juan Kattán–Ibarra

Glossary of grammatical terms

adjectives Adjectives are words which provide more information about nouns: *His / her house is very nice.* **Su casa es muy bonita.**

adverbs Adverbs are used to provide more information about verbs, adjectives or other adverbs: *He / she spoke clearly.* **Habló** claramente. *It was incredibly easy.* **Fue** increíblemente fácil. *She sang extremely well.* **Cantó** extremadamente bien.

articles There are two types of articles, *definite* and *indefinite*. Definite articles in Spanish are **el, la, los, las,** *the* in English. Indefinite articles are **un, una,** *a, an,* and **unos, unas,** *some* in English: *the book* el **libro,** *the books* los **libros,** *a chair* una **silla,** *some chairs,* unas **sillas.**

clause A clause is a group of words within a sentence which has its own verb. A *main clause* functions on its own; a *subordinate clause* is dependent on another clause. In *I'll buy it when I have money* **Lo compraré cuando tenga dinero,** *I'll buy it,* the main clause, can function on its own; *when I have money,* the subordinate clause, is dependent on the main clause.

comparative and superlative When we make comparisons we need the comparative form of the adjective. In English this usually means adding *–er* to the adjective or putting *more* in front of it. The Spanish equivalent is **más:** She is *taller* than her sister. **Es** más alta **que su hermana.** This chair is *more comfortable.* **Esta silla es** más cómoda. The most extreme version of a comparison is known as *superlative,* **el/ la más** in Spanish: e.g. this hotel is *the cheapest.* **Este hotel es** el más barato.

definite article See **articles**.

demonstratives Words like **este, esta** *this*, **esos, esas** *those*, are called demonstrative adjectives when they go before a noun: *this* boy, este **chico**, *those keys*, esas **llaves**. If these demonstratives are used instead of a noun, they are called demonstrative pronouns: *these* are nice, **estos/as son lindos/as**, **deme ese/esa** give me *that*.

direct object See **object**.

finite verb A verb form such as the one in *they work hard* is said to be *finite* because it indicates *tense*, *person* and *number*. Gerunds, infinitives and past participles are non-finite verb forms.

gender In Spanish, all nouns are either masculine or feminine. For example, el **avión**, *the aeroplane*, is masculine, while la **bicicleta**, *the bicycle*, is feminine. Nouns referring to male people are masculine and those referring to female persons are feminine.

gerund In Spanish, the word gerund refers to the forms of the verb ending in **-ando** and **-iendo**, e.g. **habl**ando, **com**iendo, **viv**iendo. Some of its uses correspond to those of the verb form ending in *-ing* in English, e.g. She *is eating* **Está comiendo**.

imperative See **mood**.

indefinite article See **articles**.

indicative mood See **mood**.

indirect object See **object**.

infinitive The basic form of the verb, as found in the dictionary, is known as infinitive. In Spanish, infinitives end

in -**ar**, -**er**, and -**ir**, for example **habl**ar *to speak,* **com**er *to eat,*
vivir *to live.*

irregular verbs Verbs which do not behave according to a set
pattern are known as irregular verbs.

mood Mood refers to the forms verbs can take depending
on how these are used. There are three moods of the
verb: *indicative mood,* normally associated with statements
of fact, e.g. He *works* here **Trabaja aquí,** *imperative mood,*
used for commands, directions and instructions, e.g. *Come*
back tomorrow **Vuelva mañana,** *and subjunctive mood,*
normally associated with doubt, possibility, wishes, etc.,
e.g. I don't think she *knows* **No creo que** sepa. See also
subjunctive.

nouns Nouns are words like *magazine* **revista,** *dog* **perro,**
beauty **belleza.**

number The word number is used to indicate whether
something is *singular* or *plural,* for example *the train* **el tren**
is singular, *the trains* **los trenes** is plural.

object In a sentence such as I gave *him the keys* Le *di las llaves,*
the phrase *the keys,* which undergoes the action of the verb
in a direct way, is said to be the direct object, while *him,*
the recipient of the giving, is the indirect object. An object
can be a noun or noun phrase, e.g. *the keys,* or a pronoun,
e.g. *him.*

personal pronouns As their name suggests, personal pronouns
refer to persons, for example *I* **yo,** *he* **él,** *she* **ella,** *we*
nosotros, *him* **lo, le,** *us* **nos.** See also **pronouns.**

plural see **number.**

possessives Words like *my* **mi,** *mine* **mío,** *her* **su,** *hers* **suyo** are
called possessives.

prepositions Prepositions are words such as *to* **a**, *in* **en**, *between* **entre**, which provide information such as direction, location, time.

pronouns Pronouns are words which stand in place of nouns or noun phrases which have already been mentioned, for example My sister went to Cuba. *She* went to Cuba. **Mi hermana fue a Cuba.** Ella **fue a Cuba.** This restaurant is cheaper. *This* is cheaper. **Este restaurante es caro.** Este **es caro.** My house is small. *Hers* is big. **Mi casa es pequeña. La** suya **es grande.**

reflexive pronouns Words such as *myself* **me**, *yourself* **te, se**, *ourselves* **nos** are known as reflexive pronouns.

reflexive verbs When the subject and the object of a verb are one and the same, the verb is said to be reflexive, for example *I enjoyed myself* very much. Me divertí **mucho.** *He washed himself*. Se lavó.

singular see number.

subject In a sentence such as, *My son finished his studies* Mi hijo **terminó** sus **estudios,** *my son*, the person performing the action denoted by the verb, is the subject of the sentence. A subject can be a single word or a group of words.

subjunctive mood The so-called subjunctive mood is used very rarely in modern English, but there are remnants of it in sentences such as the following: I insist that you *do* it. **Insisto en que lo** hagas. I wish he *were here*. **Ojalá** estuviera **aquí.** Spanish uses the subjunctive much more frequently than English.

subordinate clause See **clause.**

superlative See **comparative** and **superlative.**

tense Changes in the verb which indicate aspects of time are referred to as tenses, for example present tense, future tense, preterite tense. In She *lives* in Mexico now **Ahora** vive **en México,** the verb is in the present tense. In She *lived* here for many years Vivió **aquí durante muchos años,** the verb is in the preterite tense.

verbs Verbs are words such as *to speak* **hablar,** *to exist* **existir,** *to feel* **sentir,** which can denote actions, states, sensations.

Grammar summary

---

1 Definite and indefinite articles (Units 1 and 2)

a The word for *the* for singular nouns is **el** for masculine and **la** for feminine, e.g. **el hotel, la habitación**. The plural forms are **los, las**, e.g. **los hoteles, las habitaciones**.

b The word for *a / an* is **un** for masculine and **una** for feminine, e.g. **un señor, una señora**.

c A + el becomes **al**, e.g. **Voy al cine**, *I'm going to the cinema*.

d De + el becomes **del**, e.g. **Vengo del supermercado**, *I'm coming from the supermarket*.

---

2 Nouns

Masculine and feminine (Unit 1)

a In Spanish, all nouns are either masculine or feminine. Nouns ending in **-o** are usually masculine while those ending in **-a** are usually feminine, e.g. **el desayuno, la cena**.

b Words referring to males and females, such as occupations, must change. To form the feminine, change **-o** to **-a** or add **-a** to the consonant, e.g. **el doctor, la doctora**.

c Nouns ending in **-ista** and many of those ending in **-nte** are invariable, e.g. **el / la artista, el / la estudiante**.

d Some nouns have different forms for male and female, e.g. **el padre, la madre**.

Singular and plural (Unit 2)

e Nouns ending in a vowel form the plural by adding **-s**, e.g. **el libro, los libros**.

f Nouns ending in a consonant add -es, e.g. **la ciudad, las ciudades.**

g The masculine plural of some nouns may be used to refer to members of both sexes, e.g. **el padre, la madre, los padres.**

---

3 Adjectives (Units 1 and 5)

Number and gender agreement

Adjectives must agree in gender and number with the noun they describe.

a Adjectives ending in **-o** change **-o** to **-a** with feminine nouns, e.g. **un hotel pequeño, una habitación pequeña.**

b As a general rule, adjectives ending in a letter other than -o or -a do not change for masculine and feminine, e.g. **el vestido azul, la camisa azul.**

c Adjectives indicating nationality form the feminine by changing **-o** into **-a** or by adding **-a** to the consonant, e.g. **un amigo mexicano, una amiga mexicana.**

d To form the plural of adjectives follow the same rules as for nouns, e.g. **los carros antiguos.**

Position of adjectives

a The great majority of adjectives come after the noun, e.g. **una persona inteligente.**

b Adjectives are sometimes used before nouns for emphasis or to convey some kind of emotion, e.g. **un excelente hotel.**

c Certain adjectives, among them **grande** *big, large,* **pequeño** *small,* **bueno** *good,* **malo** *bad,* usually precede the adjective, e.g. **un pequeño problema.**

d **Grande** normally follows the noun when its meaning is *big* or *large,* but it goes before it when it means *great.* Before the noun, **grande** becomes **gran,** e.g. **una persona grande, una gran persona.**

e **Bueno** and **malo** become **buen** and **mal** before masculine singular nouns, e.g. **un buen / mal momento.**

4 Adverbs (Unit 4)

a To form an adverb from an adjective, add **-mente** to the singular form of the adjective, e.g. **posible, posiblemente**.

b If the adjective ends in **-o**, change the **-o** to **-a** and then add **-mente**, e.g. **rápido, rápidamente**.

c Many adverbs are not derived from adjectives, e.g. **ahora, mañana, aquí, bien**.

5 Pronouns

Subject pronouns (Unit 1)

singular	
yo	*I*
tú	*you* (familiar)
usted	*you* (formal)
él, ella	*he, she*

plural	
nosotros/as	*we* (m / f)
ustedes	*you* (formal / informal)
ellos/as	*they* (m / f)

Subject pronouns are usually omitted in Spanish, unless you want to show emphasis or to avoid ambiguity.

Direct and indirect object pronouns (Unit 5)

a Object pronouns can be direct, e.g. <u>La</u> invité *I invited her*, or indirect, as in <u>Le</u> dije *I said to her / him / you* (formal).

b In the first and second person singular and plural there is no distinction between direct and indirect object pronouns, e.g. <u>Me</u> invitó *He / She invited me*, <u>Me</u> dijo *He / She said to me*.

Singular		Plural	
me	*me, to me*	nos	*us, to us*
te	*you, to you* (informal)		

c In the third person, direct and indirect object pronouns differ, e.g. **Lo / la** invité *I invited him / her*, **Le dije** *I said to him / her*.

Direct object pronouns: third person

Singular	Plural
Masc. lo *you* (formal) / *him / it*	los *you* (formal / informal) / *them*
Fem. la *you* (formal) / *her / it*	las *you* (formal / informal) / *them*

Indirect object pronouns: third person

Singular	Plural
Le *(to) you* (formal) /	les (to) you (formal / informal) / him / her / itthem

Le and **les** become **se** before **lo, la, los, las, Se lo daré** *I'll give it to you / him / her / it / them.*

Position of object pronouns (Unit 5)

a Object pronouns normally precede the verb, e.g.**¿Me trae un café?** *Will you bring me a coffee?*

b In sentences with two object pronouns, the indirect one comes first,e.g. **Te las daré**, *I'll give them to you.*

c With imperatives, they follow positive forms but come before negative ones, e.g. **Dígale** *Tell him / her*, **No le diga** *Don't tell him / her.*

d In constructions with a finite verb followed by an infinitive (e.g. **llevar**) or a gerund (e.g. **haciendo**), the object pronoun can either precede the finite verb or be attached to the infinitive or gerund, e.g. **Voy a llevarlo** or **Lo voy a llevar**, *I'm going to take it,* **Estoy escribiéndola** or **La estoy escribiendo,** *I'm writing it.*

Pronouns with prepositions (Unit 11)

a With prepositions, use **mí, ti,** for the first and second person singular, and subject pronouns, **él, ella,** etc., for the remaining persons, e.g. **Un café para mí / él,** *Coffee for me / him.*
b Note the use of this construction in **A mí me gusta** *I like it.*
c Note the special use of **con** in **conmigo,** *with me,* **contigo,** *with you* (informal). But con **él / ella / usted,** etc.

Reflexive pronouns (Unit 4)

These are **me, te, se, nos, se,** and they accompany reflexive verbs such as **levantarse,** e.g. **me levanto** *I get up.*

---

6 Possessives (Unit 4)

To say *my, your, his, her,* etc. use the following set of words, which agree in number (singular and plural) with the thing possessed, not with the possessor. The first person plural, **nuestro** *our,* also agrees in gender (masculine and feminine).

mi(s)	*my*
tu(s)	*your* (informal)
su(s)	*your* (formal), *his, her, its*
nuestro / a(s)	*our*
su(s)	*your* (formal / informal), *their*

To say *mine, yours, his, hers,* etc. use the following set of words, which agree in number and gender with the thing possessed.

mío / a(s)	*mine*
tuyo / a(s)	*yours* (informal)
suyo / a(s)	*yours* (formal), *his, hers, its*
nuestro / a(s)	*ours*
suyo / a(s)	*yours* (formal / informal), *theirs*

---

7 Prepositions (Units 4, 5, 11)

Only the most common single word prepositions and meanings are given here.

a

at: a las cuatro
on: a la derecha / izquierda
per: una vez a la semana
personal a: used before the direct object when this is a person,
  e.g. Invité a Manuel

con

with: café con leche

de

from: Julio es de Granada.
made of: es de cristal.
in: la ciudad más grande de Venezuela

desde

from: desde las 2:00 de la tarde
for: desde hace cinco años

en

in: viven en Buenos Aires
on: las llaves están en la cama
at: trabaja en la Universidad de México

hasta

until: hasta las 5:00
as far as: hasta el semáforo

para

for (direction): el tren para Lima
for (with pronouns): para mí, un café
for / by: (with time phrases) para el lunes
in order to: iré a Bogotá para ver a María

por

by: por avión, por correo electrónico
during: por dos días
via: viajaron a Chile por Buenos Aires
through: pasaron por Guatemala
along: por esa calle
around: por aquí
per: por ciento
because of: lo hago por ti
by: este libro fue escrito por García Márquez

---

8 Types of verbs

a According to the ending of the infinitive, Spanish verbs may be grouped into three main categories: **-ar**, e.g. **hablar** *to speak*, **-er**, e.g. **comer** *to eat*, and **-ir**, e.g. **vivir** *to live*. (Unit 3)
b Most Spanish verbs are regular, that is, they follow a fixed pattern in their conjugation, but some very common verbs are irregular. A list of these will be found after the **Grammar summary.**
c Stem-changing verbs (see opposite)
d Reflexive verbs (Unit 4)

9 Present tense (Units 1, 2, 3, 4)

Here are the present tense forms of three regular verbs, **hablar** *to speak*, **comer** *to eat*, **vivir** *to live*.

yo	habl<u>o</u>	com<u>o</u>	viv<u>o</u>
tú	habl<u>as</u>	com<u>es</u>	viv<u>es</u>
usted / él / ella	habl<u>a</u>	com<u>e</u>	viv<u>e</u>
nosotros / as	habl<u>amos</u>	com<u>emos</u>	vivim<u>os</u>
ustedes / ellos / ellas	habl<u>an</u>	com<u>en</u>	viv<u>en</u>

Ella **habla** muy bien español. *She speaks Spanish very well.*

¿Dónde **vives?** *Where do you live?*

Stem-changing verbs (Unit 3)

Some verbs undergo a vowel change in the stem in all persons but **nosotros/as**. Their endings remain the same as for regular verbs. The main types of changes are:

a From e to ie, e.g. **empezar** *to begin, start,* **entender** *to understand,* **pensar** *to think,* **preferir** *to prefer,* e.g. **Yo empiezo,** *I start.*

b From o to ue, e.g. **acostarse** *to go to bed,* **poder** *to be able to, can,* **volver** *to come back,* e.g. ¿**Puedes hacerlo?** *Can you do it?*

c From e to i, e.g. **pedir** *to ask for,* **seguir** *to follow,* **servir** *to serve,* e.g. ¿**Le sirvo un poco más?** *Shall I give (serve) you some more?*

10 Preterite tense (Unit 9)

To say what you did at some point in the past and to talk about events which lasted over a definite period and ended in the past, you use the preterite tense. There are two sets of endings for this tense, one for **-ar** verbs and another one for verbs in **-er** and **-ir**.

hablar	comer	vivir
hablé	comí	viví
hablaste	comiste	viviste
habló	comió	vivió
hablamos	comimos	vivimos
hablaron	comieron	vivieron

Ayer **hablé** con él.   *I spoke to him yesterday*
Viví dos años allí.   *I lived there for two years.*

---

11 Imperfect tense (Unit 10)

The imperfect tense is used to talk about what you were doing, what you used to do, and to say what people, places and things were like. Unlike the preterite, the imperfect cannot be used to indicate a definite and completed action in the past. Note that verbs in –er and –ir share the same endings.

hablar	comer	vivir
hablaba	comía	vivía
hablabas	comías	vivías
hablaba	comía	vivía
hablábamos	comíamos	vivíamos
hablaban	comían	vivían

¿Con quién **hablabas**? *Who were you speaking to?*
Comíamos siempre en casa. *We always used to eat at home.*

---

12 Perfect tense (Unit 12)

The perfect tense is used for talking about recent events as well as actions which have taken place over a period of time which has not yet ended. Usage of this tense varies among Latin Americans who, by and large, tend to use the preterite tense when talking about past events, even recent ones.

The perfect tense is formed with the present tense of **haber** followed by the past participle. This ends in -**ado** for -**ar** verbs and -**ido** for -**er** and -**ir** verbs.

	hablar	*comer*	*vivir*
he	hablado	comido	vivido
has	hablado	comido	vivido
ha	hablado	comido	vivido
hemos	hablado	comido	vivido
han	hablado	comido	vivido

Todavía no **he hablado** con Juan.	*I still have not spoken to Juan.*
¿**Has comido** ya?	*Have you eaten already?*

The pluperfect tense is used to say what one had done:

Gloria **había estado** aquí antes.	*Gloria had been here before.*

---

13 Future tense (Unit 7)

The future tense is more common in the written language. In the spoken language it is normally used to make predictions, promises, and to express probability. In the spoken language, future actions and events are normally expressed with the construction **ir a** followed by the infinitive (see Unit 5).

The future tense is formed with the whole infinitive, to which the endings are added, the same set of endings for -**ar**, -**er** and -**ir** verbs.

hablar	comer	vivir
hablaré	comeré	viviré
hablarás	comerás	vivirás
hablará	comerá	vivirá
hablaremos	comeremos	viviremos
hablarán	comerán	vivirán

Te prometo que **hablaré** con él. *I promise you I'll speak to him.*
¿Dónde **vivirá**? *I wonder where he / she lives.*

14 Conditional tense (Unit 11)

The conditional is used to say what you *would* do, as in *I would go if I could*. Like the future tense, the conditional is formed with the whole infinitive, to which the endings are added, the same for **-ar**, **-er** and **-ir verbs**.

hablar	comer	vivir
hablaría	comería	viviría
hablarías	comerías	vivirías
hablaría	comería	viviría
hablaríamos	comeríamos	viviríamos
hablarían	comerían	vivirían

Yo hablaría con ella, pero no *I would speak to her, but I haven't*
tengo su número de teléfono. *got her telephone number.*
Con todo ese dinero **viviríamos** *With all that money we would live*
muy bien. *very well.*

15 Present subjunctive (Unit 13)

The subjunctive is little used in English nowadays, except in sentences such as *If I were you, I wish he were more careful*. The subjunctive is not a tense, but a different *mood* of the verb, just as the indicative (all the tenses above) and the imperative (see 16 below) are also moods of the verb (see **Glossary of grammatical terms**).

The subjunctive usually occurs in *subordinate* clauses, in sentences expressing unreality, uncertainty, or some kind of emotion, for example joy, fear, regret, hope, anger, sadness, etc. It also occurs on its own, in independent clauses.

The subjunctive has several tenses, but only the present subjunctive, the most common of all, has been covered in this book.

To form the present subjunctive, remove the -o of the first person of the present indicative tense and add the endings, one set for -**ar** verbs, another for verbs in -**er** and -**ir**.

present indicative (1st person)	present subjunctive
hablo	hable, hables, hable, hablemos, hablen
como	coma, comas, coma, comamos, coman
vivo	viva, vivas, viva, vivamos, vivan

Necesitamos una persona que **hable** español.	*We need a person who speaks Spanish.*
Espero que **viva** muchos años.	*I hope he / she lives for many years.*
No creo que **coman** esto.	*I don't think they'll eat this.*

---

16 Imperative (Units 12 and 13)

The imperative or command form of the verb is used for giving directions, instructions and commands. Spanish uses different imperative forms depending on who you are talking to – formal or familiar – and whether you are speaking to one or more than one person, singular or plural. The familiar imperative has different positive and negative forms.

With the exception of the positive form for **tú,** imperative forms are the same as the corresponding person of the present subjunctive.

Imperative forms for *usted* and *ustedes*

hable (Ud.) hablen (Uds.)
coma (Ud.) coman (Uds.)
viva (Ud.) vivan (Uds.)

Imperative forms for *tú*

Positive	*Negative*
habla (tú)	no hables (tú)
come (tú)	no comas (tú)
vive (tú)	no vivas (tú)

For irregular imperative forms see **Irregular verbs.**

---

17 The gerund (Unit 10)

Gerunds are forms like **trabajando** *working,* **comiendo** *eating,* which are used with **estar** to refer to actions in progress at the moment of speaking, e.g. **Estoy trabajando** *I'm working.*

---

18 Ser and estar *to be* (Units 1, 2, 3, 6, 7, 10)

Ser **is used**

a To give personal information such as who you are, nationality, where you are from, occupation, marital status (see also **estar**), e.g. **Ana es mexicana** *Ana is Mexican.*

b To describe people, places and things, e.g. **Cusco es una ciudad muy interesante** *Cusco is a very interesting city.*

c With the time and certain time phrases, e.g. **Mañana es domingo** *Tomorrow is Sunday.*

d To refer to the material something is made of, e.g. **Esta camisa es de algodón** *This shirt is made of cotton.*

e To denote possession, e.g. **Este es mi libro,** *This is my book.*

f To ask and say how much something is, e.g. **¿Cuánto es?** *How much is it?*

g To indicate where an event will take place, e.g. **La fiesta es aquí** *The party is here.*

h In passive sentences, e.g. **El criminal fue detenido por la policía** *The criminal was detained by the police.*

Estar **is used**

a To ask and say where something is, e.g. **La catedral está en la plaza** *The cathedral is in the square.*

b To express marital status, e.g. **Pancho está soltero** *Pancho is single.*

c To ask people how they are and respond, e.g. **¿Cómo estás? Estoy bien** *How are you? – I'm fine.*

d To denote a temporary state or condition, e.g. **Gloria está muy guapa hoy** *Gloria looks very pretty today.*

e To refer to cost when prices fluctuate, e.g. **¿A cuánto está el cambio?** *What is the rate of exchange?*

f With past participles, to denote a condition resulting from an action, e.g. **El restaurante está abierto** *The restaurant is open.*

g With gerunds, to talk about actions in progress, e.g. **Está hablando con Carmen** *He / she is speaking with Carmen.*

h With time phrases, e.g. **Estamos a 15 de julio** *It's the 15th of July.*

19 Using *se* (Units 4, 5, 8)

Se is used with the third person of the verb

a To form impersonal sentences, e.g. **¿Cómo se va al aeropuerto desde aquí?** *How does one go to the airport from here?*

b To convey the idea that something *'is done'*, e.g. **Aquí se habla español** *Spanish is spoken here.*

c With reflexive verbs (e.g. **levantarse** *to get up*), e.g. **Se levantaron a las seis** *They got up at six.*

d As an indirect object pronoun in place of **le**, before **lo(s)**, **la(s)**, e.g. **Se lo dije** *I told him / her.*

Irregular verbs

The following list includes only the most common irregular verbs. Only irregular forms are given (verbs marked with an asterisk are also stem-changing). The **vosotros** form, used in Spain, is included here.

abrir *to open*
past participle: abierto

andar *to walk*
preterite: anduve, anduviste, anduvo, anduvimos, anduvisteis, anduvieron

caer *to fall*
present indicative: (yo) caigo
present subjunctive: caiga, caigas, caiga, caigamos, caigáis, caigan
gerund: cayendo *preterite*: (él, ella, Ud.) cayó, (ellos, ellas, Uds.) cayeron

conducir *to drive*
present indicative: (yo) conduzco
present subjunctive: conduzca, conduzcas, conduzca, conduzcamos, conduzcáis, conduzcan
preterite: conduje, condujiste, condujo, condujimos, condujisteis, condujeron

cubrir *to cover*
past participle: cubierto

dar *to give*
present indicative: (yo) doy
preterite: di, diste, dio, dimos, disteis, dieron
present subjunctive: dé, des, dé, demos, deis, den

decir* *to say*
present indicative: (yo) digo
present subjunctive: diga, digas, diga, digamos, digáis, digan
preterite: dije, dijiste, dijo, dijimos, dijisteis, dijeron
future: diré, dirás, dirá, diremos, diréis, dirán
conditional: diría, dirías, diría, diríamos, diríais, dirían
imperative (familiar, singular): di
gerund: diciendo
past participle: dicho

escribir *to write*
past participle: escrito

estar *to be*
present indicative: estoy, estás, está, estamos, estáis, están
present subjunctive: esté, estés, esté, estemos, estéis, estén
preterite: estuve, estuviste, estuvo, estuvimos, estuvisteis, estuvieron
imperative (familiar, singular): está

hacer *to do, make*
present indicative: (yo) hago
present subjunctive: haga, hagas, haga, hagamos, hagáis, hagan
preterite: hice, hiciste, hizo, hicimos, hicisteis, hicieron
future: haré, harás, hará, haremos, haréis, harán
conditional: haría, harías, haría, haríamos, haríais, harían
imperative: (Ud.) haga, (tú) haz
past participle: hecho

ir *to go*
present indicative: voy, vas, va, vamos, vais, van
present subjunctive: vaya, vayas, vaya, vayamos, vayáis, vayan
imperfect: iba, ibas, iba, íbamos, ibais, iban
preterite: fui, fuiste, fue, fuimos, fuisteis, fueron
imperative: (Ud.) vaya, (tú) ve
gerund: yendo

leer *to read*
preterite: (él, ella, Ud.) leyó, (ellos, ellas, Uds.) leyeron
gerund: leyendo

morir* *to die*
past participle: muerto

oír *to hear*
present indicative: oigo, oyes, oye, oímos, oís, oyen
present subjunctive: oiga, oigas, oiga, oigamos, oigáis, oigan
preterite: (él, ella, Ud.) oyó, (ellos, ellas, Uds.) oyeron
imperative: (Ud.) oiga, (tú) oye
gerund: oyendo

poder* *to be able to, can*
preterite: pude, pudiste, pudo, pudimos, pudisteis, pudieron
future: podré, podrás, podrá, podremos, podréis, podrán
conditional: podría, podrías, podría, podríamos, podríais, podrían
gerund: pudiendo

poner *to put*
present indicative: (yo) pongo
present subjunctive: ponga, pongas, ponga, pongamos, pongáis,
  pongan
preterite: puse, pusiste, puso, pusimos, pusisteis, pusieron
future: pondré, pondrás, pondrá, pondremos, pondréis, pondrán
conditional: pondría, pondrías, pondría, pondríamos, pondríais,
  pondrían
imperative: (Ud.) ponga, (tú) pon
past participle: puesto

querer* *to want*
preterite: quise, quisiste, quiso, quisimos, quisisteis, quisieron
future: querré, querrás, querrá, querremos, querréis, querrán
conditional: querría, querrías, querría, querríamos, querríais,
  querrían

romper *to break*
past participle: roto

saber *to know*
present indicative: (yo) sé
present subjunctive: sepa, sepas, sepa, sepamos, sepáis, sepan

preterite: supe, supiste, supo, supimos, supisteis, supieron
future: sabré, sabrás, sabrá, sabremos, sabréis, sabrán
conditional: sabría, sabrías, sabría, sabríamos, sabríais, sabrían
imperative: (Ud.) sepa

salir *to go out*
present indicative: (yo) salgo
present subjunctive: salga, salgas, salga, salgamos, salgáis, salgan
future: saldré, saldrás, saldrá, saldremos, saldréis, saldrán
conditional: saldría, saldrías, saldría, saldríamos, saldríais, saldrían
imperative: (Ud.) salga, (tú) sal

ser *to be*
present indicative: soy, eres, es, somos, sois, son
present subjunctive: sea, seas, sea, seamos, seáis, sean
preterite: fui, fuiste, fue, fuimos, fuisteis, fueron
imperfect indicative: era, eras, era, éramos, erais, eran
imperative: (Ud.) sea, (tú) sé

soltar *to loosen*
past participle: suelto

tener* *to have*
present indicative: (yo) tengo
present subjunctive: tenga, tengas, tenga, tengamos, tengáis, tengan
preterite: tuve, tuviste, tuvo, tuvimos, tuvisteis, tuvieron
future: tendré, tendrás, tendrá, tendremos, tendréis, tendrán
conditional: tendría, tendrías, tendría, tendríamos, tendríais,
  tendrían
imperative: (Ud.) tenga, (tú) ten

traer *to bring*
present indicative: (yo) traigo
present subjunctive: traiga, traigas, traiga, traigamos, traigáis,
  traigan
preterite: traje, trajiste, trajo, trajimos, trajisteis, trajeron
imperative: (Ud.) traiga
gerund: trayendo

venir* *to come*
present indicative: (yo) vengo
present subjunctive: venga, vengas, venga, vengamos, vengáis,
  vengan
preterite: vine, viniste, vino, vinimos, vinisteis, vinieron
future: vendré, vendrás, vendrá, vendremos, vendréis, vendrán
conditional: vendría, vendrías, vendría, vendríamos, vendríais,
  vendrían
imperative: (Ud.) venga, (tú) ven
gerund: viniendo

ver *to see*
present indicative: (yo) veo
present subjunctive: vea, veas, vea, veamos, veáis, vean
imperfect indicative: veía, veías, veía, veíamos, veíais, veían
imperative: (Ud.) vea
past participle: visto

volver* *to go back, return*
past participle: vuelto

Glossary of Latin American terms

This glossary is intended as a reference section of Latin American Spanish usage. The words in bold under each entry correspond to those normally used in Spain, but you may also hear some of these in Latin America. There is no need for you to learn all the different terms. They are simply given as a reference of words you may hear if you are travelling in Latin America.

Transport and travel

bus
el autobús
el bus
el camión (Mex, Central Am)
la combi (Peru)
el pesero o el colectivo (Mex, minibus in which fare depends on distance you travel)
el colectivo (in Chile, Peru and Bolivia a shared taxi with a fixed route; in Argentina and Venezuela, the word refers to a city bus)
la guagua (Caribbean) (in Chile, Peru and Bolivia, **la guagua** is *a baby*)
el ómnibus
el / micro (from **el microbús**), Argentina; la micro (Chile)

to take (**a bus, train,** *etc.*)
coger (a taboo word in some Latin American countries)
tomar

underground, subway
el metro
el subte (Arg)

car
el coche
el carro
el auto (esp. Southern Cone; i.e. Argentina, Chile and Uruguay)

car park
el aparcamiento
el aparcadero
el estacionamiento
la playa de estacionamiento

to park
aparcar
estacionar

ticket (bus, train, etc.)
el billete
el boleto
el pasaje

to hire, rent
alquilar (un coche, etc.)
rentar
arrendar

ticket office
la taquilla
la boletería

petrol
la gasolina
la bencina (Chile)
la nafta (Arg)

service station
la estación de servicio
la bomba de bencina

el grifo (Perú)
la gasolinera o gasolinería (Mex)

to drive
conducir
manejar

driving licence
el carnet (or **carné**) **/ el permiso de conducir**
la licencia de conducir / manejar
el pase (Col)
el registro (de conductor) (Arg)
el brevete (Perú)

House and hotel

reservation
la reserva
la reservación

room
la habitación
el cuarto
la pieza

single room
una habitación individual
una habitación sencilla
una habitación simple
una single
un cuarto sencillo (Mex)

bedroom
el dormitorio
el cuarto
la recámara (Mex)
la alcoba

blanket
la manta
la cobija
el cobertor
la frazada

washbasin
el lavabo
el lavatorio
el lavamanos
la pileta (Arg)

water tap
el grifo
la llave (del agua)
la canilla (Arg)
la pluma (Col)
el caño (Peru)

shower
la ducha
la regadera (Mex)

bath tub
la bañera
la tina
la bañadera (Arg)

light bulb
la bombilla
el bombillo (Col, Ven)
la ampolleta (Chile)
el foco (Mex)
la bombita (River Plate, i.e. Argentina and Uruguay)
la bujía (Central Am)

swimming pool
la piscina
la alberca (Mex)
la pileta (River Plate)

flat, apartment
el piso, el apartamento (small flat, usually a holiday apartment)
el departamento

lift
el ascensor
el elevador

Restaurants and food

Words for different dishes are not given, as in this area there are many more variations within Latin America and between Latin America and Spain. With a few exceptions, most basic food and farm produce carry the same names everywhere. However, as you travel in Latin America, you will encounter many names for products which are typical of certain countries or regions, and which you may not hear anywhere else.

waiter, waitress
el camarero, la camarera
el mesero, la mesera
el mozo, la señorita (Arg, Chile, Peru)
el mesonero, la mesonera (Ven)

to have breakfast
desayunar
tomar (el) desayuno

dinner
la cena
la comida

set-price meal
el menú (del día)
el plato del día
la comida corrida (Mex)

potatoes
las patatas
las papas

beans
las judías / alubias
los frijoles / frejoles
los porotos
las caraotas (Ven)

peas
los guisantes
los chícharos (Mex, Central Am)
las arvejas

chilli
el chile
el ají (Arg, Chile, Peru)

avocado
el aguacate
la palta (Southern Cone)

peach
el melocotón
el durazno

apricot
el albaricoque
el damasco
el melocotón (Col)
el chabacano (Mex)

strawberry
la fresa
la frutilla (South America)

black coffee
un café solo
un café
un tinto (Col)

white coffee
un café con leche
un café cortado (coffee with a dash of milk)
un cortado

to drink
beber
tomar

toilets
el lavabo
el servicio / los servicios
el baño / los baños
el sanitario (Col, Ven, Mex)
los servicios higiénicos (SSHH) (Peru)

Telephone and postal services

Hello?
¿Díga(me)?
¿Sí?
¿Aló?
¿Bueno? (Mex)
¡Hola? (River Plate)

extension
la extensión
el anexo (Chile, Peru)
el interno (Arg)

call
una llamada
un llamado

a reverse-charge call
un(a) llamado/a a / con cobro revertido
un(a) llamado/a a / por cobrar/pagar (allá)

it is engaged
está comunicando
está ocupado

stamp
el sello
la estampilla
el timbre (Mex)

post office
correos
el correo
la oficina de correos
el Serpost (Peru)

post box
el apartado (de correos)
el apartado (postal)
la casilla (de correos) (Southern Cone)
el buzón

Pronunciation

The aim of this brief pronunciation guide is to offer hints which will enable you to produce sounds recognizable to a speaker from any part of the Spanish-speaking world. It cannot by itself teach you to pronounce Spanish accurately. The best way to acquire a reasonably good accent is to listen to and try to imitate native speakers.

This guide gives hints on individual sounds and it also provides an overview of main pronunciation features within certain regions of Latin America.

Vowels

Spanish vowels are generally shorter, clearer and more precise than English vowels. Unstressed vowels are not weakened as in English but are given much the same value in pronunciation as those which are stressed. For example, in the English word *comfortable*, the vowels which follow the syllable *com* are weak, while in Spanish every vowel in the word **confortable** has the same quality.

There are only five vowel sounds in Spanish:

a	like the **a** in *answer* (but shorter – British English; like the **u** in but – American English)	gracias
e	like the **e** in *end*	él
i	like the **i** in *marine*	inglés
o	like the **o** in *God*	sol
u	like the **oo** in *moon*	uno

Note:

When **i** occurs before another vowel, it is pronounced like the **y** in *yes*.	tiene
When **u** occurs before another vowel, it is pronounced like the **w** in *wind*.	b**u**eno
After **q**, **u** is not pronounced at all.	que
u is also silent in **gui** and **gue**.	g**u**ía, g**u**erra
u is pronounced in **güi** and **güe**, a very infrequent sound combination in Spanish.	lingüística vergüenza

---

Consonants

The pronunciation of Spanish consonants is generally similar to that of English consonants. But note the following features:

b and **v**	are pronounced the same; in initial position and after **n** with lips closed, like the **b** in *bar*	bien, invierno
	in other positions the lips are slightly apart.	Salvador, Cuba
c	before **a, o, u**, like the **c** in *coast*	castellano
	before **e, i**, like the **s** in *sea*	hacer, gracias
ch	like the **ch** in *chair*.	Chile
d	like the **d** in *day*.	día
	between vowels and after **r**, more like the **th** in *those*.	nada, tarde
g	before **a, o, u**, like the **g** in *government*.	hago, Guatemala
	before **e, i**, like the **h** in *hand* in Central America and the Caribbean, but more like the Scottish **ch** in *loch* in other countries.	Argentina, Sergio
j	like the **h** in *hand* in Central America and the Caribbean, but more like the Scottish **ch** in *loch* in other countries.	Juan

h	is silent.	ahora
ll	like the **y** of *yawn*, but more like the **s** in *pleasure* in Argentina and Uruguay	llamar
ñ	like the **ni** in *onion*.	mañana
q(u)	like the **c** in *cake*.	que
r	between vowels or at the end of a word, like the **r** in *very*;	caro, calor
	in initial position, strongly rolled	río
rr	always strongly rolled	perro
y	like the **y** in *yes*, but more like the **s** in *pleasure* in Argentina and Uruguay	mayo
z	like the **s** in *sale*.	Venezuela

Latin American pronunciation

In an area as large as that of Latin America great differences in pronunciation and intonation can be found between different regions and even within the same country, just as in the English-speaking world. But as with English, these differences are no obstacle to communication. There are also a few standard pronunciation features which distinguish Latin American Spanish from the Spanish of Spain. Among these we find the *seseo*, that is, the pronunciation of *z* (e.g. **González**) and c before e and *i* (e.g. **cien, quince**) as *s* and not like the *th* in *think*, which is what you will hear in most parts of Spain. Also, the distinction made in certain areas of Spain between *y* and *ll* (e.g. **yo, llamo**) where *y* is pronounced like the *y* in **yes**, and *ll* more like the *lli* in *million*, is not made in Latin America. A single sound, not unlike the *y* in *yes*, is used in both instances in most regions, including also most parts of Spain. The pronunciation of *j* and that of *g* before before *e* and *i* (e.g. **Jorge, girar**) is general much softer in most Latin American countries, not unlike the *h* in *house*.

In terms of specific areas or countries, Mexican accent and pronunciation is one of the most distinctive in Latin America. In general, there is a weakening of vowel sounds, for example in **buen(a)s noch(e)s**, unlike what happens in many other Latin American countries, where it is consonant sounds which are reduced or even omitted altogether in certain positions. The pronunciation of final *s* and *s* before a consonant, as in *buenas noches,* for example, is fully pronounced in Mexico, unlike what happens in places like the Caribbean or Venezuela, where it tends to be substituted by an aspirated *h*, rendering a pronunciation more like *buena(h) noche(h)*. The latter is also characteristic of southern Spain.

Colombians claim they speak the best Spanish in Latin America. Even if you are reluctant to accept adjectives such as *good* or *bad* regarding a particular language or dialect, one must admit that the Spanish spoken in some areas of Colombia may seem, to foreign ears at least, clearer and easier to follow than that of some other countries or areas. However, within Colombia there are wide differences between the Spanish spoken in places like Bogotá or Cali, for example, usually associated with 'good, clear Spanish', and that spoken around the Caribbean. This bears some of the characteristics of Caribbean Spanish in general, that is, weakening or even disappearance of consonant sounds in certain positions, e.g. *do(h), tre(h)*, instead of *dos, tres*, or *pe(h)cao* instead of *pescado*.

This weakening or aspiration of *s* before a consonant or in final position (e.g. *ha(h)ta* for *hasta*, *bueno(h)* for *buenos*) and the weakening or disappearance of *d* between vowels *(to(d)o* for *todo)* is also a feature of Chilean pronunciation and to a large extent also of the Argentinian accent, except in deliberate and more careful speech. Further features of Chilean accent are the pronunciation of the combination tr, which is pronounced by most people like the *tr* in *country*, and the rendering of *ch* (e.g. *Chile*), not unlike the *sh* in *ship*. The latter is particularly common among less educated speakers.

The Argentinian accent is a very distinctive one, particularly as regards the pronunciation of *y* (e.g. *yo*) and *ll* (e.g. *allá*), which are pronounced much like the *j* in *John* or the *s* in *pleasure*. In parts of Argentina, especially in the west and north, the *r* is not rolled in words such as *río* and *perro*. What you hear instead sounds more like *rj, rjío, perjo*.

Stress and accentuation

Words which end in a vowel, **n** or **s** stress the last syllable but one.

bueno, a**mi**gos

Words which end in a consonant other than **n** or **s** stress the last syllable.

ho**tel**, se**ñor**

Words which do not follow the above rules carry a written accent over the stressed syllable.

A**mé**rica, auto**bús**

Differences in meaning between certain similar words are shown through the use of an accent.

sí *yes* **si** *if*
él *he* **el** *the*, m
sé *I know* **se** *pronoun*
dé give **de** *of, from*
mí *me* **mi** *my*

Question words carry an accent, and are preceded by an inverted question mark.

¿**dónde?** *where?*
¿**cuándo?** *when?*
¿**qué?** *what?*
¿**cuál?** *which?*
¿**cómo?** *how?*

In exclamations, **que** carries an accent. Notice also the inverted exclamation mark at the beginning.

¡**Qué lindo!** *How beautiful!*
¡**Qué difícil!** *How difficult!*

Spelling

Note the following changes in spelling.

Verbs may change their spelling in certain forms in order to keep the sound of the infinitive. For example:

es**coger** *to choose* but es**cojo** *I choose*
lle**gar** *to arrive* but lle**gué** *I arrived*
pa**gar** *to pay* but pa**gué** *I paid*
bus**car** *to look for* but bus**qué** *I looked for*

Liaison

If a word ends in a vowel and is followed by a word beginning with a vowel, the two vowels are normally pronounced as though both were part of the same word. When the two vowels are the same, these are usually pronounced as one, for example:

¿Cómo está usted? No está aquí. ¿Habla español?

Pronouncing the alphabet

◆ CD2, 1, 05:40

a	a	j	jota	r	ere
b	be	k	ka	s	ese
c	c	l	ele	t	te
d	de	m	eme	u	u
e	e	n	ene	v	uve*
f	efe	ñ	eñe	w	doble uve/ve*
g	ge	o	o	x	equis
h	ache	p	pe	y	i griega
i	i	q	cu	z	zeta

Ch and ll used to have separate entries in Spanish dictionaries, but now ch comes under c and ll under l. You may, however, still hear people name them as separate letters, che and elle, respectively.

* As Spanish does not make a distinction in pronunciation between b and v, when spelling a word v is normally qualified as ve pequeña, ve chica or ve corta, depending on the country, or else, examples are given: be de bonito, or de burro, ve de Venezuela or de vaca.

* w is called doble uve in some countries and doble ve in others.

Listening comprehension transcripts

Unit 1

Practice 8

a

Entrevistador	Buenas tardes. ¿Cómo se llama usted?
Initia	Buenas tardes. Mi nombre es Initia Muñoz García.
Entrevistador	Initia, ¿de qué país es usted?
Initia	Soy de aquí de México. Soy mexicana.
Entrevistador	¿De qué parte de México?
Initia	De la ciudad de Córdoba, Veracruz.

b

Entrevistador	Buenas tardes.
Clotilde	Buenas tardes.
Entrevistador	¿Cómo se llama usted?
Clotilde	Me llamo Clotilde Montalvo Rodríguez, para servirle.
Entrevistador	Clotilde, ¿de dónde es usted?
Clotilde	Soy de aquí de Veracruz.
Entrevistador	Veracruz. ¿Es usted mexicana?
Clotilde	Sí, soy mexicana.

c

Elizabeth	Me llamo Elizabeth. Soy de Panamá, de la Ciudad de Panamá.

Unit 2

Practice 5

a

Señor	Disculpe, señorita.
Señorita	A sus órdenes.
Señor	¿Hay una casa de cambio por aquí?
Señorita	Sí, hay una en la calle Amazonas.
Señor	¿Dónde está la calle Amazonas?
Señorita	Está a cinco cuadras de aquí, a la izquierda.
Señor	Muchas gracias. Muy amable.
Señorita	Para servirle.

b

Sr. Ramos	Buenos días.
Recepcionista	Buenos días. ¿Qué desea?
Sr. Ramos	¿Está el señor Silva?
Recepcionista	Sí, sí está. Está en su oficina.
Sr. Ramos	¿Cuál es el número de la oficina?
Recepcionista	La oficina del señor Silva es la doscientos cuarenta. Está en el segundo piso, al final del pasillo, a la derecha.
Sr. Ramos	¿Dónde está el elevador?
Recepcionista	Está allá.

Practice 7

Turista	Por favor, ¿dónde está la estación?
Colombiana	Está en la carrera diecisiete, al final de la calle dieciséis.
Turista	¿Está lejos de aquí?
Colombiana	¿A pie?
Turista	Sí, a pie.

Colombiana	Está a quince minutos más o menos.
Turista	Muchas gracias.
Colombiana	De nada.

Practice 8

Jorge	Soy director de un centro de lenguas modernas.
Entrevistador	¿Dónde ... dónde está el centro?
Jorge	El Centro de Lenguas Modernas está localizado en la ciudad de Veracruz, a media cuadra de la calle principal, es decir, a una y media cuadra del parque principal de la ciudad.

Unit 3

Practice 5

En la mañana abren a las nueve de la mañana y, entonces, trabajan de nueve a una, nueve de la mañana a una de la tarde, cierran de una a cuatro, abren a las cuatro, para trabajar hasta las ocho de la noche.

Practice 8

a

| Entrevistador | Dime, ¿cuáles son las comidas principales en México, y cuál es el horario de cada comida? |
| Jorge | O.K. Las comidas principales en México son el desayuno entre las ocho y las nueve; el almuerzo entre la una y media y las tres y media; la cena, entre ocho y media y nueve; y, opcionalmente, hay una ... podríamos llamarle poscena, que puede ser a las once y media de la noche, si nos acostamos tarde. |

a

Entrevistador	Coty, buenas tardes. Coty, ¿cuáles son las comidas principales en México y cuáles son los horarios de las comidas?
Coty	Las comidas … la comida principal es la de mediodía, que varía entre una y dos de la tarde, en que se toma. El desayuno …, pues, bueno, tenemos tres en el día: desayuno, almuerzo y cena. El desayuno es temprano, a las ocho de la mañana, almuerzo entre una y dos, y cena, pues, de las siete en adelante.

Unit 4

Practice 4

Entrevistador	Coty, ¿en qué trabaja usted?
Coty	Yo soy secretaria, eh … mi horario de trabajo es …, por la mañana entro a las diez de la mañana, salgo a almorzar a la una de la tarde, regreso a las cuatro de la tarde a seguir laborando y salgo a las nueve de la noche.

Practice 6

En las vacaciones normalmente aprovecho para visitar a mis sobrinos. Tengo tres sobrinos que viven en Tijuana, Baja California. En la frontera con Estados Unidos. Es un viaje largo, porque de Veracruz hasta allá son varios días, pero lo disfruto, porque veo a la familia muy de vez en cuando.

Practice 8

Entrevistador	¿Cómo se llama usted?
Clotilde	Mi nombre es Clotilde Montalvo Rodríguez.
Entrevistador	Clotilde, ¿cuántos años tiene usted?
Clotilde	Tengo cuarenta y cuatro años.
Entrevistador	¿Está casada o soltera?
Clotilde	Estoy casada.
Entrevistador	¿Cuántos hijos tiene?
Clotilde	Tengo dos hijas, una de veintitrés años y una pequeña de seis años y medio.
Entrevistador	¿En qué trabaja usted?
Clotilde	Soy secretaria y trabajo en el Centro Cultural de Lenguas Modernas.
Entrevistador	Y su esposo, ¿qué hace?
Clotilde	Mi esposo, pues … maneja, es chofer de carretera.

Unit 5

Practice 4

Mesero	¿Qué le traigo, señorita?
Señorita	¿Qué tiene de almuerzo?
Mesero	Tenemos sopa de pollo, sopa de verduras, crema de espárragos, de champiñones …
Señorita	Tráigame una crema de espárragos. No, no, no, mire, prefiero tomar una sopa de pollo.
Mesero	¿Y qué otra cosa? Tenemos arroz con pollo, pollo en salsa de mostaza, soufflé de calabaza, carne guisada …
Señorita	¿Pescado no tiene?
Mesero	No, no queda. Le recomiendo el soufflé de calabaza. Está muy bueno.
Señorita	Sí, tráigame eso.
Mesero	¿Y para tomar? ¿Una cerveza, vino, un jugo …?
Señorita	Una cerveza.
Mesero	Muy bien, señorita.

Unit 6

Practice 3

Clienta	Buenos días.
Vendedor	Buenos días. ¿A la orden?
Clienta	¿Podría decirme cuánto valen esos zapatos?
Vendedor	¿Cuáles?
Clienta	Esos, los negros.
Vendedor	Esos valen treinta y dos mil pesos, pero hay un descuento del diez por ciento. Con descuento son veintiocho mil ochocientos pesos.
Clienta	Sí, está bien. Quisiera probármelos.
Vendedor	¿Qué número?
Clienta	Cuarenta y dos.
Vendedor	Sí, un momento, por favor.

Practice 4

Almacenes García, calidad y economía. García. Por fin de temporada todas las camisas sport manga larga y manga corta para caballeros, cuarenta por ciento de descuento. Todos los pantalones para caballero, treinta, cuarenta y cincuenta por ciento de descuento. No incluye promociones. García.

Practice 7

Cliente	¿Cuánto es todo?
Vendedora	Bueno, tenemos ciento cuarenta y siete mil … ochenta y ocho mil …ciento sesenta y cinco mil … doscientos ochenta y seis mil … quince mil … ciento noventa y ocho mil … ciento cincuenta y un mil. El total es … un millón cincuenta mil pesos.

Unit 7

Practice 5

Entre la gloria y el paraíso está Motel Miraflores, con todos los servicios para que usted disfrute cómodamente de su estancia. Habitaciones con aire acondicionado, cama de agua, jacuzzi, suites con alberca, antena parabólica y música ambiental. Motel Miraflores, el lugar al que siempre deseará volver. Carretera Boticaria-Mocambo s/n (sin número), Veracruz.

Practice 6

El hotel tiene doscientas dieciséis habitaciones, una piscina en la parte trasera con un gran espacio verde, patios bien grandes, dos restaurantes, uno de primera categoría, que es el Techo del Mundo, la otra la cafetería y muchos … y varios salones donde se hacen muchas convenciones. Es de cinco estrellas. Aparte, tiene casino y la discoteca.

Practice 8

a

Entrevistador	¿Cómo es el clima en Panamá?
Elizabeth	Hace calor. Es de una temperatura promedio de veintiocho grados centígrados todo …, durante todo el año. Es un país netamente tropical; tiene dos estaciones, la de invierno, que es lluviosa, y la de verano, que es seca.

b

Lima, la capital del Perú, es una ciudad bonita, grande, moderna, y donde en algunos lugares se conservan las características de la época colonial. También tiene bonitas playas, museos, zoológicos y, en cuanto al clima, es cálido y casi no existen las lluvias.

Unit 8

Practice 6

Guillermo	Me gustaría ir a Mendoza. No sé en qué ir, si en bus o en avión. ¿Qué me recomiendas?
Carlos	Bueno, mira, yo te recomiendo el bus, porque el viaje es mucho más interesante. El bus demora aproximadamente cinco o seis horas. El avión demora treinta minutos, pero en bus vas a ver muchísimo más. Hay buses dos o tres veces por día y el pasaje no te va a costar mucho. Ahora, si tú quieres que te recomiende algún hotel en Mendoza, te puedo recomendar un hotel bastante bueno y económico, el hotel Plaza que está a dos cuadras de la calle principal de Mendoza. Tengo la dirección y el teléfono y te los puedo dar.

Unit 9

Practice 3

a

Sra. Puig	Buenas tardes ¿Está el señor Solís, por favor?
Recepcionista	El señor Solís está ocupado. Está en una reunión. ¿Quiere dejarle algún mensaje?
Sra. Puig	Dígale, por favor, que vino Carmen Puig, de Caracas, que yo necesito hablar urgentemente con él. Dígale que me llame al hotel, al hotel Sheraton. Yo estoy en la habitación 500. Pero tiene que ser ahora, porque yo me voy a Caracas mañana.
Recepcionista	Muy bien, señora.

b

Srta. Pérez	Buenas tardes. ¿Está el señor Solís?
Recepcionista	No, el señor Solís no está. Está en una reunión en este momento.
Srta. Pérez	¿A qué hora llega?
Recepcionista	Va a llegar a las 2.00.
Srta. Pérez	Por favor, dígale que vino Marilú Pérez. Estoy en el hotel Gala, en la habitación 324. Aquí tengo el teléfono. Es el 687951.
Recepcionista	Muy bien, señorita. Yo le daré su recado.
Srta. Pérez	Gracias.
Recepcionista	De nada.

Practice 6

Marilú	En las vacaciones fui con mi familia a la costa y estuvimos dos semanas en un hotel frente a la playa. Disfrutamos mucho, ya que el lugar donde fuimos es agradable, tranquilo y tiene unas playas maravillosas, y el aire es tan puro. Salimos mucho, harto, tomamos el sol, nadamos, hicimos deportes. Y volvimos pero llenos de energía a la ciudad.

Note that **pero** (*but*) in the last sentence is emphatic.

Unit 10

Practice 4

Entrevistador	Carlos, ¿siempre has vivido en Buenos Aires?
Carlos	No, no siempre, también viví en San Pablo, Brasil.
Entrevistador	¿Y qué hacías en San Pablo?
Carlos	En San Pablo daba clases de pintura.
	(Contd)

Entrevistador	¿Y en qué parte de San Pablo vivías?
Carlos	Vivía en el barrio de Vila Mariana.
Entrevistador	¿Y qué tal era el barrio?
Carlos	Era excelente. Uno de los más arborizados y con más vegetación de San Pablo.
Entrevistador	¿Vivías en una casa o un departamento?
Carlos	Vivía en un departamento.
Entrevistador	¿Un buen departamento tenías allí?
Carlos	Sí, pequeño, pero agradable.
Entrevistador	Y tus vecinos, ¿qué tal eran?
Carlos	Muy buenos vecinos, como todos los brasileros.
Entrevistador	¿Tenías muchos amigos en San Pablo?
Carlos	Muchos, muchos que todavía tengo.
Entrevistador	¿Y por qué volviste a Buenos Aires?
Carlos	Bueno, porque extrañaba mucho la ciudad.

Practice 7

Entrevistador	Carlos, ¿cómo describirías Buenos Aires?
Carlos	Buenos Aires es una ciudad muy grande, con muchos rincones diferentes, pero con una unidad común. Es una ciudad con mucho movimiento cultural y la expresión que más … este … la representa, para mí, es que es una ciudad que tiene alma.
Entrevistador	¿Y qué es lo que más te gusta de Buenos Aires?
Carlos	Me gusta su vida nocturna, me gusta la posibilidad de expresarse que le da a la gente que vive en ella. Me gusta su movimiento cultural.
Entrevistador	¿Hay algo que no te guste de Buenos Aires?
Carlos	Sí, hay algo que no me gusta, que es la tendencia que tenemos los porteños a entristecer y a la melancolía extrema.

Unit 11

Practice 5

Entrevistador	Carlos. ¿dónde te gustaría pasar tus próximas vacaciones?
Carlos	Me gustaría pasarlas en Bariloche.
Entrevistador	¿Y por qué en Bariloche?
Carlos	Porque fui hace muchos años y su imagen quedó profundamente grabada en mí.
Entrevistador	¿Irías solo o acompañado?
Carlos	No, iría con mi familia o con amigos.
Entrevistador	¿Y por cuánto tiempo irías?
Carlos	Bueno, iría por quince días o veinte.
Entrevistador	¿Y qué harías allí?
Carlos	Recorrería todo lo que de naturaleza se pueda visitar. No me gusta demasiado la vida ... frívola del lugar.

Practice 6

Entrevistador	¿Tienes coche?
Carlos	No tengo.
Entrevistador	¿Te gustaría tener uno?
Carlos	Sí, me gustaría mucho.
Entrevistador	¿Y qué marca de coche preferirías?
Carlos	Preferiría un Ford.
Entrevistador	Un Ford ...¿Y comprarías uno grande o uno chico?
Carlos	Me gustan más los autos grandes.
Entrevistador	¿Preferirías un coche deportivo o tradicional?
Carlos	Preferiría un coche tradicional.

(Contd)

Entrevistador	¿Y qué color comprarías?
Carlos	Un color gris o azul.
Entrevistador	¿Lo usarías para ir al trabajo o para salir a pasear?
Carlos	Por supuesto, para las dos cosas.
Entrevistador	¿Y adónde irías, por ejemplo, a pasear el fin de semana o en las vacaciones?
Carlos	Iría a lugares cercanos, pero donde abunde la naturaleza.

Unit 12

Practice 3

Entrevistador	Karina, ¿has estado en Cusco alguna vez?
Karina	Sí, estuve cuando yo tenía once años de edad.
Entrevistador	¿Y qué tal es la ciudad?
Karina	Es muy bonita. Es muy tradicional, pues (que) conserva las características de la cultura incaica.
Entrevistador	¿Y está…? ¿Cómo se puede ir desde Lima al Cusco?
Karina	Bueno, se puede viajar mediante bus, avión o tren.
Entrevistador	¿Y el avión cuánto demora?
Karina	Aproximadamente dos horas.
Entrevistador	Dos horas. Y para ir a Machu Picchu desde Cusco, ¿está muy lejos?
Karina	Exactamente, no sé a cuánto tiempo está. Está lejos de Machu Picchu y la única forma de llegar es mediante el tren.

Unit 13

Practice 4

a

Señor	Señorita, mire, yo pedí un asiento en la sección de no fumadores.
Azafata	Lo siento, tanto, señor, pero no es culpa nuestra. Inmediatamente voy a ver qué puedo hacer para cambiarlo.
Señor	Gracias.

b

Señora	¡Epa, muchacho!
Mesero	Sí, señora.
Señora	Mire, yo le pedí pescado con puré y usted … usted me trajo pescado con papas fritas, ¿vale?
Mesero	Disculpe, se lo cambio ahorita.

c

Señorita	¡Mozo!
Mozo	Señorita, ¿sí?
Señorita	Mire por favor, hace quince minutos que pedí una sopa de mariscos y todavía no me la traen. ¿Qué pasa?
Mozo	Perdone, señorita, pero estamos tan ocupados hoy día. Hay tantos clientes. Mire, voy a ver lo que pasó. Se la traigo enseguida.

Practice 6

Turista	Buenas tardes. Para ir al Teatro Segura, por favor.
Recepcionista	Sí, cómo no. Al salir de aquí, doble por la calle Ucayali, camine de frente hacia Abancay. Ahí doble a la mano izquierda, camine dos cuadras y media, y ahí está el Teatro Segura.
Turista	Gracias.
Recepcionista	De nada.

Practice 8

Doctor Manuel Loyo de Valdés, fracturas, luxaciones, cirugía, traumatología y ortopedia. Doctor Manuel Loyo de Valdés. Consultas, de 11.00 a 13.00 horas y de 18.00 a 21.00 horas, en González Pajés 1016, entre Iturbide y Mina. Teléfono 325228, en Veracruz.

Practice 9

Paciente	Quisiera pedir hora con el doctor Martínez, por favor. ¿Qué días atiende?
Recepcionista	Atiende los lunes, miércoles y viernes. Los lunes atiende de cuatro a seis y los miércoles y viernes de once de la mañana a una de la tarde.

Key to the activities and to Test yourself

Unit 1

Dialogues

4 a Me llamo (*your name*). **b** Soy de (*country or city*). **5 a** ¿Cómo te llamas? **b** ¿De dónde eres?

Practice

1 Buenos días. / Tengo una reservación. / Mi nombre es … *or* Me llamo … (*name*). / Gracias. **2** Buenas tardes. / No, no soy Emilio/a Zapata. Soy … (*your name*). / No se preocupe. **3** Mi nombre es … *or* Me llamo … (*name*), soy de … (*place where you come from*). / Mucho gusto *or* Encantado/a. / Siéntese, por favor. **4** No, no soy americano/a. Soy inglés / inglesa (*or* Sí, soy americano/a). / Soy de (*city*). / Me llamo … (*name*). ¿Y tú? / Mucho gusto *or* Encantado/a. **5 a** Buenas tardes. **b** ¿Cuál es su nombre? *or* ¿Cómo se llama Ud.? **c** ¿De dónde es (usted)? **d** ¿Es usted mexicano/a? **e** ¿De qué parte de México es? **7** Pablo Miranda Frías es venezolano. Pablo es de Caracas. **8 a** Initia is from Córdoba in Veracruz. **b** ¿De qué país es Ud.? **c** Clotilde is from Veracruz. **d** ¿De dónde es Ud.? **e** Elizabeth is from Panama City. **f** Hola, me llamo Elizabeth.

Test yourself

1 a es **b** eres **c** llamo **d** son **e** somos; **2 a** Tengo una reservación/ reserva. **b** ¿Cómo se llama usted?/¿Cuál es su nombre? **c** ¿De dónde es usted? **d** Soy de Santiago. **e** Encantado/a, Mucho gusto.

Unit 2

Dialogues

3 La oficina del señor Martínez. 4 ¿Cómo le va? 5 a ¿Hay una casa de cambio por aquí? b ¿Hay un banco por aquí? c Está a tres cuadras de aquí, a la izquierda. d Está a cuatro cuadras de aquí, a la derecha.

Practice

1 habitación doscientos veinte, en el segundo piso; habitación cuatrocientos treinta, en el cuarto piso; habitación quinientos cincuenta, en el quinto piso (*follow the model to complete the dialogues*). 2 Hola, ¿cómo estás? *or* ¿cómo te va? / Estoy muy bien. Siéntate. Me alegro mucho de verte. / ¿Cómo están tus papás? 3 Buenos días, ¿cómo está usted? *or* ¿Cómo le va? / Bien, gracias. Siéntese, por favor. Me alegro mucho de verla. 5 a He is looking for a bureau de change. b There is one in the calle Amazonas. c Five blocks away. d He is in his office. e 240 f On the second floor. g At the end of the corridor, on the right. 6 a ¿Hay una (*or* alguna) estación (de metro) por aquí? b ¿Dónde está? *or* ¿Está lejos? c ¿Hay un (*or* algún) hotel por aquí? d ¿Está lejos? e ¿Dónde está el Banco Nacional, por favor? f ¿Dónde está la calle Pánuco? *or* ¿Está cerca / lejos la calle Pánuco? 7 a F. b F. c V. 8 a It is half a block from the main street. b It is one and a half blocks from the main park. 9 a It is in a valley, at an altitude of 2,240 m. b It has a rich cultural and artistic life, and is the intellectual centre of Latin America. c It is a modern city, with wide avenues and lively squares, elegant districts, popular markets, futuristic buildings, colonial buildings and barroque churches.

Test yourself

a ¿Hay una casa de cambio por aquí? b ¿Dónde está la calle Bolívar? c ¿Dónde están los teléfonos? d There's one two blocks from here. e It's at the end of the corridor, on the left. f Hola, ¿cómo estás?/¿cómo te va? g estoy h está i cuál j cómo

Unit 3

Dialogues

1 a ¿Qué hora es? Son las dos y media. b Son las seis y media.
c Son las diez y media. d Son las doce menos cuarto. e Son las doce.
f Es la una y cuarto. **3** a ¿A qué hora abren el banco? Abren a las
nueve. b ¿A qué hora abren el museo? Abren a las nueve y media.
c ¿A qué hora abren la oficina de turismo? Abren a las diez. **4** a ¿A
qué hora cierran los bancos? b ¿A qué hora cierran los museos?
c ¿A qué hora cierran las casas de cambio? **5** a ¿A qué hora es el
desayuno? Es a las siete y media. b ¿A qué hora es el almuerzo?
Es a la una. c ¿A qué hora es la salida? Es a las ocho. **6** a Rosa has
breakfast at 8.30 a.m. b Raúl has breakfast at 7.00 a.m. c Raúl has
lunch between 12.30 and 1.00 p.m. d Rosa has lunch at 2.00 p.m.

Practice

1 a Es la una y media. b Son las seis y veinticinco. c Son las siete y
cuarto. d Son veinte para las nueve. *or* Son las nueve menos veinte.
e Es un cuarto para las diez. *or* Son las diez menos cuarto. f Son las
once. **2** a Son las diez. b Son las cinco. c Es la una. d Son las seis.
3 a Está detrás del Auditorio Nacional. b El viernes quince hay una
función. c Es a las ocho de la noche. d Es a las doce. **4** a ¿A qué
hora abren las tiendas? b ¿A qué hora abre(n) el supermercado?
c ¿A qué hora cierra(n) el correo? d ¿A qué hora cierran los
museos? **5** a F. b V. c F. **6** Disculpe, ¿qué hora tiene? / Son las dos y
media. / ¿A qué hora abren las casas de cambio? / Abren a las
cuatro. / ¿Hay una casa de cambio por aquí? / Sí, La Internacional
está a dos cuadras de aquí ... **7** a Tomo el desayuno (*or* Desayuno)
a las ... (*time*). b Almuerzo a las ... (*time*). c Almuerzo en (casa / la
oficina / una cafetería / un restaurante / un bar). d No, no muy tarde.
or Sí, bastante / muy tarde. Ceno a las ... (*time*). **8** a Breakfast
between 8.00 and 9.00 a.m., lunch between 1.30 and 3.30 p.m. and
dinner between 8.30 and 9.00 p.m. b It is at 11.30 p.m. c mediodía.
d 1.00 y 2.00. e de las 7.00 en adelante.

1 **a** Son las diez y veinticinco. **b** Son las doce menos cuarto/Es un cuarto para las doce. **c** Son las doce y media. **d** Son las dos y cuarto. **e** Son las diez y diez. **2 a** toma, desayuno **b** almuerzan, almuerza **c** como, come **d** cenamos, cenas **e** Abre, cierra.

Unit 4

Dialogues

1 a ¿Cómo estás? Pues, un poco cansado. b Tengo mucho trabajo. c Está aquí de vacaciones. d Este es Juan. e Trabajo en una agencia de viajes. 2 a Because it is a beautiful place and it has a good climate. b She starts at nine in the morning and finishes at seven. 3 a Sometimes he goes out of Santiago, to the beach or the countryside. When he stays in Santiago he goes to the cinema or eats out with friends. b She normally watches television, reads or listens to music. 4 a She has two children. b They are aged twelve and ten.

Practice

1 Hola, Raúl. Te presento a mi mamá. Este es Raúl. / Encantada. 2 *Ud.*: Buenas tardes, señor Molina. ¿Cómo está Ud.? *Sr. Molina*: Muy bien, gracias. ¿Y Ud.? *Ud.*: Bien, gracias. Le presento a mi colega John Evans. Este es el señor Molina. *Sr. Molina*: Encantado. *J. Evans*: Mucho gusto. *Sr. Molina*: Siéntense, por favor. 3 a ¿Dónde vives? / Vivo en ... (*place*). ¿En qué trabajas? / Soy ... (*occupation or profession*) *or* Trabajo en ... (*place of work*). b ¿De dónde son ustedes? / Soy de ... (*country*). ¿Dónde viven (ustedes)? / ¿Y en qué trabajan? / Yo soy ... (*occupation or profession*) *or* Trabajo en ... (*place of work*). 4 a F. b V. c F. 5 Soy ... (*occupation*) *or* Trabajo en ... (*place of work*) *or* Estudio en ... (*place where you are studying*). Trabajo de lunes a viernes *or* Voy a la universidad / al colegio de lunes a viernes. Empiezo a las ... (*time*) y termino a las ... (*time*).

Generalmente almuerzo en … (*place*). Cuando salgo del trabajo / de la universidad / del colegio, generalmente (veo la televisión / leo el periódico / escucho música / estudio / visito a mis amigos/as / riego el jardín / cocino, etc.). Los fines de semana (me levanto tarde / trabajo en casa / salgo de compras / juego al tenis / voy al cine / salgo a caminar / salgo a correr, etc.). **6** a She visits her nephews in Tijuana. b Because she very rarely sees her family. **7** Antonio Fernández es nicaragüense y trabaja como técnico en una empresa textil. Antonio es casado y tiene tres hijos, Adela, Mario y Domingo. Su hija Adela tiene veinticuatro años, su hijo Mario tiene veintiún años y su hijo Domingo tiene diecinueve (años). La esposa de Antonio se llama María Rosa Poblete. María (Rosa) es ama de casa. **8** *Age*: 44 *Marital status*: Married. *Profession*: Secretary. *Husband's profession*: Coach or lorry driver. *No of children*: 2. *Ages*: 23, 6½. **9** a Soy casado/a *or* Soy soltero/a. b Tengo (dos) hijos. / No tengo hijos. c Tengo (tres) hermanos. / No tengo hermanos. d (John) tiene (doce) años, (Anne) tiene (siete). e Vivo en … (*city or town*).

Test yourself

1 a vivo, vive, viven b empiezo, termino c tengo, soy, tengo d hace, es, trabaja e haces, voy **2** a Te presento a mi esposa/mujer – Este es Carlos – Encantado/Mucho gusto. b Me levanto a las siete y generalmente/por lo general/normalmente me acuesto a las once. c Normalmente/Generalmente/Por lo general me quedo en casa, veo (la) televisión, leo o escucho música. d Tenemos tres hijos/niños. Nuestro hijo mayor tiene seis años y nuestra hija menor tiene cuatro. e Soy ingeniero y trabajo en una empresa/compañía. Mi esposa/mujer es enfermera y trabaja en un hospital.

Unit 5

Dialogues

1 Prefiero filetes de pescado / Quiero … / Quiero (café / té).
2 a ¿Tiene una mesa para tres? b Quiero un aperitivo. c ¿Nos trae

una botella de vino tinto, por favor? 3 a ¿Me trae una sopa de verduras? b Quiero pollo asado con puré. c ¿Nos trae una ensalada mixta? d Para mí, café, por favor. 4 ¿Tiene helados? / Prefiero de … y quisiera / quiero un café también.

Practice

1 Buenos días, quisiera reservar una mesa para dos (personas). / Sí, para hoy. / Para la una y media. / A nombre de … (*your name*).
2 Buenas tardes, tengo (*or* tenemos) una reservación para la una y media. / Mi nombre es … *or* Me llamo … (*your name*). 3 *Mesero:* ¿Qué van a comer? Para empezar tenemos… También tenemos sopas y cremas / *Ud.* Para empezar yo quiero … / *Colega* Y para mí… / *M* ¿Y qué más? / *Ud.* Yo quisiera… *M* ¿Con qué lo / la quiere? *Ud.* Lo / la quiero con … *M* ¿Y usted señor/a? *C* Yo quiero / prefiero … con … *M* ¿Qué van a tomar? *Ud.* Tráiganos … *M* ¿Qué desean de postre? *Ud.* Tráigame… *C* Para mí … *M* ¿Van a tomar café? *Ud.* Yo sí / no, gracias. *C* Yo… 4 a Sopa de pollo. b Soufflé de calabaza. c Una cerveza. 5 a Because the food tastes good, the service is good, the prices are low and it's a nice place. b They serve fish, seafood and meat. 6 a Potatoes and tomatoes b It is difficult to imagine European cuisine without these products. 7 a Tortillas, like maize bread. Another basic ingredient in Mexican food is chilli. b The staple food in Central America is maize. c A typical dish in many Caribbean and South American countries is chicken and rice. d Argentinians and Uruguayans prefer to eat beef.

Test yourself

1 a lo, Lo b las, Las c me d se la e nos 2 a Chuletas de cerdo con legumbres mixtas para mí. b Quiero pescado a la plancha con puré. c Un agua mineral y una cerveza, por favor. d ¿Nos trae un helado de vainilla y una ensalada de fruta? e ¿Me puede traer un café, por favor?

Unit 6

Dialogues

1 a Quisiera ver esa maleta. b Es un poco cara. ¿Tiene una / otra más barata? c Esa no me gusta mucho. d Voy a llevar la negra. e ¿Puedo pagar con cheques de viaje? **2** Quisiera ver los / esos pantalones que están en la vitrina / el escaparate / Sí, esos / Talla (*size*) / Los quiero en (*colour*) / ¿Me los puedo probar? **3** a ¿Cuánto valen / cuestan los tomates? / ¿Qué precio tienen …? b ¿Qué precio tienen los mangos? c Deme dos libras / kilos. d Quiero un kilo y medio. **4** a ¿Dónde está la oficina de correos? b ¿Cuánto vale / cuesta enviar una carta a (*destination*)? c Quisiera tres estampillas / sellos de ochocientos pesos.

Practice

1 Quisiera ver ese 'bolso' que está en la vitrina. / Ese, el café (*or* marrón). / Es muy bonito. ¿Es de cuero? / ¿Cuánto cuesta? / ¿(No) tiene otro más barato? / Me gusta mucho. / Lo voy a llevar. ¿Puedo pagar con tarjeta de crédito? / Sí, es para regalo. **2** Quisiera ver (una chaqueta), por favor. / Talla … (*your size*). / ¿Qué colores tiene? / La prefiero en blanco. / No me gusta mucho el modelo. ¿Tiene otras? / Sí, esas me gustan más. / ¿Me la puedo probar? / Me queda muy bien. ¿Cuánto cuesta (*or* vale)? / Sí, la voy a llevar. / Voy a pagar en efectivo. **3** *Precio sin descuento*: 32,000 pesos. *Precio con descuento*: 28,800 pesos. *Color*: negro. *Número*: 42. **4** a Long and short sleeved sport shirts are on offer. b Men's trousers have a 30, 40 and 50% discount. c Todos los pantalones para caballeros. No incluye promociones. **5** a ¿Cuánto valen (*or* cuestan) los aguacates? b ¿Tiene mangos? c ¿Qué precio tienen los duraznos? d Quiero un kilo de zanahorias. e Deme una lechuga. f Quiero dos repollos. g Eso es todo. h ¿Cuánto es? **6** mandar *or* enviar; a; pesos; estampilla; de; Eso; es; tres mil cuatrocientos; buzón; a. **7** A bedroom suite, a double sofabed, a 10-foot refrigerator, a washing machine, a TV table, a stereo system, a 14" TV. The total is 1,050,000 pesos.

Test yourself

1 a esos b ese c eso d esas 2 a todo b toda c otra d otro
3 a Me gustan todos. Son más baratos también. b Me gusta ese
bolso/esa cartera. ¿Y a ti? c A Ema le gusta jugar al tenis, y a mí
también. d (A nosotros) No nos gusta mucho ese hotel. El otro
es mejor.

Unit 7

Dialogues

1 Iré a Cuba con un amigo / Vamos a estar cuatro días en La
Habana y tres días en Santiago de Cuba. Y tú, ¿qué piensas
hacer? / Es un país muy lindo. Espero que lo pases muy bien.
2 a No, not at this time of the year. b She proposes to take
something for the rain.

Practice

1 Pienso ir a México y Quito. / No, voy a estar allí doce días en
total. / Sí, es un tour y no es muy caro. Cuesta mil quinientos
dólares. / Sí, incluye el pasaje aéreo (or el vuelo), hoteles de cuatro
estrellas, excursiones y traslados. / No, voy a viajar con un colega
(or amigo/a). Y tú ¿qué vas a hacer este verano? 2 a Coyoacán
is a typical district, with good restaurants and some important
monuments. b You will be able to visit the Frida Khalo Museum.
c Cuernavaca and Taxco. d No. 3 a It is quite pleasant. b It is a
little cold. c It does not rain much. d A sweater for the mornings
and evenings. 4 está; tiene; hay; tiene. 5 Facilities include air
conditioning in the rooms, water bed, jacuzzi, suites with a pool,
satellite TV and piped music. 6 a It has 216 rooms. b It has two
restaurants. c It has a swimming pool, conference rooms, a casino
and a disco. 7 a Voy a ir (or Iré) al banco. b Voy a tener (or Tendré
or Tengo) una reunión con el director de producción. c No, voy

a almorzar con el gerente. d Voy a estar (*or* Estaré *or* Estoy) libre entre las dos y las tres. 8 a F. b V. c V. d She says Lima is a nice, big and modern city, which retains some of the characteristics of colonial culture. e Lima has nice beaches, museums and zoos. f The weather is warm and there is almost no rain. 9 a Es una ciudad grande / mediana / pequeña / moderna / antigua / industrial / agrícola. b Tiene ... habitantes. c (No) hace mucho frío. *or* (No) llueve mucho. *or* En verano (generalmente) hace calor (*or* sol). 10 a No, en México está nublado. b En Londres está despejado. c No, en París está despejado. d En Madrid está lloviendo (*or* lluvioso). e La temperatura mínima será de doce grados. La máxima será de veintidós.

Test yourself

1 a saldrán, nos quedaremos b harás, podré, tendré c enviaré, invitaré d llegarán, estarán e venderá, comprará 2 a ¿Qué piensas hacer este sábado? b Pablo y Sara van a pasar unos días con nosotros. c Llegan el próximo viernes/viernes próximo. d Pensamos viajar a Ecuador. e ¿Cuánto tiempo se van a quedar/ van a quedarse?

Unit 8

Dialogues

1 a ¿A qué hora sale el tren? b ¿A qué hora llega? c ¿Cuánto cuesta un boleto de ida y vuelta? d ¿Tiene boletos para el viernes 12? Quiero dos. 2 a El desayuno es aparte. b ¿Cuántos días van a quedarse? c Dos días solamente. d Nos vamos el martes. 3 a ¿Tiene una habitación individual / sencilla? b ¿Tiene baño la habitación? / ¿La habitación tiene baño? c Tiene agua caliente? d ¿Sirven desayuno? 4 a ¿Qué haces aquí? b Estoy aquí de vacaciones. c Nos vamos pasado mañana. d Llevamos dos días (aquí) solamente.

Practice

1 Buenos días. ¿A qué hora sale el próximo bus a/para Valparaíso? –
¿Cuánto cuesta el pasaje/boleto de ida y vuelta? – Quiero dos
pasajes/boletos de ida y vuelta. – ¿A qué hora llega el bus a
Valparaíso? **2** Voy a viajar a Concepción. – Me voy el veinte de
noviembre. – Voy a viajar en tren y (en) bus. – Demora cinco horas
a Chillán y de Chillán a Concepción es una hora en bus. – Voy a
volver el veinticinco. **3** *Ud*: Buenos días. ¿Tiene una habitación?
Recepcionista: Sí, sí tenemos. ¿Quiere una habitación doble o
sencilla? *Ud*: Sencilla. ¿Cuánto vale? *R*: Veinticinco mil pesos.
Ud: ¿Está incluido el desayuno? *R*: No, el desayuno es aparte.
¿Cuánto tiempo va a quedarse? *Ud*: Cinco días solamente. *R*: Bien,
me da su nombre, por favor. *Ud*: (*Say your name.*) *R*: ¿Cómo se
escribe? *Ud*: (*Spell your name.*) *R*: ¿Y la dirección? *Ud*: (*Give your
address.*) *R*: Gracias. Su habitación es la 320, en el tercer piso.
Aquí tiene la llave. El ascensor está al fondo. **4** a They are weekly
departures. b By plane. c By bus. d Four nights. e All meals, rafting
equipment and bilingual Spanish-English guides. **5** a ¿Cuánto
tiempo llevas en Santiago?, Llevo un año en Santiago. b ¿Cuánto
tiempo hace que vives en esta casa?, Hace seis meses que vivo en
esta casa/Vivo en esta casa desde hace seis meses. c ¿Cuánto tiempo
hace que practicas yoga?, Hace un año que practico yoga/Practico
yoga desde hace un año. d ¿Cuánto tiempo llevas estudiando
inglés?, Llevo tres años estudiando inglés. e ¿Cuánto tiempo hace
que conoces a Mario?, Hace cuatro años que conozco a Mario/
Conozco a Mario desde hace cuatro años. f ¿Cuánto tiempo llevas
trabajando en esta empresa?, Llevo ocho meses trabajando en esta
empresa. **6** a F. b F. c V. d F. **7** a Most people in Latin America
travel by bus. b In Mexico, there is a first-class bus service with air
conditioning and toilet. Seats can be booked in advance, and the
service is much more comfortable than the second-class service.
c During holiday time you have to book in advance because many
people travel by bus.

Test yourself

a sale b llega c boletos/pasajes, ida d para, para e escribe f puede,
hablo g desde h que i llevas j llevo

Unit 9

Dialogues

1 a ¿Puede repetir su nombre? **b** ¿Cuándo hizo la reserva? **c** No la hice yo. **2 a** ¿Aló? **b** She went out to have lunch with a client. **c** He says he arrived in Santiago yesterday and that he is at the hotel Santiago Park Plaza. **3** Buenas tardes / noches. ¿Podría decirme si volvió Alfonso? / De parte de (*your name*) **4** Estuve en Santiago hace dos años. Me gustó mucho. / Llegué el sábado en la mañana. / Fue un poco largo.

Practice

1 *Ud*: Buenas tardes. Mi nombre es … (*name*). Tengo una habitación reservada. *Recepcionista*: Perdone, ¿puede repetir su nombre, por favor? *Ud*: (*Say your name again and spell it.*) *R*: ¿Cuándo hizo la reserva (*or* reservación)? *Ud*: No la hice yo, mi secretaria reservó la habitación por teléfono desde (*town*) hace cinco días más o menos. *R*: Ah sí, aquí está. Es la habitación número cincuenta en el quinto piso. ¿Podría llenar esta ficha, si es tan amable? **2 a** ¿Aló? **b** Quiero el anexo dos, cinco, cinco, dos (*or* veinticinco cincuenta y dos), por favor. **c** Quisiera hablar con el señor Juan Miguel García, por favor. *or* ¿Está el señor …? **d** ¿De parte de quién? – De parte de (*your name*). **e** Encantado de conocerlo, señor García. **f** Por favor, dígale que llamó … (*your name*). Llegué a Santiago hace dos días y estoy en el hotel Plaza, en la habitación número cincuenta. **3 a** Carmen Puig, from Caracas, needs to speak to señor Solís urgently. She wants him to phone her at the Sheraton Hotel, room 500, where she is staying. But it has to be now, as she is leaving for Caracas tomorrow. **b** Marilú Pérez came to see señor Solís. She is staying at the Gala Hotel, in room 324. The telephone number is 687951. **4** fue, fui, estuvimos, entramos, gustó, levanté, tomé. **5 a** ¿Cuándo llegó (usted)? **b** ¿Qué tal el viaje? **c** ¿Volvió (ya) la señorita Alonso? **d** ¿Es la primera vez que viene (usted) a Santiago? **e** ¿Le gustó Chile? **f** ¿Cenó (usted) ya? **6 a** She went to the coast with her family. **b** They stayed in a hotel opposite the beach. **c** She says the place is pleasant, quiet, has wonderful beaches and that the air is very clean. d Salimos mucho, tomamos el sol, nadamos, hicimos deportes. **7** a Fui a ... (*place*). b Fui solo/a / acompañado/a. c Me quedé en ... (*place*). d Estuve ... (*length of time*) allí. e *Possible replies*: nadé, tomé el sol, salí a pasear, fui a bailar, comí mucho, bebí mucho, etc. f Volví hace (una semana).

Test yourself

a llegó, llegaron, llegué b pasamos, pasaron c bebí, bebió d hiciste, hice e tuve, tuvo f fuimos, fueron, fueron g vinieron, vine h quisieron, quiso i dijimos, dijo j vi, viste

---

Unit 10

Dialogues

1 a-3, b-1, c-4, d-2. **2** era, estaba, era, era, tenía, compartía, estudiaba, era, trabajaba, era.

Practice

1 vivía; trabajaba; viajaba; pasaba; compartía; se llamaba; vivían; era; tenía; estaba; gustaba; había. **2** a Ella vivía en Bariloche. b Trabajaba como guía en una agencia de viajes. c Era muy agradable. d Estaba frente al lago. e La vida era muy tranquila y a veces un poco monótona. f Porque ella extrañaba a su familia. **3** a Tenía dos dormitorios. b Tenía dos baños. c La cocina estaba entre el dormitorio dos y el estar-comedor. d Había una cama. **4** a V. b F. c F. d V. e F. **5** a Hace cinco/diez años yo vivía en ... (*town or old address*). b Estaba soltero/a / casado/a. c Vivía con ... (mis padres / mi novio/a / mi marido / mujer / mis hijos, etc.). d Estudiaba / Trabajaba. e Estudiaba / Trabajaba en ... (*place*). *or* Trabajaba en una empresa / compañía / un colegio que se llamaba ... (*name*). f (No) me gustaba (mucho). g Mi casa / departamento / apartamento era grande / chico / agradable / cómodo, etc. **6** a ¿Dónde

vivías antes? b ¿En qué parte de Ecuador vivías? c ¿Qué hacías allá?
d ¿Y qué estás haciendo acá? 7 a He describes Buenos Aires as a
very large city, with many different corners, but with a unity. A city
with a cultural life, a city which has 'a soul'. b He likes its nightlife,
and the possibility it gives its people for expressing themselves.
He likes its cultural life. c He does not like the tendency the
'porteños' have towards sadness and melancholy. 8 Él era guapo. /
Ella era bonita / linda. Era trigueño/a (moreno/a *in certain
countries*), alto/a y delgado/a. Tenía pelo negro y ojos verdes.
Tenía unos … años Era de mi edad y era muy simpático/a.

Test yourself

1 a vi, estaba b era, tenía c conocí, presentó d llamó, invitó e
estaba, pude 2 a Ella me llamaba todos los días. Me gustaba
mucho. b Vivía con un/a amigo/a no lejos de mi casa. Tenían un
lindo/bonito departamento/apartamento. c Su amigo/a trabajaba
en un hospital. Era médico/a. d Yo los visitaba de vez en cuando.
e Vive en París ahora. Está estudiando francés.

Unit 11

Dialogues

1 a Nos gustaría / Quisiéramos alquilar / arrendar un coche / auto /
carro. b ¿Podría recomendarnos una agencia? c Está a media
cuadra de aquí. d Está cuatro cuadras más abajo, a la izquierda.
2 a A car with room for four people, comfortable and economical.
b 90 dollars per day. c It includes tax and insurance. c He wants it
for two days. 3 a He asks the attendant to fill the petrol tank and
to check the tyre pressure. b ¿Me podría decir …? 4 a ¿Podrían
repararme …? b ¿Para cuándo la quiere? c Se la puedo tener lista.
5 a Llamo desde la habitación veinticinco. b ¿Sería posible hacer
una llamada a (*place*) desde mi habitación? c Es una llamada de
persona a persona, al número (*number*). El nombre de la persona
es (*name*) *or* La persona se llama (*name*).

Practice

1 *Ud*: Buenos días. Quisiera alquilar un coche. ¿Me podría recomendar una agencia? *Recepcionista*: Sí, en la calle Agustinas, frente al cerro Santa Lucía, hay una agencia. *Ud*: ¿Frente al cerro Santa Lucía me dijo? *R*: Sí, dos cuadras más abajo por calle Moneda, después a la izquierda en Santa Lucía y a la izquierda otra vez en calle Agustinas. *Ud*: Gracias. **2** Quisiera alquilar un coche. ¿Qué me recomienda? / Quiero un coche chico, no demasiado caro. / ¿Cuánto cuesta el alquiler por día? / ¿Y por semana? / ¿Es con kilometraje ilimitado? / ¿El IVA y el seguro están incluidos? / Está bien. Lo llevaré (*or* Me lo llevo) / Sí, aquí está. / ¿Sería posible dejar el coche en otra ciudad? Me gustaría viajar al sur y dejar el coche allí. Quiero volver en tren. **3** a ¿Hay una estación de servicio por aquí? b Me lo llena, por favor. *or* ¿Podría llenármelo? c ¿Podría revisar el aceite y la presión de las ruedas, por favor? *or* Me revisa … d ¿Podría limpiar el parabrisas, por favor? *or* Me limpia … e ¿Me podría reparar esta llanta (*or* este neumático), por favor? *or* Me repara … f ¿Falta mucho para llegar a Santa Isabel?
4 *Telefonista*: ¿Dígame? *or* ¿Aló? *or* ¿Hola? *or* ¿Bueno? *Ud*: ¿Sería posible hacer una llamada internacional con cobro revertido desde mi habitación? *T*: Sí, cómo no. ¿Adónde quiere llamar? *Ud*: A … (*place*). *T*: ¿Y a qué número? *Ud*: (*telephone number*). *T*: ¿Y con quién desea hablar? *Ud*: Con … (*name*). *T*: ¿Su nombre, por favor? *Ud*: Me llamo *or* Mi nombre es … (*name*). *T*: Un momento, por favor. Cuelgue y yo lo vuelvo a llamar. **5** a Because he went there many years ago and its image is deeply engraved in him. b He would go with his family or friends, for fifteen or twenty days.
6 a grande b tradicional c gris o azul d ir al trabajo y salir a pasear.
7 a Me gustaría llamar a David en Nueva York. Tú tienes su número. ¿Me lo das? b Telefonista, quisiera hacer una llamada internacional desde mi habitación. ¿Sería posible? c Quiero llamar con cobro revertido. d ¿Le doy el nombre y el número de teléfono? e ¿Le dice que soy Nora Vargas y que lo llamo desde México? f ¿Podría decirme cuánto salió la llamada?

Test yourself

a Quisiéramos arrendar / alquilar un auto / coche / carro.
b ¿Cuánto es el alquiler / cuesta / arrendamiento? c Tax and
insurance are included. d There are still 2 km to get to the city.
e Shall I fill it up for you? f 2 g conmigo; contigo h ¿Me lo podría
reservar para mañana? i haría j sería.

Unit 12

Dialogues

1 a F b F c V 2 a Lléveme al aeropuerto, por favor. b Llévenos a la
calle San Martín, por favor. 3 a ¿Me da la cuenta de la habitación
ciento cincuenta? Me voy mañana en / por la mañana. b ¿Me
despierta a las siete y media? Tengo que estar en el aeropuerto a
las nueve. 4 Sí, tengo una maleta. Sí, tengo una mochila pequeña/
chica. Prefiero un asiento junto a la ventanilla. ¿Está retrasado
el vuelo?

Practice

1 Sí, es la primera vez. Me gusta mucho. Es un país bonito, aunque
todavía no he visto mucho. / No, todavía no he ido a Cusco (or
Todavía no he estado en ...), pero espero ir la próxima semana.
Voy a visitar Machu Picchu también. Me han dicho que es muy
interesante. ¿Usted ha estado en Europa alguna vez? / Sí, he estado
allí varias veces. Me gusta mucho España, especialmente el sur. /
Gracias. Estudié español en el colegio. ¿Usted habla inglés? / Está
bien. / No, gracias. Ya he tomado dos. Es suficiente. Y, además,
mañana tengo que levantarme temprano, así que debo volver
pronto al hotel. 2 a Sí, ya estuve allí. b No, todavía no lo he
visitado. c Sí, ya lo vi. d No, todavía no lo he conocido. 3 a She
was there when she was 11 years old. b She says the city is very
beautiful. It is a traditional city, as it still retains the characteristics
of Inca culture. c From Lima, you can travel to Cusco by bus, train

or plane. d The only way of getting to Machu Picchu is by train.
4 a Deme (*or* Me da) la cuenta, por favor b Escriba c Haga
d Díganos e Ilámeme f Suba g cierra / cierre. 5 a 6 b 3 c 1 d 5
e 2 f 4. 6 Recommendations for tourists. For your own security,
the National Tourist Service in our country makes the following
suggestions: Change your money and travellers cheques only in
banks or at authorised bureaux de change. Do not change money
in the street. Leave your valuables in the safe deposit box at your
hotel. Do not go out carrying large sums of money. When you
take a taxi, see what the meter shows, as that is the amount that
you will have to pay. In our country, there are no additional
surcharges. If possible, use the taxi services of your own hotel.
7 tu seguridad – te hace – cambia – no cambies – deja tus – tu
hotel – no salgas – observa – deberás – utiliza – tu propio.

Test yourself

a visto, tenido b hecho, estado, venido c vuelto, pasado d dicho,
escrito e deme, tengo f envíenos g se lo digas, se lo cuentes
h llámelo i dígale j tienes, dame

Unit 13

Dialogues

1 a Hizo escala en París. b por error. c Yo misma me encargaré
de buscarla. 2 a ¿En qué puedo servirle? b ¿No tendría una
(habitación) más tranquila? c Veré qué habitación puedo darle.
d Ahora mismo. e Acaba de irse la persona que estaba allí. 3 a It's
three or four blocks from the cathedral, on the left. b Go straight
on as far as the park, and then turn right. c Turn left at the corner
and continue as far as the end of that street. d When you reach the
square you will see a large yellow building. That is the museum.
4 a No dormí en toda la noche. b Fiebre no tengo. c No me siento
bien. d No creo que sea nada serio.

Practice

1 Recién llegué (*or* Acabo de llegar) en el vuelo trescientos diez de Hispanair que venía de … (*city or country*), pero desgraciadamente mi equipaje no ha llegado (*or* no llegó). / Traía dos maletas, una grande y una chica. Aquí tengo los tickets (*or* talones) del equipaje. Las dos maletas tenían etiquetas con mi nombre (*say your name*). / Espero que las encuentren. Tengo toda mi ropa en ellas y también unos regalos que traía para unos amigos.
2 a vayamos, b pasen, c envíen, d llegue, e haga, f venga, g guste, h llueva. **3** a El aire acondicionado no funcionó. b No había agua caliente. c El lavatorio estaba tapado / atascado. d En el baño no había toallas. e La habitación es muy ruidosa. No pude dormir anoche. f Quiero cambiarme a una habitación más tranquila.
4 a The man had asked for a seat in the non-smoking section of the plane. b The Venezuelan lady in the restaurant had ordered fish with mashed potatoes and the waiter brought her fish with fried potatoes instead. c The young Chilean lady ordered a seafood soup 15 minutes ago and it still hasn't arrived. **5** b **6** ir; salir; doble; doble; mano; cuadras; de nada. **7** No me siento bien. Tengo dolor de estómago (*or* Me duele el estómago) y tengo diarrea. / Empezó anoche. Salí a comer (*or* cenar) con unos amigos y comí pescado y papas fritas. Seguramente fue eso. Más tarde, cuando volví al hotel empecé a sentirme mal. / Sí, he vomitado y parece que tengo fiebre también. / Espero que sí. **8** a 11.00 a 13.00; 18.00 a 21.00.
b 1016 c 325228 **9** Surgery days and hours are Mondays from 4.00 to 6.00 p.m. and Wednesdays and Fridays from 11.00 a.m. to 1.00 p.m. **10** a Espero que podamos encontrar/que encontremos una habitación. b No creo que sea importante. c Estoy seguro/a de que vendrán. d Puede que llueva. e Creo que está en la oficina. f La invitaremos para que la veas. g Nos quedaremos aquí hasta que terminemos. h Cuando llegue Sara, por favor dile que quiero hablar con ella.

Test yourself

1 a salir b encontrará c sea d llegue e reserven **2** a siga b doble c llegar d siento, duele e tengo.

Spanish–English vocabulary

a *to, at, on*
a la derecha *on the right*
a la izquierda *on the left*
a partir de *starting in / on*
a pesar de *although, despite, in spite of*
a sus órdenes *at your service*
a veces *sometimes*
abajo: más – *further down*
abrazar *to embrace, hug*
abrir *to open*
abuelos *(m, pl) grandparents*
abundar *to be plentiful*
acá *here*
acabar de *to have just*
aceite *(m) oil*
acerca de *about*
acogedor/a *welcoming*
acompañado/a *accompanied*
acostarse *to go to bed*
activar *to activate*
acuerdo: de – *fine, OK, agreed*
adelante *see:* **en adelante**
además *besides*
adentro *inside*
adicional *additional*
adiós *goodbye*
aeropuerto *(m) airport*
afuera *outside*
agencia *(f) agency*
agencia de viajes *(f) travel agency*
agradable *pleasant*

agua *(f) water*
aguacate *(m) avocado*
ahí *there*
ahora *now*
ahora mismo *right now*
ahorita *right now (diminutive)*
aire *(m) air*
aire acondicionado *(m) air conditioning*
al (a + el) *to the, on the, at the*
al final de *at the end of*
al fondo de *at the end of*
al lado de *next to*
alberca *(f) swimming pool (Mex)*
alcoba *(f) bedroom*
alegrarse *to be glad*
alegre *lively*
algo *something*
algún *(m) some, any*
alguna *(f) some, any*
alguna vez *ever*
algunos/as *some*
alimento *(m) food*
allá *there*
allí *there*
alma *(f) soul*
almacenes *(m, pl) department store*
almíbar: en – *in syrup*
almorzar *to have lunch*
almuerzo *(m) lunch; –*
de negocios *business –*
aló *hello (on the phone)*

alojamiento *(m) accommodation*
alquilar *to rent*
alquiler *(m) rent*
altitud *(f) altitude*
alto/a *tall; top; upper*
alubias *(f, pl) beans (Spain)*
ama de casa *(f) housewife*
amable *kind*
amarillo/a *yellow*
ambiente *(m) atmosphere*
ambos/as *both*
América del Sur *South America*
americano/a *American*
amigo/a *(m/f) friend*
amplio/a *wide*
andén *(m) platform*
anexo *(m) extension (Chile)*
animado/a *animated*
año *(m) year*
año pasado *(m) last year*
anoche *last night*
antelación: con *– in advance*
antena *(f) aerial, antenna*
antes *before*
antiquísimo/a *very ancient*
anunciar *to announce*
apacible *peaceful*
aparecer *to appear*
aparte *separate*
apellido *(m) surname, family name*
aperitivo *(m) aperitif, appetizer*
aprender *to learn*
aprovechar *to take the opportunity, take advantage*
aproximadamente *approximately*

aquí *here*
arborizado/a *with trees*
arquitecto *(m) architect*
arquitectónica *architectural*
arquitectura *(f) architecture*
arroz *(m) rice*
artículo *(m) article*
arvejas *(f, pl) peas*
asado/a *roast*
ascensor *(m) lift/elevator*
así *thus*
asiento *(m) seat*
asistir *to attend*
atender *to see (a patient)*
atendido/a *served*
aunque *although, even though*
auto *(m) car*
autobús *(m) bus*
autorización *(f) permission*
autorizado/a *authorized*
avenida *(f) avenue*
aventura *(f) adventure*
avión *(m) plane*
ayer *yesterday*
azafata *(f) stewardess*
azteca *(m / f) Aztec*
azul *blue*

bajar *to go down*
bajo/a *low, lower*
balsa *(f) raft*
bañarse *to take a bath*
banco *(m) bank*
baño *(m) toilet, bathroom*
bar *(m) bar*
barato/a *cheap*
barrio *(m) district, area*
barroco/a *baroque*

base: a – de containing
bastante quite
beber to drink
bebida gaseosa (f) fizzy drink
bien well; ¡qué – ! great!
bienvenido/a welcome
bistec de lomito (m) fillet steak
blanco/a white
blusa (f) blouse
boleto (m) ticket
bolso (m) handbag, bag
bonito/a pretty
botella (f) bottle
brasileño/a Brazilian
brasilero/a Brazilian
brevedad: a la – as soon as possible
buen día good morning
buenas noches good evening/ night
buenas tardes good afternoon/ evening
bueno well
bueno/a good
buenos días good morning
bulla (f) noise
bus (m) bus
buscar to look for
buzón (m) post box

caballero (m) gentleman
cacahuete (m) peanut
cada each, every
caer mal to be ill (from food)
café (m) coffee, café
caja de seguridad (f) safe-deposit box
calabaza (f) pumpkin

calidad (f) quality
cálido/a warm
caliente hot
calle (f) street
calor (m) heat; (adj) warm, hot
cama (f) bed
cama de agua (f) water bed
camarones (m, pl) prawns, shrimps
cambiar to change
cambiarse to move
caminar to walk
camino (m) road
camión (m) bus (Mex), lorry, truck
camioneta (f) van
camisa (f) shirt
campo (m) countryside
cansado/a tired
cantidad (f) amount, quantity
capacidad (f) room
Caribe (m) Caribbean
carne (f) meat; – **de vaca** beef
carne asada roast / grilled meat
carnet de conducir (m) driving licence, driver's license
caro/a expensive
carrera (f) street (Colombia)
carretera (f) highway
carro (m) car
carta (f) menu, letter
casa (f) house, home
casa de cambio (f) bureau de change
casado/a married
caso (m) case; **en todo –** in any –
castellano (m) Castilian

catalán/catalana *from Catalonia*
catedral *(f) cathedral*
categoría *(f) category*
cena *(f) dinner*
cenar *to have dinner*
centro *(m) centre*
centro cívico *(m) town hall*
Centroamérica *Central America*
cerca *near*
cerdo *(m) pig, pork*
cerrado/a *closed*
cerrar *to close*
cerveza *(f) beer*
chamarra *(f) jacket (Mex)*
champiñones *(m, pl) mushrooms*
chao *goodbye*
chaqueta *(f) jacket*
cheque de viaje *(m) traveller's cheque, traveler's check*
chícharos *(m, pl) peas*
chico/a *boy, girl*
chico/a *small*
chileno/a *Chilean*
chofer *(m) driver*
chuleta *(f) chop;* **– de ternera/ cerdo** *veal/pork –*
cine *(m) cinema*
cirugía *(f) surgery*
ciudad *(f) city*
claramente *clearly*
claro (que sí) *certainly, of course*
clases: dar – *to teach*
cliente *(m / f) client*
clima *(m) climate*
coche *(m) car*
coche dormitorio *(m) sleeping car*
cocinar *to cook*
colega *(m / f) colleague*

colegio *(m) school*
colgar *to hang up*
colombiano/a *Colombian*
color *(m) colour*
combinación *(f) combination*
comedor *(m) dining room*
comer *to eat*
comida *(f) meal, food, dinner*
cómo *how?, what?*
como *such as, like, as*
cómo no *certainly*
como también *as well as*
cómodo/a *comfortable*
compañero/a de trabajo *colleague*
compañía *(f) company*
comparación *(f) comparison*
compartir *to share*
completo/a *complete, full*
compra *(f) shopping*
comprar *to buy*
computadora *(f) computer*
computarizado/a *computerized*
con *with*
concierto *(m) concert*
concluyendo *finishing*
conectar *to connect*
conmigo *with me*
conocer *to know*
conseguir *to get*
conservar *to retain*
consultas *(f, pl) surgery hours*
contar *to tell*
contar con *to have, depend on*
contento/a *happy*
contigo *with you (fam sing)*
continuar *to continue*
contribución *(f) contribution*

convertirse to become
copa (f) glass
correo (m) post office
correr to run
corto/a short
costa (f) coast
costar to cost
costoso/a expensive
creer to believe, think
crema (f) soup; cream
crema de espárragos (f)
  asparagus soup
crema del día (f) soup of the day
creo que sí I think so
cuadra (f) block
cuál what?, which?
cuando when
cuándo when?
cuánto how much?
cuánto tiempo how long?
cuanto: en – a as regards
cuántos how many?
cuarto (m) quarter, room
cuarto/a fourth
cuenta (f) bill
cuero (m) leather
culpa (f) fault
cultura (f) culture
curso (m) course
cuyo/a whose

damasco (m) apricot
danza (f) dance, dancing
dar paseos to walk
dar to give
de of, from, on
de nada don't mention it, not at all
¿de qué parte? what part of?

de vez en cuando from time to
  time
deber must, to have to
debido a due to
decidir to decide
decir to say
decorado/a decorated
dejar to leave
dejar de: no – not to fail
del (de + el) of the
demasiado/a too, too much
deme give me
demora (f) delay
demorar to take (time)
dentro de within
departamento (m) flat,
  apartment, (train) compartment
dependiente/a shop assistant,
  salesclerk
deporte (m) sport
deportivo/a sport (adj)
derecha (f) right
desayunar to have breakfast
desayuno (m) breakfast
descansar to rest
describir to describe
descuento (m) discount
desde from
desea: ¿qué – ? what would you
  like?, can I help you?
desear to wish, to want
despejado/a clear
despertar to wake up
después after, afterwards
destino (m) destination
detenerse to stop
detrás behind
devolver to return (something)

día *(m) day*
día siguiente *(m) following day*
día: al *– valid*
diario *per day*
diarrea *(f) diarrhoea*
días de semana *(f, pl) week days*
diciembre *December*
dieta *(f) diet*
diferente *different*
difícil *difficult*
dígale *tell him/her*
dígame *Hello (on the phone), Can I help you?*
digamos *let's say*
digas: ¡no me – *! you don't say!*
dinero *(m) money*
dirección *(f) address*
director/a de producción *production manager*
discoteca *(f) disco*
disculpe/a *I am sorry, excuse me*
disfrutar *to enjoy*
distancia *(f) distance;* **viaje de larga** *– long distance travel*
Distrito Federal *(m) Federal District (Mexico City)*
doblar *to turn*
doler *to hurt, feel pain*
dolor *(m) pain*
dolor de estómago *(m) stomach ache*
domingo *(m) Sunday*
dónde *where?*
donde *where*
dormir *to sleep*
dormitorio *(m) bedroom*
durante *during*
durazno *(m) peach*

e *and (before i)*
económica: clase – *(f) economy class*
edad *(f) age*
edificio *(m) building*
efectivo *see:* **en efectivo**
eficiente *efficient*
ejecutivo/a *executive*
el *(m) the*
electrodomésticos *(m, pl) household electrical goods*
elevador *(m) lift, elevator*
ello *this, that*
embarcar *to board*
empanada *(f) pasty, turnover*
empezar *to begin*
empleado/a *employee, clerk*
empresa *(f) company*
empresa constructora *(f) construction company*
en *in, on, at*
en adelante *onwards*
en efectivo *in cash*
en todo caso *in any case*
encantado/a *pleased to meet you*
encantar *to love, like*
encargarse *to be responsible, see to*
encontrar *to find*
encontrarse *to be, be situated*
energía *(f) energy*
enero *January*
enfrente *in front*
enorme *huge*
ensalada *(f) salad*
ensalada de fruta *(f) fruit salad*
ensalada mixta *(f) mixed salad*
enseguida *right away*

enseñar *to show, teach*
entonces *then*
entrar *to begin, start*
entre *between, among*
entrevista *(f) interview*
entristecer *to grow sad*
enviar *to send*
época *(f) time*
equipaje *(m) luggage, baggage*
equipaje de mano *(m) hand luggage/baggage*
equipo *(m) equipment*
equipo *(m)* **de sonido** *stereo system*
error: por – *by mistake*
es decir *that is to say*
escala: hacer – *to stop over*
escalera *(f) stairs*
escribir *to write, spell*
escritorio *(m) desk*
escuchar *to listen*
ese/a *that*
esos/as *(pl) those*
espárragos *(f, pl) asparagus*
especialmente *especially*
especie *(f) kind*
esperar *to hope, wait, expect*
esposo/a *husband, wife*
esquina *(f) corner*
establecimiento *(m) establishment*
estación *(f) station, season*
estación de metro *(f) underground/subway station*
estación de servicio *(f) petrol station*
estadía *(f) stay*
Estados Unidos *(m, pl) United States*

estampilla *(f) stamp*
estancia *(f) stay*
estar *to be*
estar seguro/a *to be sure*
este/a *this*
estomacal *stomach (adj)*
estómago *(m) stomach*
estos/as *(pl) these*
estrella *(f) star*
estudiante *(m / f) student*
estudiar *to study*
estudios *(m, pl) studies*
estupendo/a *very good, fantastic*
etiqueta *(f) label*
europeo/a *European*
excitante *exciting*
experimentado/a *experienced*
explicadas *explained*
expreso *(m) express train*
extrañar *to miss*
extremadamente *extremely*

falda *(f) skirt*
faltar *to be lacking*
familia *(f) family*
famoso/a *famous*
favorito/a *favourite*
febrero *February*
felicitar *to congratulate*
feria *(f) fair*
ferrocarril *(m) railway*
ficha *(f) registration form*
fiebre *(f) fever*
filete de pescado *(m) fillet of fish*
fin *(m) end*
fin *(m)* **de temporada** *end of season*
fin de semana *(m) weekend*

final: al – de *at the end of*
finalmente *finally*
fino/a *good, of good quality*
firma *(f) signature*
flan *(m) creme caramel*
fondo *see: al fondo de*
fono *(m) telephone*
forma *(f) way*
fractura *(f) fracture*
frente a *opposite*
frente: de – *straight on*
fresa *(f) strawberry*
frijoles *(m, pl) beans*
frío *(m) cold*
frito/a *fried*
fritura *(f) fried dish*
frívolo/a *frivolous*
frontera *(f) border*
fruta *(f) fruit*
frutilla *(f) strawberry*
fuera *outside*
fumador *smoker*
fumar *to smoke*
fundamentalmente *essentially*

galleta *(f) biscuit*
ganar *to earn, win*
general: en – *generally*
general: por lo – *usually*
generalmente *generally, usually*
gente *(f) people*
gerente *(m / f) manager*
gesticular *to gesticulate*
gloria *(f) glory*
gobierno *(m) government*
goma pinchada *(f) flat tyre*
gozar de *to enjoy*
gracias *thank you*
grado *(m) degree*

gran *big*
grande *big, great*
grave *serious*
gris *grey*
guía *(m / f) guide (person)*
guisado/a *stewed*
guisantes *(m, pl) peas (Spain)*
gustar *to like*
gusto: buen – *(m) good taste*
gusto: mucho – *pleased to meet you*

habas *(f, pl) broad beans*
había *there was / were*
habitación *(f) room*
habitante *(m) inhabitant*
habla: países de – hispana *Spanish-speaking countries*
hablar *to speak*
hace *for, ago*
hace sol *it is sunny*
hacer *to do, make*
hacer deportes *to practise sports*
hacer escala *to stop over*
hacer frío / calor *to be cold / warm*
harto *a lot*
hasta *until, as far as*
hasta luego *good bye*
hay *there is, there are*
helado *(m) ice-cream*
hermano/a *brother / sister*
hermanos *(m, pl) brothers and sisters*
hijo/a *son, daughter*
hijos *(m, pl) children*
Hispanoamérica *Spanish-speaking countries in the Americas*

hispanoamericano/a *Spanish American*

historia *(f) history*

hola *hello*

hora *(f) time, hour*

hora: a la *– on time*

horario *(m) times, timetable*

horario de trabajo *(m) working hours*

hotelería *(f) hotel trade/business*

hoy *today*

hoy en día *nowadays*

huésped *(m / f) guest*

ida *(f) single (ticket)*

ida y vuelta *(f) return (ticket), round trip ticket*

idioma *(m) language*

iglesia *(f) church*

ilimitado/a *unlimited*

imaginar *to imagine*

importar: si no le importa *if you don't mind*

impuesto *(m) tax*

incluido/a *included*

incluir *to include*

independiente *independent*

individual *(adj) single*

infección *(f) infection*

informe *(m) report*

ingeniería *(f) engineering*

ingeniero/a *engineer*

Inglaterra *England*

inglés *(m) English*

inglesa *(f) English*

inmediatamente *immediately*

inmediato: de *– immediately*

inmensamente *immensely*

instituto de idiomas *(m) school of languages*

interesante *interesting*

interesar *to be interested*

interior *at the back*

interrupción *(f) interruption*

invierno *(m) winter*

invitar *to invite*

ir *to go*

ir de compras *to go shopping*

irse *to leave*

izquierda *(f) left*

jardín *(m) garden*

jefe *(m) boss, manager*

judías *(f, pl) beans (Spain)*

jugo *(m) juice*

junto a *next to*

juntos *together*

juvenil *young (adj)*

kilometraje *(m) mileage*

kilometraje ilimitado *(m) unlimited mileage*

la *(f) the, it, her*

laborar *to work*

lado *see:* **al lado de**

lago *(m) lake*

largo/a *long*

las *(f, pl) the, them*

lástima *(f) pity, shame*

lavabo *(m) washbasin; toilet, restroom*

lavadora *(f) washing machine*

le *to him, to her, to you (pol)*

lechuga *(f) lettuce*

leer *to read*

legumbre (f) vegetable, pulse
lejos far
lengua (f) language, tongue
lento/a slow
levantarse to get up
leve slight
libra (f) pound
libre free
licencia de conducir (m) driving licence
limpiar to clean
lindo/a pretty, beautiful
listo/a ready
liviano/a light
llamada (f) telephone call
llamados/as called, so called
llamar to call
llamarse to be called
llave (f) key; water tap
llegada (f) arrival
llegar to arrive, get to
llenar to fill in
lleno/a full
llevar to carry, take, have
llevar to take
llevarse bien to get on well
llover to rain
lluvia (f) rain
lluvioso/a rainy
lo you (pol), him, it
lo siento I am sorry
localizar to trace, look for
Londres London
los (m, pl) the
lugar (m) place
luna (f) moon
lunes (m) Monday
luxación (f) dislocation

madre (f) mother
maestro/a teacher
mal bad
maleta (f) suitcase
maletín (m) briefcase
mamá (f) mother
mañana tomorrow
mañana (f) morning
mandar to send
manejar to drive
manga (f) sleeve
mantequilla (f) butter
manzana (f) apple
mar (m) sea
maravilla (f) marvel
maravilloso/a marvellous
marca (f) make
marcar to indicate, show
marido (m) husband
mariscos (m, pl) seafood
marrón brown
más more, else; ¿**qué** – ? what else?
más o menos more or less
materno/a maternal
mayor elder, eldest, bigger
mayoría (f) majority
me me, to me, myself
mediano/a medium sized
mediante through
médico/a doctor
medio/a half
mediodía (m) midday
mejor better
mejor: el/la – the best
melocotón (m) peach
menor younger, youngest
mensaje (m) message

menú del día (m) set menu
menudo: a – often
mercado (m) market
mes (m) month
mesa (f) table
mesero/a waiter / waitress
metro (m) underground railway/ subway
mexicano/a Mexican
mezcla (f) mixture
mí me
mi my
millón (m) million
minuto (m) minute
mira look (fam)
mirar to look
mire look (pol)
mismo/a same, itself
mitad (f) half
mixto/a mixed
mochila (f) rucksack
modelo (m) model
momentito (m) moment (diminutive)
moneda (f) coin
monedero (m) purse
monótono/a monotonous
montaña (f) mountain
monumento (m) monument
mostaza (f) mustard
mostrador (m) desk
mostrar to show
movimiento (m) movement
mozo (m) waiter
muchas gracias thank you very much
mucho gusto pleased to meet you

mucho/a much, a lot
muchos/as many
mueble (m) furniture
mundialmente world wide
mundo (m) world
museo (m) museum
música (f) music
música ambiental (f) piped music
muy very
muy bien very well

nacional national
nacionalidad (f) nationality
nada nothing
nadar to swim
naranja orange (colour)
naturaleza (f) wild life, nature
negocio (m) business
negro/a black
neumático (m) tyre
nevar to snow
nevera (f) refrigerator
ni nor
niño/a boy/girl, child
niños (m, pl) children
no dejar de not to fail to
no me digas you don't say
no me importa I don't mind
noche (f) night
nocturno/a night (adj)
nombre (m) name
nombre completo (m) full name
normalmente normally
norte (m) north
Norteamérica North America
nos us, to us

nublado/a cloudy
nuestro/a our
Nuevo Mundo (m) New World
número (m) number
número de teléfono (m)
  telephone number
nunca never

o or
objetos de valor (m, pl)
  valuables
observar to observe
ocupado/a occupied, engaged
ocurrir to happen, occur
oferta (f) offer
oficial official
oficina (f) office
ofrecer to offer
ojalá let's hope so
ómnibus (m) bus
opcionalmente optionally
oportunidad (f) opportunity,
  chance
orden: a la – / a sus órdenes
  can I help you?
oscuro/a dark
otoño (m) autumn
otra vez again
otro/a other, another
otros/as others

padre (m) father
padres (m, pl) parents
pagar to pay
país (m) country
paisaje (m) landscape
palacio (m) palace
pan de maíz (m) maize bread

pantalones (m, pl) trousers,
  pants
papa (f) potato
papá (m) father
papás (m pl) parents
papas doradas / fritas (f, pl)
  golden potatoes / chips
papaya (f) papaya, pawpaw
par (m) pair
para for, to, in order to
para que so that
para servirle at your service,
  you're welcome
paralela parallel
parecer to seem
pariente (m / f) relative
parque (m) park
parte (f): **¿de – de quién?** who is
  speaking?
partir to depart, leave
pasado past
pasado mañana the day after
  tomorrow
pasaje (m) ticket
pasaje aéreo (m) air fare
pasaporte (m) passport
pasar to come in, spend (time)
pasar: ¿qué le pasa? what's the
  matter with you?
pasarlo bien to have a good
  time
pasear to go for a walk/ride
paseo (m) walk, avenue
pasillo (m) corridor
paso (m) step
pasos: a pocos – near
pastel (m) pie, cake
pastel de queso (m) cheesecake

pastilla *(f) tablet, pill*
patata *(f) potato (Spain)*
pedir *to ask for*
pedir hora *to ask for an appointment (doctor, etc.)*
película *(f) film*
pensar *to think*
pensión *(f) boarding house*
pequeño/a *small*
perdón *excuse me, sorry*
perdone/a *excuse me, I'm sorry (pol/fam)*
periódico *(m) newspaper*
periodista *(m / f) journalist*
pero *but*
persona *(f) person*
persona a persona *personal (telephone call)*
pescado *(m) fish*
pescado frito *(m) fried fish*
peso *(m) Latin American currency*
pie *(m) foot*
pieza *(f) room*
pinchazo *(m) puncture*
pintura *(f) painting*
pirámide *(f) pyramid*
piscina *(f) swimming pool*
piso *(m) floor*
plancha: a la *– grilled*
planta alta *(f) upper floor*
planta baja *(f) ground floor*
plata *(f) money, silver*
plato *(m) dish, plate*
plato del día *(m) today's special*
playa *(f) beach*
plaza *(f) square*

plazoleta *(f) small square*
plebeyo/a *commoner*
poco *a little*
pocos/as *few*
poder *to be able, can*
podríamos *we could*
policía *(f) police*
pollo *(m) chicken*
pollo asado / rostizado *roast chicken*
por *for, by, along, per*
por aquí *near here, nearby;* **pase** *– come in this way*
por ciento *per cent*
por ejemplo *for example*
por error *by mistake*
por favor *please*
por la noche *in the evening, at night*
por lo general *usually, generally*
por qué *why?*
por semana *per week*
por si acaso *just in case*
por supuesto *of course, certainly*
porotos *(m, pl) beans*
porque *because*
porteño/a *(m/f) inhabitant of Buenos Aires*
posgrado *postgraduate*
posible *possible*
posiblemente *possibly*
postal: tarjeta *– (f) postcard*
postre *(m) dessert*
precio *(m) price*
precioso/a *very beautiful*
predominar *to predominate*
preferentemente *mainly*

preferir *to prefer*
preguntar *to ask*
preocuparse *to worry*
presentar *to introduce*
presente *(m) present*
presión *(f) pressure*
primavera *(f) spring*
primero/a *first*
príncipe *(m) prince*
privado/a *private*
probador *(m) fitting room, changing room*
probar *to try on*
procedencia *(f) place of origin*
programa *(m) programme, program*
promedio *(m) average*
prometer *to promise*
pronto *soon*
propio/a *itself, own*
proporcionar *to provide*
próximo/a *next*
psicólogo/a *psychologist*
puerta *(f) gate, door*
puerta de embarque *(f) boarding gate*
pues *well*
puré de papa *(m) mashed potatoes*
puro/a *pure*

que *than, that*
qué *what?, which?, who?, how?*
quedar *to be left*
quedar *to fit*
quedar bien *to fit well*
quedarse *to stay*

querer *to want, love*
querido/a *dear*
queso *(m) cheese*
quien *who*
quién *who?*
quinto/a *fifth*
quisiera *I would like*
quizá(s) *perhaps*

rápidos *(m, pl) rapids*
razón: por esta *– for this reason*
realidad: en *– really*
realizar *to carry out*
realmente *really*
recado *(m) message*
recargo *(m) surcharge*
recepción *(f) reception*
recepcionista *(m/f) receptionist*
receta *(f) prescription*
recién *just (now)*
recomendar *to recommend*
reconfirmar *to reconfirm*
recorrido *(m) tour*
recuerdos *(m, pl) memories*
red ferroviaria *(f) railway network*
regalo *(m) gift, present*
regar *to water*
regresar *to come back*
reparar *to repair*
repetir *to repeat*
repollo *(m) cabbage*
reserva *(f) reservation*
reservación *(f) reservation, booking*
reservado/a *booked, reserved*
reservar *to book, reserve*
residencia *(f) house, residence*

retrasado/a *delayed*
retraso *(m) delay*
reunión *(f) meeting*
revisar *to check*
rey: a cuerpo de – *like a king*
rincón *(m) corner*
rodeado/a *surrounded*
rojo/a *red*
ropa *(f) clothing*
rueda *(f) wheel*
ruido *(m) noise*
ruidoso/a *noisy*

sábado *(m) Saturday*
saber *to know*
sala de conferencia *(f) conference room*
saldo *(m) sale, bargain*
salida *(f) departure*
salir *to go out*
salir *to leave; to work out, cost*
salir a *to go to*
salón *(m) railway carriage with wider and more comfortable seats (Chile)*
salsa *(f) sauce*
sanitario *(m) toilet, restroom*
se *to you*
se *yourself (pol), himself, herself, one*
sección *(f) area, section*
secretario/a *secretary*
seguir *to continue, follow, go on*
seguir derecho *to go straight on*
segundo/a *second*
seguramente *surely*
seguridad *(f) security*
seguro *(m) insurance*

seguro: estar – *to be sure*
seleccionado/a *chosen, of your choice*
semana *(f) week*
sencillez *(f) simplicity*
sencillo/a: habitación – *single room*
señor *Mr, sir*
señora *(f) lady, Mrs, wife*
señorita *(f) young lady, Miss*
sentarse *to sit*
sentirse *to feel*
ser *to be*
serio/a *serious*
servicio *(m) service*
servir *to serve*
servirse *to help oneself*
si *if, whether*
sí *yes*
siempre *always*
siéntate *sit down (fam)*
siéntense *sit down (pl)*
siguiente *following*
simpático/a *nice*
simplemente *simply*
sin *without*
situación *(f) situation*
situado/a *situated*
sobrino/a *nephew, niece*
sofá-cama *(m) sofa bed*
sol *(m) sun; Peruvian currency*
solamente *only*
soler: suele ser *it usually is*
sólo *only*
solo/a *alone*
soltero/a *single*
sopa *(f) soup*
sopa de pollo *(f) chicken soup*

sopa de verduras *(f) vegetable soup*
sorpresa *(f) surprise*
sos *you are (fam, Arg)*
su *your (pol), his, her*
suave *mild*
sueldo *(m) salary*
suerte *(f) luck*
suéter *(m) sweater*
suficiente *enough, suficient*
sugerencia *(f) suggestion*
sugerir *to suggest*
suma *(f) amount, sum*
supuesto: por *– of course*
sur *(m) south*

tableta *(f) tablet*
tal: ¿qué (–)? *how are you? (fam), how about it?*
talla *(f) size (clothes)*
talón *(m) receipt*
tamaño *(m) size*
también *also, too*
tampoco *neither*
tan *so*
tan amable *so kind*
tantos/as *so many*
tarde *late*
tarde *(f) afternoon, early evening*
tarjeta *(f) card*
tarjeta de crédito *(f) credit card*
tarjeta de embarque *(f) boarding card*
taxímetro *(m) taximeter*
te *you, to you, yourself (fam)*
té *(m) tea*
teatro *(m) theatre*
técnico *(m/f) technician*

teléfono *(m) telephone*
teléfono celular *(m) cell / mobile phone*
templo *(m) temple*
temporada *(f) season*
temprano *early*
tendencia *(f) tendency*
tener *to have*
tener que *to have to*
tercero/a *third*
terminar *to finish*
ternera *(f) veal*
terrestre *land (adj)*
ti *you (fam)*
tiempo *(m) weather; time*
tiempo libre *(m) spare time*
tienda *(f) shop, store*
tienda de regalos *(f) gift shop, gift store*
tinto *red (wine), coffee (Colombia)*
típico/a *typical*
todavía *still, yet*
todo/a *all, every*
tomar *to drink, to have; to take, to catch (bus, train, etc.)*
tomar (el) sol *to sunbathe*
tomar el desayuno *to have breakfast*
tomate *(m) tomato*
torcer *to turn*
tortilla *(f) flat maize pancake (Mex), omelette*
tostadas *(f, pl) toast*
tostado: pan *– toast (Mex)*
trabajar *to work*
trabajo *(m) work*
traer *to bring*
tráfico *(m) traffic*

tranquilo/a *quiet*
traslado *(m) transfer*
tratar de *to try to*
tratarse de *to have to do with,*
  to be a question of
traumatología *(f) orthopaedics*
tren *(m) train*
tú *you (fam)*
tu *your (fam)*

último/a *last*
único/a *only*
universidad *(f) university*
uno/a *a, one*
urgentemente *urgently*
usar *to use*
usted *you (pol)*
ustedes *you (pl)*
utilizar *to use*

vacaciones *(f, pl) holidays*
vainilla *(f) vanilla*
valer *to cost*
valija *(f) suitcase (Arg)*
valle *(m) valley*
valor *(m) cost, value*
variado/a *varied*
variar *to vary*
varios/as *several*
veces *(f, pl) times;* **a** *– sometimes*
vecino/a *neighbour*
vegetación *(f) vegetation*
vender *to sell*
venir *to come*
ventana *(f) window*
ver *to see*
verano *(m) summer*

verdad *true*
verdadero/a *true, real*
verde *green:* – **oscuro** *dark –*
verdura *(f) vegetable*
vez *(f) time;* **primera** *– first –*
viajar *to travel*
viaje *(m) journey, trip*
viaje: cheque de *– (m) traveller's*
  cheque
vida *(f) life*
viento *(m) wind*
viernes *(m) Friday*
vino *(m) wine;* – **tinto/blanco**
  red/white –
visitar *to visit*
vista *(f) view*
vitrina *(f) shop window*
vivienda *(f) housing, house*
vivir *to live*
volver *to come back*
vómito *(m) vomiting, being sick*
vos *you (fam, Arg)*
vuelo *(m) flight*
vuelta *(f) return*

y *and*
ya *already, soon*
ya que *since, as, for*
ya regreso *I'll be right back*
yo *I*
yo mismo/a *I myself*

zanahoria *(f) carrot*
zapallo *(m) pumpkin*
zapato *(m) shoe*
zócalo *(m) plaza (Mexico)*
zona *(f) district, zone*

English–Spanish vocabulary

a **un/a; uno**
able: to be – **poder**
about **acerca de**
accommodation **alojamiento** *(m)*
accompanied **acompañado/a**
activate: to – **activar**
additional **adicional**
address **dirección** *(f)*
adventure **aventura** *(f)*
aerial **antena** *(f)*
after **después**
afternoon **tarde** *(f)*
afternoon: good – **buenas tardes**
afterwards **después**
again **otra vez, de nuevo, nuevamente**
agency **agencia** *(f)*
ago **hace**
air **aire** *(m)*
air conditioning **aire acondicionado** *(m)*
airport **aeropuerto** *(m)*
all **todo/a**
alone **solo/a**
along **por**
already **ya**
also **también**
although **aunque, a pesar de**
always **siempre**
American **norteamericano/a, americano/a, estadounidense**
among **entre**
ancient **antiguo**
ancient: very – **antiquísimo/a**

and **y, e (***before* **i, hi)**
animated **animado/a**
announce: to – **anunciar**
another **otro/a**
apartment **departamento** *(m)*, **apartamento** *(m)*
appear: to – **aparecer**
April **abril**
architect **arquitecto/a**
area **barrio** *(m)*, **sección** *(f)*
Argentinian **argentino/a**
arrival **llegada** *(f)*
arrive: to – **llegar**
article **artículo** *(m)*
as **ya que, como**
as far as **hasta**
as regards **en cuanto a**
as soon as possible **a la brevedad, lo más pronto posible, lo antes posible**
as well as **como también**
ask: to – *for* **pedir**
asparagus **espárragos** *(m, pl)*
asparagus soup **crema de espárragos** *(f)*
at **en**
attend: to – **asistir**
August **agosto**
avenue **avenida** *(f)*
average **promedio** *(m)*
Aztec **azteca** *(m / f)*

bad **mal, malo/a**
bank **banco** *(m)*

bar **bar** *(m)*
bath: to take a – **bañarse**
bathroom **baño** *(m)*
be: to – **ser, estar**
beach **playa** *(f)*
beautiful **lindo/a, bonito/a**
beautiful: very – **precioso/a**
because **porque**
bed **cama** *(f)*
bed: to go to – **acostarse**
bedroom **dormitorio** *(m)*
beer **cerveza** *(f)*
before **antes**
begin: to – **empezar; entrar a**
  (to begin work)
believe: to – **creer**
besides **además**
better **mejor**
between **entre**
big **gran, grande**
bigger **más grande, mayor**
bill **cuenta** *(f)*
black **negro/a**
block **cuadra** *(f)*
blue **azul**
board: to – **embarcar**
boarding card **tarjeta de
  embarque** *(f)*, **pase de
  abordar** *(m)*
boarding house **pensión** *(f)*
book: to – **reservar**
booked **reservado/a**
booking **reservación** *(f)*,
  reserva *(f)*
border **frontera** *(f)*
boss **jefe/a** *(m / f)*
bottle **botella** *(f)*
boy **niño, chico, muchacho**

Brazilian **brasileño/a,
  brasilero/a**
breakfast **desayuno** *(m)*
breakfast: to have – **tomar (el)
  desayuno, desayunar**
briefcase **maletín** *(m)*,
  portafolio *(m)*
bring: to – **traer**
brother **hermano**
brothers and sisters
  hermanos *(m, pl)*
brown **marrón, café**
building **edificio** *(m)*
bureau de change **casa / oficina
  de cambio** *(f)*
bus **autobús** *(m)*, **ómnibus** *(m)*,
  camión *(m Mex)*, **colectivo**
  (m Arg)
business **negocio** *(m)*,
  empresa *(f)*
but **pero**
butter **mantequilla** *(f)*, **manteca**
  (f) (Arg)
buy: to – **comprar**
by **por**

cafe **café** *(m)*
call: telephone – **llamada** *(f)*,
  llamado *(m)*
called: to be – **llamarse**
can **poder**
car **carro** *(m)*, **auto** *(m)*, **coche** *(m)*
card **tarjeta** *(f)*
carry: to – out **realizar**
case **caso** *(m)*
case: just in – **por si acaso**
cash **efectivo**
cash: in – **en efectivo**

Castilian **castellano** *(m)*
catch: to – **tomar, coger**
  (bus, train, etc.)
category **categoría** *(f)*
cathedral **catedral** *(f)*
cell phone **teléfono celular** *(m)*
Central America **Centroamérica**
centre **centro** *(m)*
certainly **por supuesto**
chance **oportunidad** *(f)*
change: to – **cambiar**
cheap **barato/a**
check: to – **revisar**
chicken **pollo** *(m)*
chicken soup **sopa de pollo** *(f)*
child **niño/a, chico/a, hijo/a**
children **niños/as, chicos/as,**
  hijos/as
Chilean **chileno/a**
chosen **seleccionado/a,**
  escogido/a
church **iglesia** *(f)*
cinema **cine** *(m)*
city **ciudad** *(f)*
clear **despejado/a**
clerk **empleado/a**
client **cliente/a**
climate **clima** *(m)*
close: to – **cerrar**
clothing **ropa** *(f)*
cloudy **nublado/a**
coast **costa** *(f)*
coffee **café** *(m)*, **tinto** *(m*
  Colombia)
cold **frío** *(m)*
cold: to be – **hacer/sentir frío**
colleague **colega** *(m / f)*,
  compañero/a de trabajo

Colombian **colombiano/a**
colour **color** *(m)*
come: to – **venir**
come: to – back **volver, regresar**
come: to – in **pasar, entrar**
comfortable **cómodo/a**
company **empresa** *(f)*,
  compañía *(f)*
comparison **comparación** *(f)*
complete **completo/a**
computerized **computarizado/a**
conference room **sala de**
  conferencia *(f)*
congratulate: to – **felicitar**
connect: to – **conectar**
continue: to – **continuar, seguir**
corner **esquina** *(f)*, **rincón** *(m)*
corridor **pasillo** *(m)*
cost: to – **costar, valer**
country **país** *(m)*
countryside **campo** *(m)*
course **curso** *(m)*
course: of – **por supuesto**
credit card **tarjeta de crédito** *(f)*
culture **cultura** *(f)*

dark **oscuro/a**
daughter **hija** *(f)*
day **día** *(m)*
day: following – **día siguiente** *(m)*
dear **querido/a, estimado/a**
December **diciembre** *(m)*
decide: to – **decidir**
degree **grado** *(m)*
delay **demora** *(f)*, **retraso** *(m)*
delayed **retrasado/a**
depend on: to – **depender de,**
  contar con

describe: to – **describir**
desk **escritorio** (m), **mostrador** (m)
despite **a pesar de**
dessert **postre** (m)
destination **destino** (m)
diarrhoea **diarrea** (f)
different **diferente**
difficult **difícil**
dining room **comedor** (m)
dinner **cena** (f), **comida** (f)
dinner: to have – **cenar**
disco **discoteca** (f), **disco** (f)
discount **descuento** (m)
district **barrio** (m), **zona** (f)
do: to – **hacer**
doctor **médico/a**
door **puerta** (f)
down: **abajo:** – further **más abajo**
drink: to – **tomar, beber**
drive: to – **manejar, conducir**
driver **conductor/a, chofer** (m)
driving licence **carnet de conducir** (m), **licencia de manejar** (f)
due to **debido a**
during **durante**

each **cada**
early **temprano**
earn: to – **ganar**
eat: to – **comer**
elder **mayor**
eldest: the – **el / la mayor**
else **más**
employee **empleado/a**
end **fin, final** (m)
end: at the – of **al final de, al fondo de**

energy **energía** (f)
engaged **ocupado/a**
engineer **ingeniero/a**
engineering **ingeniería** (f)
England **Inglaterra**
English **inglés** (m) (language); **inglés / inglesa** (m / f)
enjoy: to – **disfrutar**
equipment **equipo** (m)
establishment **establecimiento** (m)
even though **aunque**
evening **tarde** (f early), **noche** (f late)
ever **alguna vez**
every **cada, todo/a**
example: for – **por ejemplo**
exciting **excitante**
excuse: – me **disculpe/a** (pol / fam), **perdone/a** (pol / fam)
executive **ejecutivo/a**
expect: to – **esperar**
expensive **caro/a, costoso/a**
experienced **experimentado/a, con experiencia**
explain: to – **explicar**
extension **extensión** (f), **anexo** (m Chile), **interno** (m River Plate)

fail: not to – to **no dejar de**
family **familia** (f)
famous **famoso/a**
fantastic **estupendo/a**
far **lejos**
fare: air – **pasaje aéreo** (m)
father **padre, papá**
fault **culpa** (f)
February **febrero**

Federal District **Distrito Federal** **(m)** *(Mexico City)*
feel: to – **sentirse**
fever **fiebre** *(f)*
fifth **quinto/a**
fill: to – in **llenar**
finally **finalmente**
find: to – **encontrar**
finish: to – **terminar**
first **primero/a**
fish **pescado** *(m)*
fish: fillet of – **filete de** **pescado** *(m)*
fit: to – well **quedar bien**
fizzy drink **bebida gaseosa** *(f)*
flat **departamento** *(m),* **apartamento** *(m)*
flight **vuelo** *(m)*
floor **piso** *(m)*
follow: to – **seguir**
following **siguiente**
food **alimento** *(m),* **comida** *(f)*
for **por, para**
free **libre**
French **francés** *(m) (language);* **francés/francesa**
Friday **viernes**
fried **frito/a**
fried: – dish **fritura** *(f)*
friend **amigo/a**
from **de, desde**
fruit **fruta** *(f)*
fruit: – salad **ensalada de fruta** *(f)*
full **completo/a, lleno/a**

gate **puerta** *(f),* **salida** *(f)*
generally **generalmente, por lo** **general, normalmente**

gentleman **caballero** *(m)*
German **alemán** *(m) (language);* **alemán/alemana**
get to: to – **llegar**
get up: to – **levantarse**
get: to – **conseguir**
gift **regalo** *(m)*
gift shop **tienda de regalos** *(f)*
girl **niña, chica, muchacha**
give me **deme**
give: to – **dar**
glad: to be – **estar contento/a**
glass **copa** *(f),* **vidrio** *(m)*
glory **gloria** *(f)*
go: to – **ir**
go: to – down **bajar**
go: to – on **seguir**
go: to – out **salir**
good **bueno/a, fino/a**
goodbye **adiós, hasta luego;** **chao, chau** *(fam)*
grandparents **abuelos** *(m, pl)*
green **verde** *(m / f)*
grey **gris**
guest **huésped** *(m / f)*
guide **guía** *(m / f person)*

half **medio/a; mitad** *(f)*
hand luggage **equipaje de** **mano** *(m)*
hang: to – up **colgar**
happen: to – **ocurrir, pasar,** **suceder**
happy **contento/a**
have: to – **tener, tomar, contar** **con**
have: to – just **acabar de**
heat **calor** *(m)*

hello **hola**; (on the phone) **aló,
  bueno** (Mex), **holá** (River Plate)
help **ayuda** (f)
help: Can I – you? **¿Dígame?**
help: to – **ayudar**
help: to – oneself **servirse**
her **la, le** (pronouns), **su, sus**
  (possessives)
here **aquí**
herself **se**
highway **carretera** (f)
him **lo, le** (pronouns)
himself **se**
his **su, sus, suyo/a**
history **historia** (f)
holidays **vacaciones** (f pl)
home **casa** (f), **hogar** (m)
hope: to – **esperar**
hot **caliente** (m)
hot: to be – **hacer calor, tener
  calor**
house **casa** (f)
housing **vivienda** (f)
how many? **¿cuántos/as?**
how much? **¿cuánto/a?**
how: are you? **¿cómo está
  (usted)?**; **¿cómo estás?, ¿qué
  tal?** (fam)
how? **¿cómo?**
husband **marido, esposo**

I **yo**
ice cream **helado** (m)
if **si**
immediately **inmediatamente,
  de inmediato**
in **en, dentro**
in any case **en todo caso**

in order to **para**
in spite of **a pesar de**
include: to – **incluir**
included **incluido/a**
independent **independiente**
  (m / f)
infection **infección** (f)
inhabitant **habitante** (m)
inside **adentro**
insurance **seguro** (m)
interested **interesado/a**
interesting **interesante**
interruption **interrupción** (f)
interview **entrevista** (f)
introduce: to – **presentar**
Irish **irlandés/irlandesa**

January **enero**
journey **viaje** (m)
juice **jugo** (m)
July **julio**
June **junio**

key **llave** (f)
kind **amable**
know: to – **conocer, saber**

label **etiqueta** (f)
lacking: to be – **faltar**
lady **señora**
lady: young – **señorita**
lake **lago** (m)
land (adj) **terrestre**
landscape **paisaje** (m)
language **idioma** (m),
  lengua (f)
last **último/a**
last night **anoche**

last year **el año pasado** *(m)*
late **tarde**
Latin American
  latinoamericano/a
learn: to – **aprender**
leather **cuero** *(m)*
leave: to – **irse, dejar**
left **izquierda** *(f)*
left: on the – **a la izquierda**
letter **carta** *(f),* **letra** *(f)*
lettuce **lechuga** *(f)*
licence: driving – **licencia de**
  conducir *(f)*
life **vida** *(f)*
lift **elevador** *(m),* **ascensor** *(m)*
light **liviano/a**
like **como**
like: to – **gustar**
like: to – very much **encantar**
listen: to – **escuchar, oír**
little **poco/a**
live: to – **vivir**
long **largo/a**
look: to – at **mirar**
look: to – for **buscar, localizar**
lot: a – **mucho/a**
love: to – (to like very much)
  encantar
low **bajo/a**
luck **suerte** *(f)*
luggage **equipaje** *(m)*
luggage: hand – **equipaje de**
  mano *(m)*
lunch **almuerzo** *(m),* **comida** *(f)*
lunch: to have – **almorzar**

majority **mayoría** *(f)*
make: to – **hacer**

manager **gerente** *(m / f),* **jefe/a**
many **muchos/as**
many: so – **tantos/as**
March **marzo**
market **mercado** *(m)*
married **casado/a**
marvellous **maravilloso/a**
mashed potatoes **puré** *(m)* **de**
  papas
matter: what's the – with you?
  ¿qué le / te pasa? *(pol / fam)*
May **mayo**
meal **comida** *(f)*
meat **carne** *(f)*
medium sized **mediano/a**
meeting **reunión** *(f)*
memories **recuerdos** *(m pl)*
mention: don't – it **de nada**
menu **carta** *(f)*
message **mensaje** *(m),* **recado** *(m)*
Mexican **mexicano/a**
midday **mediodía** *(m)*
mild **suave**
mileage **kilometraje** *(m)*
mileage: unlimited – **kilometraje**
  ilimitado *(m)*
million **millón** *(m)*
mind: I don't – **no me importa**
mind: if you don't – **si no le/te**
  importa *(pol / fam)*
minute **minuto** *(m)*
Miss **señorita**
miss: to – **extrañar, echar de**
  menos; *(bus, train)* **perder**
mistake: by – **por error**
model **modelo** *(m)*
moment **momento** *(m),*
  (diminutive) **momentito** *(m)*

Monday **lunes** *(m)*
money **dinero** *(m)*, **plata** *(f)*
month **mes** *(m)*
moon **luna** *(f)*
more **más**
more or less **más o menos**
morning **mañana** *(f)*
morning: good – **buenos días**
mother **madre** *(f)*, **mamá** *(f)*
move: to – **cambiarse, mudarse**
Mr **señor**
Mrs **señora**
much **mucho/a**
museum **museo** *(m)*
mustard **mostaza** *(f)*
my **mi / mis** *(sing, pl)*
myself **me**
myself: I – **yo mismo/a**

name **nombre** *(m)*
nationality **nacionalidad** *(f)*
near **cerca**
near here **por aquí**
nearby **por aquí**
neighbour **vecino/a**
neither **tampoco**
nephew **sobrino**
never **nunca**
next **próximo/a**
next to **al lado de, junto a**
niece **sobrina**
night **noche** *(f)*; **nocturno/a** *(adj)*
night: at – **en/por la noche**
noise **ruido** *(m)*
noisy **ruidoso/a**
nor **ni**
normally **normalmente,
  generalmente, por lo general**

north **norte** *(m)*
North America **Norteamérica**
not at all **de nada**
nothing **nada**
November **noviembre**
now **ahora**
number **número** *(m)*
nurse **enfermero/a**

occupied **ocupado/a**
occur: to – **ocurrir, pasar, suceder**
October **octubre**
of **de**
offer: to – **ofrecer**
office **oficina** *(f)*
official **oficial**
oil **aceite** *(m)*
on **en, sobre, encima de**
one **uno/a**
only **sólo, solamente**
onwards **en adelante**
open: to – **abrir**
opportunity **oportunidad** *(f)*
opportunity: to take the –
  aprovechar
opposite **frente a, enfrente de**
or **o (u** *before* **o, ho)**
orange **naranja** *(f)*
origin: place of – **procedencia** *(f)*
other **otro/a**
others **otros/as**
our **nuestro(s)/a(s)**
outside **fuera, afuera**

pain **dolor** *(m)*
painting **pintura** *(f)*
pair **par** *(m)*
palace **palacio** *(m)*

parallel **paralelo/a**
parents **padres** *(m pl)*
park **parque** *(m)*
passport **pasaporte** *(m)*
past **pasado**
pay: to – **pagar**
peach **durazno** *(m)*
per **por**
per cent **por ciento**
per day **diario, por día**
perhaps **quizá(s)**
permission **autorización** *(f)*
person **persona** *(f)*
personal call (telephone) **llamada**
  (f) **de persona a persona**
petrol station **estación de**
  servicio *(f)*; **gasolinera** *(f)*
pity **lástima** *(f)*
place **lugar** *(m)*
place of origin **procedencia** *(f)*
plane **avión** *(m)*
pleasant **agradable**
please **por favor**
pleased to meet you **mucho**
  gusto, encantado/a
police **policía** *(f)*
possible **posible**
post box **buzón** *(m)*
post office **(oficina de) correos**
  (f), **correo** *(m)*
potato **papa**
potato: mashed – **puré** *(m)*
  (de papa)
prefer: to – **preferir**
prescription **receta** *(f)*
present **regalo** *(m)*, **presente** *(m)*
pressure **presión** *(f)*
pretty **bonito/a, lindo/a**

price **precio** *(m)*
private **privado/a**
programme **programa** *(m)*
promise: to – **prometer**
provide: to – **proporcionar**
psychologist **psicólogo/a**
pumpkin **calabaza** *(f)*, **zapallo** *(m)*
puncture **pinchazo** *(m)*
pure **puro/a**
purple **púrpura, violeta, morado**

quality **calidad** *(f)*
quality: of good – **fino/a**
quarter **cuarto** *(time (m))*
quiet **tranquilo/a**
quite **bastante**

raft **balsa** *(f)*
rain **luvia** *(f)*
rain: to – **llover**
rainy **lluvioso/a**
read: to – **leer**
ready **listo/a**
real **verdadero/a**
receipt **talón** *(m)*, **recibo** *(m)*
reception **recepción** *(f)*
receptionist **recepcionista** *(m / f)*
recommend: to – **recomendar**
reconfirm: to – **reconfirmar**
red **rojo/a**
registration form **ficha** *(f)*
relative **pariente** *(m / f)*
rent **alquiler** *(m)*
rent: to – **alquilar, rentar,**
  arrendar
repair: to – **reparar**
repeat: to – **repetir**
report **informe** *(m)*

reservation **reservación** *(f)*, **reserva** *(f)*

reserve: to – **reservar**

reserved **reservado/a**

residence **residencia** *(f)*

responsible: to be – **encargarse**

rest: to – **descansar**

return (something): to **devolver**

return ticket **boleto de ida y vuelta** *(m)*

rice **arroz** *(m)*

right **derecha** *(f)*

right away **enseguida**

right now **ahora mismo / ahorita** *(diminutive)*

right: on the – **a la derecha**

road **camino** *(m)*

roast **asado/a**

room **habitación** *(f)*, **cuarto** *(m)*; **capacidad** *(f)*, **pieza** *(f)*

rucksack **mochila** *(f)*

salad **ensalada***(f)*

salary **sueldo** *(m)*, **salario** *(m)*

same **mismo/a**

Saturday **sábado** *(m)*

sauce **salsa** *(f)*

say: to – **decir**

school **escuela** *(f)*, **colegio** *(m)*, **instituto** *(m)*

Scottish **escocés/escocesa**

seafood **mariscos** *(m pl)*

season **estación** *(f)*, **temporada** *(f)*

seat **asiento** *(m)*

second **segundo/a; segundo** *(m time)*

secretary **secretario/a**

section **sección** *(f)*

security **seguridad** *(f)*

see: to – **ver**

seem: to – **parecer**

sell: to – **vender**

send: to – **enviar, mandar**

separate **aparte**

September **septiembre**

serious **serio/a**

serve: to – **servir**

service **servicio** *(m)*

shame **lástima** *(f)*

share: to – **compartir**

shirt **camisa** *(f)*

shoe **zapato** *(m)*

shop **tienda** *(f)*

shop assistant **dependiente/a**

shopping: to go – **ir de compras**

short **corto/a**

show: to – **mostrar, enseñar**

since **ya que, desde**

single (person) **soltero/a**

single: ticket **boleto de ida** *(m)*

sister **hermana**

sit: to – **sentarse**

situated **situado/a**

size **tamaño** *(m)*; **talla** *(clothes f)*

sleep: to – **dormir**

sleeping car **coche dormitorio** *(m)*

small **pequeño/a**

smoke: to – **fumar**

smoker **fumador/a**

snow: to – **nevar**

so **tan; entonces; así que**

so that **para que**

some **algún / alguna** *(m / f)*, **algunos/as** *(m / f pl)*

something **algo**

sometimes **a veces, algunas veces**

son **hijo**

soon **pronto, ya**

sorry: I am – **disculpe/a** *(pol / fam);* **perdone/a** *(pol / fam),* **lo siento**

soup **sopa** *(f),* **crema** *(f)*

soup of the day **crema / sopa del día** *(f)*

south **sur** *(m)*

South America **Sudamérica, Suramérica**

Spanish American **hispanoamericano/a**

Spanish **español** *(m) (language);* **español/a**

spare time **tiempo libre** *(m)*

speak: to – **hablar**

speaking: who is –? **¿de parte de quién?**

spell: to – **escribir**

spend: to – *(time)* **pasar;** *(money)* **gastar**

sport **deporte** *(m)*

square **plaza** *(f)*

square: small – **plazoleta** *(f)*

stairs **escalera** *(f)*

star **estrella** *(f)*

start: to – **empezar, comenzar; entrar** *(to start work)*

station **estación** *(f)*

stay **estadía** *(f),* **estancia** *(f)*

stay: to – **quedarse**

step **paso** *(m)*

stewardess **azafata** *(f)*

stewed **guisado/a**

still **todavía**

stomach **estómago** *(m); (adj)* **estomacal**

stomachache **dolor de estómago**

stop over **escala** *(f)*

stop: to – **hacer escala**

store: department – **tienda de departamentos** *(f)*

straight: to go – on **seguir derecho**

strawberry **fresa** *(f),* **frutilla** *(f)*

street **calle** *(f)*

student **estudiante** *(m / f)*

studies **estudios** *(m pl)*

study: to – **estudiar**

subway: **metro** *(m),* **subte** *(m Arg)*

such as **tal(es) como**

suggest: to – **sugerir**

suggestion **sugerencia** *(f)*

suitcase **maleta** *(f),* **valija** *(f Arg)*

summer **verano** *(m)*

sun **sol** *(m)*

sunbathe: to – **tomar (el) sol**

Sunday **domingo** *(m)*

sunny: it is – **hace sol**

sure **seguro**

sure: to be – **estar seguro/a**

surely **seguramente**

surname **apellido** *(m)*

surprise **sorpresa** *(f)*

sweater **suéter** *(m)*

swim: to – **nadar**

swimming pool **piscina** *(f),* **alberca** *(f Mex),* **pileta** *(River Plate)*

table **mesa** *(f)*

tablet **tableta** *(f)*

take: to – **tomar, llevar;** *(time)* **demorar**

tall **alto/a**

tap: water – **grifo** *(m),* **llave** *(f),* **canilla** *(f, River Plate)*

tax **impuesto** *(m)*

tea **té** *(m)*

teacher **maestro/a, profesor/a**

telephone **teléfono** *(m)*

telephone number **número de teléfono** *(m)*

tell: to – **contar**

temple **templo** *(m)*

tendency **tendencia** *(f)*

than **que**

thank you (very much) **(muchas) gracias**

that **ese** *(m)*, **esa** *(f)*, **eso** *(neuter)*; **que**

that is to say **es decir**

the **el** *(m sing)*, **la** *(f sing)*, **los** *(m pl)*, **las** *(f pl)*

them **los** *(m)*, **las** *(f)*; **les**

then **entonces**

there **allá, allí, ahí**

there is / are **hay**

these **estos** *(m)*, **estas** *(f)*

think: I (don't) – so **creo que sí (no)**

think: to – **creer, pensar**

third **tercero/a**

this **este / esta; esto** *(neuter)*; **ello** *(neuter)*

those **esos / esas** *(pl)*

Thursday **jueves**

thus **así**

ticket **boleto** *(m)*, **pasaje** *(m)*

time **hora** *(f)*; **tiempo** *(m)*; **vez** *(f)*; **época** *(f)*

time: from – to – **de vez en cuando**

time: on – **a la hora**

time: to have a good – **pasarlo bien**

times **veces** *(f / pl)*

times: several – **varias veces**

timetable **horario** *(m)*

tired **cansado/a**

today **hoy**

together **juntos / juntas**

toilet **baño** *(m)*; **servicios** *(m pl)*, **sanitario** *(m)*

tomato **tomate** *(m)*; **jitomate** *(Mex)*

tomorrow **mañana**

tomorrow: the day after – **pasado mañana**

too (much) **demasiado/a**

tour **tour** *(m)*, **recorrido** *(m)*

trace: to – **localizar**

traffic **tráfico** *(m)*

train **tren** *(m)*

transfer **traslado** *(m)*

travel agency **agencia de viajes** *(f)*

travel: to – **viajar**

trip **viaje** *(m)*

trousers **pantalones** *(m, pl)*

true **verdad** *(f)*; **verdadero/a** *(adj)*

try: to – **tratar, intentar**

try: – to on **probarse**

Tuesday **martes**

turn: to – **doblar**

typical **típico/a**

tyre **neumático** *(m)*

underground station **estación** *(f)* **de metro/subte** *(Arg)*

United States **Estados Unidos** *(m pl)*

university **universidad** *(f)*

unlimited **ilimitado/a**

until **hasta**

us **nosotros/as; nos**

use: to – **usar, utilizar**
usually **generalmente, por lo general, normalmente**

van **camioneta** (f)
vary: to – **variar**
vegetable **verdura** (f)
vegetable soup **sopa / crema de verduras** (f)
Venezuelan **venezolano/a**
very good – **muy bueno/a, estupendo/a**
very **muy**
visit: to – **visitar**

wait: to – **esperar**
waiter **mesero, camarero, mozo**
waitress **mesera, camarera**
wake up: to – **despertar**
walk: to – **caminar, andar**
walk: to go for a – **pasear, dar un paseo, ir a caminar**
want: to – **querer, desear**
warm **cálido/a**
warm: to be – **hacer / sentir calor**
water **agua** (m)
weather **tiempo** (m)
Wednesday **miércoles**
week **semana** (f)
week: per – **por semana**
weekend **fin de semana** (m)
welcome **bienvenido/a**
well **bien; bueno; pues**
well: very – **muy bien**
what **qué; cuál/ cuáles; cómo**
wheel **rueda** (f)
when **cuando**

where **donde**
which **cual / cuales**
white **blanco/a**
who **quien / quienes, que**
whose **cuyo/s** (m), **cuya/s** (f)
why? **¿por qué?**
wide **amplio/a**
wife **mujer, esposa, señora**
wind **viento** (m)
window **ventana** (f)
wine **vino** (m)
wine: red – **vino tinto**
winter **invierno** (m)
wish: to – **desear**
with **con**
within **dentro de**
without **sin**
work: to – **trabajar, laborar; trabajo** (m)
working hours **horario de trabajo** (m)
world **mundo** (m)
worry: to – **preocuparse**
write: to – **escribir**

year **año** (m)
yellow **amarillo/a**
yes **sí**
yesterday **ayer**
yet **todavía**
you **tú, usted, ustedes** (subject pronouns)
young **joven**
younger **menor**
youngest: the – **el / la menor**
your **su/s** (pol), **tu/s** (fam)
yourself **se** (pol); **te** (fam)

zone **zona** (f)

Taking it further

Further study

The following recommended textbooks may help you to expand your knowledge of Spanish grammar:

Batchelor, R., *A Student Grammar of Spanish*, Cambridge University Press, 2006

Butt, J., *Spanish Grammar*, Oxford University Press, 2000

Butt, J., and Benjamin, C., *A New Reference Grammar of Modern Spanish*, Hodder Education, 4th edition, 2004.

Kattán-Ibarra, J. and Howkins, A., *Spanish Grammar in Context*, Hodder Education, 2nd edition, 2008.

Kattán-Ibarra, J. and Pountain, C. J., *Modern Spanish Grammar*, Routledge, 2nd edition, 2003

Muñoz, P. and Thacker, M., *A Spanish Learning Grammar*, Hodder Education, 2nd edition, 2006

Ortega, Beaven, Garrido and Scrivener, *¡Exacto! A Practical Guide to Spanish Grammar*, Hodder Education, 2009

Turk, P. and Zollo, M., *¡Acción gramática!*, Hodder and Stoughton, 1993

Sources of authentic Spanish

Latin American newspapers and magazines
Latin American newspapers and magazines are difficult to find outside each country, but if you have access to the Internet you will be able to find their websites, although they may be special net versions. The following is a list of some main Latin American newspapers:

Argentina: *La Nación* (http://lanacion.com.ar/)
Clarín (http://www.clarin.com)

Chile: *El Mercurio* (http://www.elmercurio.cl/)

Colombia: *El Espectador* (http://www.elespectador.com/)

Cuba: *Granma* (http://www.granma.cu/)

México: *El Universal* (http://www.el-universal.com.mx/)

Perú: *El Comercio* (http:/elcomercioperu.com.pe/); *Correo* (http://www.correoperu.com.pe/)

Spanish newspapers and magazines

El País (http://www.elpais.es); *El Mundo* (http://www.el-mundo.es/); *La Vanguardia* (http://www.lavanguardia.es); *ABC* (http://www.abc.es); *El Periódico* (http://www.elperiodico.es/)

For general information, including Spanish current affairs and world news, try the following magazines: *Cambio 16, Tiempo, Tribuna, Época, etc.*

For light reading and entertainment you might like to look at *Hola, Cosas, Quo, Mía, etc.* These, together with *Marca*, a sports magazine, are by far the most popular amongst Spaniards and, as a beginner, you may find some of the articles easier to follow. Some of these magazines have Latin American editions.

Radio, television and internet news

An excellent way to improve your understanding of spoken Spanish is to listen to radio and watch television. On medium wave after dark (in Europe) and via satellite you will be able to gain access to Radio Nacional de España, Televisión Española (TVE) and other stations. For Spanish language news on internet you may like to go to BBC Mundo.com, or to Podcast BBC Mundo Radio, which offers a 15-minute world news summary from Monday to Friday, with a special focus on Latin America. The main Website is http://www.bbc.co.uk/mundo/

Travelling in Latin America and Spain

Travelling in a Spanish-speaking country is probably the best way to practise what you have learnt and improve your command of the spoken language. If you are planning to do this, there are a number of good guidebooks which will help you to plan your journey. The well-known *Lonely Planet* covers not just specific countries, but also main regions and cities, including Spain and Latin America. For the latter, the *Mexico and Central American Handbook* and the *South American Handbook* have a long tradition amongst travellers in the region. *Time Out, Michelin, Fodor's,* among several others, are well established in the travelling market.

Travellers in Latin America will find useful information in:

Travel.org – Latin America: http://www.travel.org/latin.htm/;

Latin America – travel notes: http://www.travelnotes.org/LatinAmerica/index.htm

For travellers in Spain, the following websites may prove useful, with information such as tourist attractions, accommodation, travel, restaurants, etc.:

Travelling to Spain: http://www.SiSpain/english/ travelli/

Spain Today (local section of the *Europe Today* travel guide): http://www.wtg-online.com/data/esp/esp.asp

All about Spain: http://www.red2000.com/

Páginas amarillas del viajero (yellow pages for travellers): http://www.spaindata.com/data/1index.shtml

Spanish National Tourist Office: http://www.tourspain.co.uk

Spanish language, culture and history

For Spanish language, the *Instituto Cervantes* (http://cervantes.es), a worldwide organization, offers courses in Spanish and promotes Spanish culture in general; the *Hispanic and Luso Brazilian Council*, in the United Kingdom, based in London, may be able to help you with enquiries about Spanish language courses and aspects of life in Latin America and Spain. For information on Latin American Spanish you can contact the embassy of the country you are interested in. There are also numerous websites where you can find information on cultural aspects related to Latin America and on Latin American Spanish, including study abroad programmes or even improve your Spanish through online courses. Some of these include:

http://www.spanish.about.com
http://www.spanish-language.org
http://www.spanishabroad.com
http://planeta.com/schoolist.html

About.com – Latin American culture:
http://Latin American culture.about.com/

Internet users interested in Spain may like to try the following sites:

Sí – Spain: http://www.sispain.org/spanish/index.htm/
Historia – Sí Spain: http://www.sispain.org/spanish/history
About.com – Spanish culture: http://spanishculture.about.com/

Working in Latin America and Spain

For an overview of job prospects in Latin America and Spain, including teaching go to:

http://www.transitionsabroad.com/listings/work/esl/articles/workinlatinamerica.html
http://www.transitionsabroad.com/listings/work/esl/teachingenglishinspain.html
http://www.tefllogue.com/finding-a-job/working-in-latin-america-an-overview.html
http://www.4icj.com/Latin-America

The publisher has used its best endeavours to ensure that the URLs for external websites referred to in this book are correct and active at the time of going to press. However, the publisher has no responsibility for the websites and can make no guarantee that a site will remain live or that the content is or will remain appropriate.

Index to grammar

Where references take the form 13.5, the first number is the unit and the second a section within the unit. 'G' before the section number refers to a Grammar section.

Other abbreviations used:

GS   Grammar summary
GGT Glossary of grammatical terms
IV   Irregular verbs
P   Pronunciation